Contributions to Finance and Accounting

The book series 'Contributions to Finance and Accounting' features the latest research from research areas like financial management, investment, capital markets, financial institutions, FinTech and financial innovation, accounting methods and standards, reporting, and corporate governance, among others. Books published in this series are primarily monographs and edited volumes that present new research results, both theoretical and empirical, on a clearly defined topic. All books are published in print and digital formats and disseminated globally. This book series is indexed in Scopus.

Anatol Melega

Geopolitical Risks in Financial Reporting and Transfer Pricing

Springer

Anatol Melega
Ştefan cel Mare University of Suceava
Suceava, Romania

ISSN 2730-6038 ISSN 2730-6046 (electronic)
Contributions to Finance and Accounting
ISBN 978-3-031-76599-5 ISBN 978-3-031-76600-8 (eBook)
https://doi.org/10.1007/978-3-031-76600-8

This Springer imprint is published by the registered company Springer Nature Switzerland AG
The registered company address is: Gewerbestrasse 11, 6330 Cham, Switzerland

Introduction

The intensity of recent geopolitical changes, amplified by overlapping crises (economic, health, energy, and military) has created a new economic reality with direct repercussions on the national and international business environment. Major geopolitical shifts, accentuated by the military conflict in Ukraine, have divided the world into two opposing poles, East and West. These negative effects have been particularly felt by the economic environment, which has been severely affected by the changing market conditions, price volatility, inflation rises, disruptions to the supply chains and, last but not least, by several factors with a direct impact on companies' performance. Against this backdrop, foreign direct investment (FDI) and socially responsible investment (SRI) inflows are declining, while investment risk is increasing. At the same time, worsening geopolitical and economic tensions *over* the last year have led to *over-regulation* and increased controls imposed on companies by national governments, especially for those operating in countries directly affected by the crisis. In these circumstances, there is an increase in compliance costs and risk of financial penalties for companies that breach these regulations.

Therefore, we can state that the new global economic and geopolitical context may constitute an impediment to the reporting process of companies, in the sense that the provided financial and non-financial information may have lower quality, with some characteristics being visibly affected, such as credibility and accurate representation. In such circumstances, given that companies rely on many estimates and assumptions in preparing their annual accounts, some situations of uncertainty and risk for investors and stakeholders may become increasingly pronounced. To avoid such problems, it is recommended that companies' management should be aware of the potential impact of the current geopolitical crisis, which generates several vulnerabilities and risks, with a predominantly indirect impact on financial reporting. Therefore, to prevent these situations, strategies need to be built in advance, including the establishment of an effective risk management system and the strengthening of relationships with the stakeholders. The main consequences of geopolitical risks for multinational companies include supply disruptions, loss of sales opportunities, currency and price fluctuations, and last but not least, increased legal and reputational risk.

The process of globalisation of national economies and the internationalisation of companies is a multidimensional phenomenon influenced by various factors, including geopolitical risks. The amplification of geopolitical risks in recent times has disrupted the global economic system, generating an unprecedented economic and political crisis, which in turn has divided the major powers and has highlighted the weaknesses and vulnerabilities of the globalisation process of national economies and the internationalisation of companies. Against the backdrop of the military conflict in Ukraine and the economic sanctions imposed on Russia, we are witnessing the consolidation and the imposition on the political and international stage of a new political and economic power—the BRICS group (Brazil, Russia, India, China, South Africa, and India).

At the beginning of the twenty-first century, geopolitical risks were not emphasised in the high-level category of risk management policy for large multinational corporations. These assumptions began to change with the arrival of the *Arab Spring* and the *Occupy Movement*, culminating in the *Crimean conflict*. There is now a common consensus in academia, as well as in politics and economics, that geopolitical strategies often underpin the competitive business environment and that multinational corporations can be perceived as extensions of state borders and interests abroad, which increases exposure to geopolitical events.

In this vein, we believe that a possible process of decentralisation of the world's economies will redefine the global political and economic balance, leading to the redefinition of the International Financial Reporting Framework (IFRS), which will inevitably be exposed to the risk of divergence in some countries of the world, concerning their affinity or membership in certain international structures (economic, geopolitical, cultural, or other interests). The creation of new political and economic blocs at the international level will lead to a new regrouping of national economies in relation to social and regional interests, with an emphasis on developing intra-group relations and maintaining relations with countries outside the group according to its interests. The creation of these geo-economic aggregates will facilitate access to flows of investment, raw materials, and labour. To smooth the flow of intra-group capital, member countries need to develop fiscal, financial, accounting, and other regulations and to set up common supervisory bodies. At the same time, in order to meet the needs of intra-group investors for common, *comparable* and *verifiable financial reporting* requirements, these countries may be tempted or even induced to develop common accounting rules that will be valid only within the group. It can therefore be argued that the redefinition of the geopolitical context will also lead to the redesign of companies' financial reporting, as they will have to adapt to the policies and regulations of the group in which they operate or the jurisdictions in which they have subsidiaries. In the aftermath of the COVID-19 pandemic, the geostrategies of multinational corporations play a significant role in the process of recovery and re-establishing power in the globalised economy, as they can lead to the strengthening of business relationships and the pursuit of more sustainable partnerships built around public health improvement and digital resilience.

In this context, it's normal to ask *How will things evolve in terms of the financial reporting system? To what extent will deglobalisation or the shift from a single pole of power, concentrated in the US, to an economic multipolarity, where the BRICS countries will dominate and affect the financial reporting journey*?

At the same time, as the geopolitical scenario tends to escalate, the business environment is increasingly confronted with new risks and challenges that may affect its ability to attract foreign direct investments and achieve long-term investment returns. In other words, paradigm shifts in the current global context call for analysing the impact of geopolitical risks and overlapping crises on the predictability of FDI flows and transfer pricing (TPs) which, in turn, will influence financial reporting information, both quantitatively and qualitatively. Such an approach requires an examination of the ramifications of geopolitical risks on the process of internationalisation of companies and implicitly on the international accounting referential, or even the creation of a new concept: "geographic accounting".

We believe that it is now essential to carefully monitor the geopolitical changes that have taken place, as well as the successive and overlapping crises impacting the international financial reporting framework, as companies are facing unprecedented situations, with no possibility of evading from the geopolitical equation of the world. As a result, we can expect trade sanctions, increased tariffs, disrupted supply chains, more and more regulations and barriers to new investments, and we may soon see the formation of regional alliances that will give preferential treatment to countries with the same geopolitical affinity. In response, companies may need to diversify and localise their supply chains and rethink their cross-border strategies.

The book is structured in four chapters. The first chapter provides an overview of geopolitical risks and their influence on the internationalisation process of companies, sources of financing, volatility of financial assets and stock markets, and threats to the International Financial Reporting Framework (IFRS). The chapter also discusses the pros and cons of the need to adapt the international financial reporting system to global geopolitical changes, as well as ideas on the definition and development of the concept of geo-accounting, as a result of the separation of the world's economies and the emergence of new economic and political powers such as the BRICS group of emerging economies. The second chapter analyses new opportunities for attracting foreign direct investment and building the transfer pricing case by capitalising on financial and non-financial information. At the same time, in this scientific endeavour, the stakeholder theory has been discussed, especially from the perspective of the positioning of investors in relation to other users of financial accounting information, with a focus on the contribution of this information in attracting FDI.

The increasing emphasis on the international political and economic arena of the emerging BRICS economies was the premise for the development of Chap. 3, where a comparative analysis of the financial reporting framework of companies in the emerging BRICS economies was carried out, highlighting the peculiarities of the applied accounting policies and practices, while also inventorying the effects of financial reporting on attracting foreign direct investment.

In the fourth chapter, accounting and tax policies related to transfer pricing applied by BRICS companies are examined. To complement the literature and to draw new research directions, a bibliometric and statistical analysis of scientific publications on the topic of "transfer pricing" was conducted.

We can easily see that the topics discussed in this book are relevant not only for macro-level decision-makers but also for reporting entities that are and will be confronted with novel situations characterised by uncertainty and even lack of predictability. This is because, as the global economic environment becomes increasingly complex and difficult to manage, financial information may increasingly lack accuracy, timeliness, verifiability, and comparability, which will alter the confirmation and predictability values. Therefore, the changing political and economic landscape makes it difficult to accurately forecast and assess the performance and sustainability of companies.

Contents

1 Internationalisation of Companies: From Geopolitics to Geo-Accounting 1
1.1 Geopolitical Risks: Factors Influencing the Internationalisation of Companies 3
1.2 Threats to the IFRS Benchmark Due to Increasing Geopolitical Risks 6
1.2.1 Influence of Geopolitical Risks on Funding Sources 8
1.2.2 Volatility of Financial Assets and Stock Markets Under Risk Conditions 10
1.2.3 Effects of Geopolitical Risks on the Performance of Internationalised Companies 12
1.3 International Financial Reporting Framework and the New Global Geopolitical Structure 14
1.4 Geo-Accounting: A New Concept or Paradigm for Investors and Other Stakeholders 16
1.5 Summary Conclusions 18
References 19

2 Opportunities to Attract Foreign Direct Investments by Leveraging Financial Accounting Information 23
2.1 Stakeholder Theory and Other Users of Financial and Accounting Information 24
2.1.1 Objectives of Financial Statements in Relation to the Information Transparency 28
2.1.2 Limits and Obstacles in Meeting Stakeholders' Information Needs with a Focus on Investors 32
2.1.3 Prospects for Developing Stakeholder Theory in the Current Global Geopolitical Context 36
2.2 Quality of Financial Statement Information and Attracting Foreign Direct Investment 38

2.2.1 Impact of Accounting Policies on the Quality of Financial Statements and Attracting FDI. 44
2.2.2 Opportunities to Reduce Information Asymmetries 48
2.3 Adopting IFRS and Attracting Foreign Direct Investment in BRICS Economies. 54
2.4 Summary Conclusions 56
References. 58

3 Financial Reporting Framework in Emerging Economies: BRICS 65
3.1 Particular Features of Accounting Policies and Practices Applied by BRICS Economies 67
3.2 Objectives and Structure of Financial Reporting by Companies in the BRICS Economies. 71
3.3 Strengths and Weaknesses of Financial Reporting by Companies in BRICS Economies. 74
3.4 Comparative Analysis of the Financial Reporting Structure of BRICS Economies. 77
3.5 IFRS Financial Reporting and Attracting Foreign Direct Investment in BRICS Economies 81
3.6 Summary Conclusions 89
References. 90

4 Accounting and Tax Policies Applied to Transfer Pricing in BRICS Economies. 93
4.1 Bibliometric Analysis of the Term "Transfer Pricing" 94
4.1.1 Bibliometric Analysis of the Transfer Pricing Literature 99
4.1.2 Modelling the Behaviour of Research Clusters. 103
4.2 Accounting, Legal, and Fiscal Approaches to Transfer Pricing 107
4.3 Determinants in Building the Transfer Pricing Case and Attracting Foreign Direct Investment 112
4.4 Transfer Pricing Documentation 114
4.5 Transfer Pricing Assessment Policies and Methods According to OECD Guidelines 118
4.6 Tax Policies Applied to Transfer Pricing in BRICS Economies . . . 125
4.7 Summary Conclusions 133
References. 133

Conclusions 143

Chapter 1
Internationalisation of Companies: From Geopolitics to Geo-Accounting

The process of globalisation of the world's economies is constantly on the rise, which is confirmed by the formation of a growing number of multinationals and the intensification of economic relations between countries, which has led to the creation of new economic relations and new supply chains, thus fluidising the movement of capital and labour. The removal of economic barriers between countries has facilitated the development of multinational companies through the opening of new subsidiaries, giving at the same time access to the international market for all national economies, which brings them several advantages, especially for those emerging or developing economies that are perceived as a magnetic pole for investors from developed countries due to the abundance of cheap resources like raw materials and labour. In turn, they benefit from a relatively constant flow of foreign investment in key areas of the economy, which contributes to the country's economic and social development through job creation, human capital development, transfer of know-how, etc.

Over the last two decades, the process of internationalisation of companies has intensified, mainly due to market liberalisation in several countries with controlled economies, which have opened access for foreign investors to the domestic market. At the same time, various international bodies have begun to emerge or consolidate in the political arena, to strengthen bilateral and multilateral relations between states and facilitate access for all national economies to the global market. One of the positive effects of the internationalisation of companies and the increase in cross-border investment flows is the highlighting of the political, economic, fiscal, social, environmental, and economic problems faced by these entities in their efforts to enter a new market. Thus, the problem raised by potential investors wishing to open a business in a new jurisdiction is access to information, both macroeconomic information on the country's economic and social indicators and microeconomic information on the economic and social behaviour of enterprises. In these circumstances, it is up to the political factor to intervene in eradicating these problems by creating

A. Melega, *Geopolitical Risks in Financial Reporting and Transfer Pricing*,
Contributions to Finance and Accounting,
https://doi.org/10.1007/978-3-031-76600-8_1

a regulatory framework that facilitates access to quality information for all stakeholders on fair terms. An important step in this direction is the harmonisation of national accounting standards with the International Financial Reporting Standards (IFRS). The progress in this direction varies from country to country and is strongly influenced by political, cultural, and social factors. As a rule, it is the political factor that has all the levers to push through the accounting reforms, there being several emerging or underdeveloped countries where this process is stagnating.

Due to the intensification of political dissent at the level of geopolitical and economic groupings, some countries or groups of countries have been excluded from certain economic and political alliances, affecting this way the global economy and thus the foreign direct or socially responsible investments flows. Political and economic disagreements have risen as a result of the intensification of the monopoly of countries such as Russia, China, and India on the raw materials market, which was initially severely affected by the COVID-19 pandemic and later by the military conflict at the borders of the European Union. Russia's increasing appetite to flaunt its power in the international political arena led to the outbreak of the military conflict in Ukraine in February 2022, thus intensifying the global energy crisis. At the same time, as the main supplier of energy to several European countries, Russia has halted its deliveries to EU countries that have imposed economic and political sanctions because of the invasion of Ukraine, as well as to other countries that have condemned its actions. To this end, Russia has summoned the BRICS member countries (Brazil, Russia, India, China, South Africa, India, China) to strengthen bilateral relations and to condemn the imposed economic sanctions. The BRICS group was set up in the wake of the 2008 financial market crisis as a new geopolitical and geo-economic power competing on the world stage alongside the US and the EU. The dominance of the world economy by the BRICS countries has led to their incorporation into various international economic bodies, and the group has always managed to express a unified position in different international economic and political forums. These countries have also changed the architecture of the international financial system with the creation of the New Development Bank, thus strengthening their economic and financial relations and reducing their dependence on other international financial institutions. China's foreign ministry spokesperson said that "*BRICS member countries agree to strengthen cooperation with emerging markets and ensure that these governments can make their voice heard on major international issues. China actively supports the enlargement process, promotes the formulation of standards and procedures to this end, and looks forward to the accession of like-minded BRICS partners*".

In this vein, we believe that we are currently witnessing a process of decentralisation of the world's economies that will redefine the global political and economic balance, leading to the redefinition of the international financial reporting system. The consolidation of political and economic groupings such as the BRICS will lead to their isolation from the global economic and political context by reorienting policies towards intra-group development while maintaining a reduced multipolarity in relations with countries outside the group. Thus, the creation of these geo-economic aggregates facilitates access to intra-group investments as well as the transfer of raw materials and labour. To facilitate the flow of intra-group capital, member countries are already developing tax, financial, and accounting regulations and setting up joint supervisory bodies. To meet the requirements of intra-group investors for "*single and comparable reporting*", these countries are likely to develop common accounting and financial reporting standards that will be valid within the group. It should therefore be borne in mind that the redefinition of the political context will also lead to the redefinition of the financial reporting system of companies, which will have to adapt to the policies and regulations of the countries in which they operate, in which they wish to maintain their existing subsidiaries or possibly open new subsidiaries. In this context, it is natural to wonder how things will evolve in terms of the financial reporting system and to what extent deglobalisation or the shift from a single pole of power, concentrated in the US, to an economic multipolarity with the BRICS countries as dominant players, will affect the financial reporting evolution.

The present research adds value to accounting and financial reporting theory by analysing geopolitical factors and their influence on the sources of enterprise financing, long-term return on investment, return on current assets and, last but not least, the performance of internationalised companies and the sustainability of their business. The current topicality of the addressed issues is given by the intensification of the effects of the multiple crises (health, economic, social, social, military, and energy) on the world's economy, but also by the political divergences caused by the conflict in Ukraine.

1.1 Geopolitical Risks: Factors Influencing the Internationalisation of Companies

The political power of a country is the main factor that influences the development of the national economy and strengthens international economic relations with other countries. Using the tax levers, the governments can manage to create an attractive regulatory environment for businesses, the political decision-makers being directly responsible for attracting and protecting investment in their own country. In other words, the role of the political factor in the economy is to provide the economic and legal framework for the activities of all participants in the economic life so that they take place under optimal conditions, being also a regulating factor in the national and international economy. It is therefore up to the political factor to create a favourable and secure environment for investors, which can be achieved by extending cooperation relations with various countries, joining various economic and trade bodies, and drawing up regulations that provide investment security and predictability of investment risk. The development of political, economic, and trade relations between states is the main prerequisite for the internationalisation of companies, contributing to the free movement of foreign investment flows, goods, and labour. In practice, it is the political apparatus that opens the doors of companies to the international market, being a promoter of internationalisation and economic globalisation. The current geopolitical changes in relations between the world's major powers are having an impact on the development of the business environment and are decisive factors in the allocation of investment.

However, geopolitical shifts are also a risk factor for investors, as frequent geopolitical shocks such as military attacks, terrorism, and wars lead to economic downturns, which jeopardise the business of companies. According to the systemic risk barometer developed by the Depository Trust and Clearing Corporation (2021), geopolitical risk has overtaken cyber risk to enter the top five of the risk rankings and is considered the main threat to international economic stability. The geopolitical risk landscape tends to evolve from one period to the next due to political dissensions between major powers that have significant effects on the economic and social environment.

According to the data in Fig. 1.1, there is a permanent fluctuation in geopolitical risk at the global level, which was mainly influenced by the terrorist attacks in London and Paris, and the military interventions of the U.S. and Russia. In the period 2014–2022, the geopolitical risk recorded high values determined by Russia's military interventions in Ukraine, which came with a wave of economic and political sanctions, strongly affecting the international economy, especially the energy market.

The problem of geopolitical risk for multinational companies is that it is unpredictable and can take different forms in different areas. Political and military dissensions—as mentioned above—are associated with significant economic downturns, with negative effects on trade and global economic welfare. According to Nikkinen and Vahamaa (2010), geopolitical turmoil can cause investors to postpone their investments, which further fuels the uncertainty in the global economy. Therefore, changes related to the domestic and international political environment significantly affect economic and corporate investment behaviour (Wolfers & Zitzewitz, 2009) and the activity of multinational companies is strongly affected by geopolitical changes. The amplification of geopolitical risks may lead to a reduction in the number of subsidiaries or the reallocation of investments to environments that offer

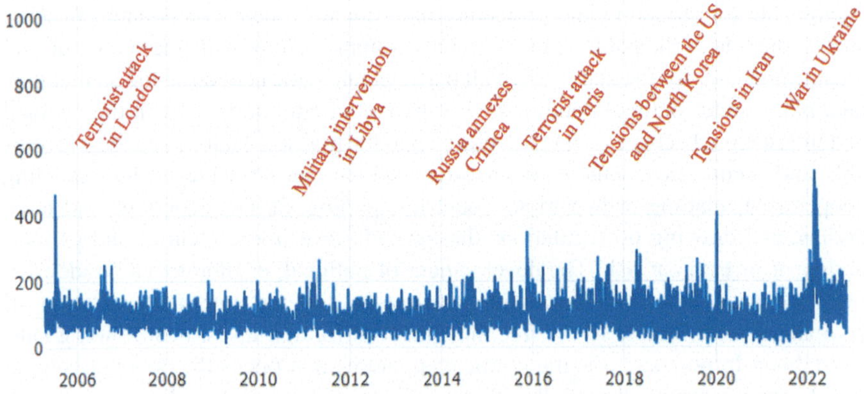

Fig. 1.1 Global geopolitical risk trends. Source: Adapted from Caldara and Iacoviello (2022)

higher security for the invested capital. To mitigate geopolitical risks, international bodies may resort to severe economic sanctions on the aggressor state, which has several negative effects on the business environment and may also lead to a period of economic recession and financial instability characterised by rising inflation and reduced flows of foreign direct and socially responsible investments. The severing of economic and political ties with partner countries harms the internationalisation of companies, considering that the imposed sanctions target first the foreign-owned companies, especially those in which the shares are held by third parties in the political sphere.

Economic sanctions are a range of economic and financial tools aimed at limiting a country's access to the international, regional, or local economic circuit. Typically, such sanctions are used when a country does not comply with economic, political, and social agreements between states or economic and political organisations. Whang (2011) defines them as *"trade and financial sanctions applied by one or more countries against a self-governing state, group or individual"*. Therefore, economic sanctions are a way of punishing those who violate certain rules, these being lifted when the sanctioned countries comply with all the requirements imposed by the sanctioner. However, even if economic sanctions are intended to punish a single state, they have repercussions for other countries too, including the ones that establish them (Smeets, 2018). An eloquent example is the EU sanctions on Russia that led to the halting of gas supplies and triggered an unprecedented energy crisis. The severity of economic sanctions is determined by their impact on the economy of the targeted state.

The geopolitical changes harm the development of the business environment, affecting business performance due to the severing of economic ties, reduced exports, currency depreciation, rising inflation, and others. Political and economic instability has always been a determinant of sustainable economic, social, and environmental development. The literature has provided solid evidence on the negative impact of geopolitical changes on firm performance in sanctioned countries. For example, Huynh et al. (2023) analysed the effects of economic sanctions over the past 20 years on firms in Russia and the research revealed that the performance of firms in the energy sector did not suffer from economic sanctions, while the performance of firms in other sectors was undermined. In particular, it was found that the negative impact of economic sanctions is strongly felt on capital expenditures, leading to an increase in the cost of capital and undermining R&D activity. Sun et al. (2022) who analysed the effects of economic sanctions on firm performance in Zimbabwe, concluded that economic sanctions reduce firm performance. Economic sanctions also have effects on other macroeconomic indicators that are determinants of sustainable business development such as inflation, foreign investment inflow circuit, levels of exports and imports, supply chain system, etc. The evolution of the above-mentioned factors is in a close correlation with the level of business performance, while also affecting the internationalisation process of companies. For example, following the invasion of Ukraine by Russia, several multinationals stopped their operations in Russia, leading to a mass exodus of the largest multinationals such as Mercedes-Benz, General Motors, Volkswagen, Apple,

Boston Consulting Group, Grant Thornton, Total Energies, British Petroleum, and others. The mass exodus of multinationals was also caused by the exclusion of several Russian banks from the SWIFT international payments system, limiting Russia's access to the international financial market. At the same time, several Russian-owned companies in the EU and the US have been subject to sanctions, with the EU so far applying sanctions on 116 such companies. In practice, multinationals are caught up in the geopolitical web, which is why economic sanctions can be applied and have their effects, given their strong connectivity with the political factor. Most multinationals are active in key sectors of the international economy, such as the energy, food, and metals industries, making a significant contribution to the creation of national and international GDP. Some authors consider that multinationals are an international system for the private sector that is simultaneously caught between the geopolitical mechanism and international markets (Abdelal, 2015), and the effects of geopolitical risks that they experience are transmitted to domestic enterprises. In other words, the business environment is strongly connected to the geopolitical context, and geopolitical changes can be fatal for some businesses.

In this vein, we believe that geopolitical risks represent a real challenge for businesses, affecting their internationalisation process. In this respect, companies must constantly assess this risk and be aware of its potential negative impact on their operational activity, and consequently on their economic, social, and environmental performance. We must not ignore the fact that geopolitical risks are triggers of other risks that come in a chain, and the lack of management skills to foresee these can lead to bankruptcy. Geopolitical risk assessment is essential, especially for those companies who wish to enter a new market, as it can efficiently complete the investment risk profile that is economy-specific.

1.2 Threats to the IFRS Benchmark Due to Increasing Geopolitical Risks

The geopolitical risks manifested at a global level are tending to widen due to the amplification of the conflict at the borders of the European Union and the energy crisis. The disruption of the West's economic, political, and social relations with Russia and its other allies is leading to a global economic recession and is a real threat to the international business environment. The effects of geopolitical risks are devastating for the economy, affecting the main distribution channels of international foreign direct investment flows, as well as the process of internationalisation of the world's companies. At the same time, the prolonged geopolitical shocks of recent times and the slow economic growth determined by the health and energy crises are leading to a collapse of financial markets and the regrouping of the world's economies. Therefore, the business environment must constantly assess its strategies in light of geopolitical risk, which in turn is made up of several risk types with different intensities, being a threat to sustainable business development.

The intensification of geopolitical risks and their effects on the international economy have channelled academic attention to monitoring the impact on macroeconomics (Zhang & Hamori, 2022), price dynamics (Caldara & Iacoviello, 2022), investment decisions (Lee & Wang, 2021), and stock market fluctuations (Smales, 2021). However, the impact of geopolitical risks on the international financial reporting framework (IFRS) was ignored when the BRICS countries decided to create their own intra-group payments system because Russia was excluded from the SWIFT system. The recent changes in the geopolitical landscape, the increasingly fierce competition between nations, and the assertion of national interests represent a real challenge for the IASB. Camfferman (2020) considers geopolitics to be a relevant angle in international financial reporting standard setting because *"on the one hand, the IASB presents itself, not without justification, as a technical, expertise-based, politically neutral organisation and its accounting standards as a universal language that can be applied worldwide regardless of national boundaries, and on the other hand, it is also widely accepted that there is a political dimension to international accounting standard setting, even if, as is normal for any political subject, there is a diversity of views as to where accounting ceases to be a technical activity and where, and in what sense, it starts to be political"*. Two essential elements are present in the design of international financial reporting standards, namely the political—which legitimises the standards—the business environment and the accounting profession that implement and enforce them. Geopolitics is thus one of the most important factors in the development and implementation of IFRS at the international level. Rising political and economic tensions between countries could be a real threat to the international accounting framework. The same assent is presented by Camfferman (2020) who argues that increased rivalry between nations could emerge as a threat to IFRS, as its intensification leads to their regrouping and the consolidation of new, narrower economic relationships with third countries to ensure the development of a new economic core. An illustrative example of this is the BRICS group, which might develop a common set of financial reporting standards to ensure the circulation of intra-group investment flows, and the likelihood of this scenario materialising is quite high, especially because of Russia's exclusion from the SWIFT system and the UN council, and its possible exclusion from the Group of 20 (G20). At the same time, Russia has adopted a policy of rejecting everything from the West as a result of the sanctions to which it has been subjected. Therefore, being a construct of the West, IFRS could be refused by some states as a protest. Russia's progress in converging its national accounting standards to the international accounting benchmark is minimal and slow, once again showing that its interests in accounting regulations for financial reporting are different. China, another economic power, is geared towards building a "China-centric network of economic, political, cultural, and security relations" consisting of neighbouring countries, leading to the reconstruction of the regional order with new ideas of governance, norms, and rules (Callahan, 2016). The adoption of the International Financial Reporting Standards by the BRICS countries could be seen as an element of symbolism, a recognition of the West's economic power in the international arena, their adoption is also constrained by their membership in the Group of 20, and the exclusion of one of them could jeopardise the process of financial reporting internationalisation. The new geopolitical context would reconfigure power into four blocs: BRICS, the US, the EU, and other countries—which would affiliate to a group according to their political affinities and interests pursued, which would rewrite international financial reporting practices. A similar previous geopolitical context gave rise to the idea of creating a single set of international financial reporting standards for strengthening economic and political relations between countries in the 1980s–2000. Taking the US GAAP as a benchmark was also a political element, as the US is one of the largest economic and political powers, with a growing financial market and businesses, and is taken as an example of best practice in financial reporting policies and practices. As in the present case, the current geopolitical changes could redirect some countries towards new financial reporting practices. National interests have always been and will always be paramount, and if a country sees IFRS as a threat, it will always move away from it and implement its own set of standards. Accounting policies and practices are internal policies specific to a country or jurisdiction, and the interference of an outside third party could be considered a violation of national sovereignty. Each country, therefore, is free to choose its future directions of development in any area according to its internal rules and principles of functioning. Therefore, IFRS are not and cannot be imposed on a country and cannot be a binding element for access to the international market, and the creation of regional financial reporting standards must be taken into account in the current context, especially by multinationals.

Financial georeporting could be a new paradigm for companies, representing financial reporting under regional accounting standards based on the geographical location of the subsidiary or enterprise, or it could be a reconfiguration of the IFRS, based on geopolitical factors. Therefore, the IASB should consider geopolitical changes to achieve its goal of *"developing in the public interest a single set of high-quality, understandable, globally applicable and accepted financial reporting standards based on clearly established principles"* (IASB, 2022). At the same time, the IFRS framework should provide additional clarification on the treatment of issues related to the effects of geopolitical risks on the return on investments, the return on current assets, the volatility of financial assets and more generally, on the performance and sustainability of the enterprise. This information is of paramount importance to investors in assessing the risk and return of investments over the short, medium, and long term. International Financial Reporting Standards need to be adapted not only to geopolitical changes but also to any event that affects or may affect the business environment, thus supporting stakeholders by providing them with quality information in line with economic reality.

1.2.1 Influence of Geopolitical Risks on Funding Sources

Geopolitical changes pose a real threat to companies' access to sources of finance and at the same time to the attraction of foreign investment by countries involved in conflicts of any kind. The disruption of economic, trade, and political relations between states determines a stagnation of foreign direct investment flows or their redirection to more stable economic environments. The geopolitical risk, which is composed of several other risks, represents a bottleneck for access to sources of financing, with investors being more vigilant in periods of major geopolitical changes that are also characterised by a slowdown in business activity due to changes in consumer behaviour, as they postpone their consumption and investments, generating a state of uncertainty in the national and international economy. Thus, it can be stated that geopolitical risk is a threat to the financial stability of companies since it determines the reduction of the financing sources for the economy, considering the uncertainties in the global economic circuit. The impact of geopolitics on companies' financing sources is undeniable, especially for multinational companies whose operational activity is largely conditioned by geopolitical changes. In other words, multinationals are connected to the international business environment through the "geopolitical tightrope", because as political frictions in the international political arena increase in intensity, the likelihood that they will affect companies' domestic and foreign operations increases too. Their impact can be manifested with blocked shares, prohibitions on the transfer of capital or even on the activity of foreign-owned companies.

The strategic competition between developed and emerging economies puts geopolitical risk at the forefront of the risks in terms of the circuit of FDI flows between economies, as they are considered one of the main sources of financing for both companies and the country (especially for emerging economies that are growing mainly due to a large inflow of FDI) and show high sensitivity in crisis contexts. After a period of growth, the COVID-19 pandemic has stagnated its evolution, with a drastic drop of 49% globally (UNCTAD, 2022). The negative trend continued in the following period characterised by major geopolitical changes: the tensions in Iran and the war in Ukraine, which is the largest military conflict in Europe since the Second World War. According to a study by the EY European Attractiveness Survey (2022), investors have become more vigilant in their investment activity, with their trust falling by 79% in 2022 due to the conflict at the EU borders which jeopardised the European economy, as Russia halted energy supplies and a multinationals' exodus happened. UNCTAD's forecasts for the investment environment are gloomy, as the geopolitical risk has changed the investment climate, and companies have tighter financing sources. According to them, even though multinationals have recorded high profits, the "investment in new projects abroad was still a fifth below pre-pandemic levels" (UNCTAD, 2022). Geopolitical shocks have a considerable impact on the financing sources of emerging and developing economies, which for the most part originate from developed economies. Thus, geopolitical tensions between the West and the East are a threat to emerging and developing economies, especially the BRICS ones, which are the main recipients of foreign direct investments. In this respect, they need to reorient their intra-group or regional financing policy. Emerging economies have taken important steps to ensure the financial stability of the group with the establishment in 2014 of the New Development Bank, which is seen as a competitor to the main global financial structures such as the International Monetary Fund (IMF) and the World Bank. At the same time, the BRICS emerging economies plans to break away from the global economy were foreseeable as early as 2014, when at the Fortaleza summit, the Russian foreign minister stated that *"just as the West isolates Russia outside its economic system as punishment for its policies towards Ukraine, Russia is getting involved in the financial superstructures of the new generation of global economic heavyweights"* (Russian Ministry of Finance, 2014). The establishment of this financial superstructure of the BRICS economies strengthens the sources of financing of these economies, thus reducing their influence and financial dependence on the EU and the US.

Existing studies provide strong evidence regarding the dependence of international financing sources on geopolitical changes. Based on a sample of G8 countries and using Kónya's (2006) causality test, Ceyhan and Gulcan (2022) analysed the impact of geopolitical risks on FDI and financial development, concluding that there is causality between the analysed elements: "rising geopolitical risks amplify political and economic uncertainties and cause significant fluctuations in financial investment and capital movements". In the same assent, Thi et al. (2022) analysed the impact of geopolitical factors on FDI inflows for 18 emerging economies, arguing that geopolitical stability is essential to enhance the economic progress of emerging economies. As noted above, emerging economies are the main recipient of FDI inflows and their economic development is closely linked to the evolution of FDI inflows. In practice, geopolitical risk is pushed to the forefront when it comes to investment decisions, with increased geopolitical risk leading to a decrease in FDI flows. Typically, the most significant geopolitical risks for investment are military attacks, wars, and, of course, sanctions imposed on states considered as aggressors. Findings from the literature show that geopolitical risks have become an important dimension of the international economy, being an essential element in ensuring the flow of foreign direct investment between economies.

The sustainable development of an economy is therefore dependent on geopolitical changes, and the diversification of sources of finance is crucial for both the economy and multinationals.

1.2.2 Volatility of Financial Assets and Stock Markets Under Risk Conditions

Stock markets are the most sensitive to geopolitical changes, and the effect on them is direct and immediate, i.e. the intensification of geopolitical tensions also increases stock market volatility. The effects of geopolitical risks on the economy are protracted and differ depending on the intensity of their fluctuations, which are also characterised by a high level of uncertainty regarding their future trend. Studies in the literature have focused on assessing the impact level of geopolitical tensions (Hudson & Urquhart, 2016) on several economic factors such as recession, demand, supply, inflation, labour force, and others (Pástor & Veronesi, 2013). According to Ha et al. (2021), heightened geopolitical risk may *"increase financial market volatility and induce lags in investment decisions and as a result, negatively impact macroeconomic outcomes"*. Geopolitical threats are characterised by a shift of investors towards areas of interest that offer higher safety of the invested capital, as they seek to minimise their risks to investment returns. At the same time, periods of heightened geopolitical risk also lead to a fall in consumption and hence market demand. In particular, during periods of political, economic, and military uncertainty, consumers are more reluctant to purchase goods and services, thus worsening the "supply and demand balance". For stock markets, geopolitical risks are a real constraint, with liquidity, market, credit, and operational risks amplifying as they escalate. Because of the geopolitical crisis amplified by the war in Ukraine, an ESMA report (2022) estimated a rather high level of risks for investors in the coming period *"as a result of possible significant market corrections, in the context of rising volatility and high inflation eroding potential gains"*. The volatility in the prices of financial instruments is also determined by the energy crisis, as well as the severing of trade ties between countries, which has affected most EU economies.

The European Securities and Markets Authority forecasts (Fig. 1.2) that the current border conflict in the EU tends to amplify stock market volatility. The political uncertainty over Russia's invasion of Ukraine is identified by ESMA as a major risk (red), considering its major impact on the volatility of European stock markets and the uncertainty about further developments. Financial market instability, rising inflation, and energy, political, military, and social crises are a real threat to the sustainability of the global economy. The continued volatility of financial assets is also an effect of inflation, which has reached exorbitant levels in some economies. The high volatility of stock markets is also associated with major investment risk, especially in the case of long-term investments, because the evolution of certain risks—such as geopolitical risks—is difficult to predict, as is their impact on financial assets. Therefore, in periods of major geopolitical changes, there is a withdrawal or reluctance of investors, or a migration of investments to safer investment environments. At the same time, another phenomenon during periods of high price volatility is an increase in short-term investments, as they are considered less risky compared to long-term ones.

RISKS			
Risk categories		**Sources of risk**	
Level	**Outlook**		**Outlook**
Overall, ESMA's mission	→	Geopolitical risks, especially following the conflict in Ukraine	↗
Liquidity risks	→	Macroeconomic environment	↗
Market risks	→	Inflation and interest rate environment	↗
Credit risks	↗	Sovereign and private debt markets	↗
Risks of contagion	→	Market infrastructure disruptions	↗
Operational risks	→	Other political risks and events	↗
Environmental risks	↗		

Fig. 1.2 The European Securities and Markets Authority's level of stock market risks. Source: ESMA (2022). ESMA Report on Trends, Risks, and Vulnerabilities

The connection between geopolitical changes and financial asset volatility has been confirmed by several researchers. For example, Yang et al. (2021) analysed the effects of geopolitical risk on the Chinese stock market and concluded that global geopolitical risk has a significant impact on the Chinese stock market, and the authors attributed this risk a key role in explaining and forecasting the volatility of market returns in China. Balcilar et al. (2018)—using non-parametric quantile causality tests—analysed the effect of geopolitical changes on the dynamics of stock market returns and volatility in emerging BRICS stock markets, concluding that *"the effect of geopolitical risks is heterogeneous across BRICS stock markets, suggesting that news about geopolitical tensions does not affect the dynamics of returns in these markets in a uniform way, with Russia bearing the highest exposure to geopolitical risks in terms of both returns and volatility, and India being the most resilient BRICS nation in the group"*. Given the expansionist nature of Russian policy, its involvement in many military conflicts, and the economic sanctions to which it has been subjected, high volatility is generated in the financial assets. In general, the Russian stock market is considered by investors as a politically controlled market with a major investment risk. For example, with the invasion of Ukraine in February 2022, the Russian stock market saw the most volatile trading in decades. In the same vein, Choi (2022) analysed the effects of geopolitical risks on the volatility of stock indexes in Northeast Asian countries (South Korea, Japan, and China), arguing that there is a strong interdependence between geopolitical risk and volatility of the three stock markets in the short run, i.e. the geopolitical risk index and volatility have a time-dependent relationship. Thus, geopolitical changes harm financial markets, contributing to higher price volatility and higher investment risks, respectively. In particular, the effects of geopolitical risks are felt more by stock markets in countries directly involved in political, military, economic, and social conflicts.

An eloquent example of this is the Russian stock market, which, with the escalation of the conflict in Ukraine in February 2022, recorded its most volatile prices in decades.

1.2.3 Effects of Geopolitical Risks on the Performance of Internationalised Companies

In a world where globalisation has reached its peak and the number of multinationals has increased dramatically, the dependence of economies on each other is now stronger than ever, with geopolitical shocks having an octopus effect and affecting all branches of the international economy. The breakdown of economic, political, social, and trade relations between states threatens the performance and sustainability of internationalised companies. One of the main effects of geopolitical risks on the sustainability of companies is the reduction of financing channels. As mentioned above, the intensification of geopolitical risks leads to a reduction in investment flows, especially long-term investments that are associated with high risks during periods of price volatility. The sustainability and performance of companies in emerging economy countries are highly dependent on FDI inflows, the reduction of which may lead to a financial collapse for these companies.

The global escalation of geopolitical risks as a result of Russia's invasion of Ukraine has a direct impact on companies that have operations or agreements in or with Russia, Belarus, and Ukraine, due to import and export restrictions, limited availability of local services, and access to local resources needed to conduct business. The effects of geopolitical changes are practically correlated with the operational and financial activity of the enterprise, with direct implications on the performance and sustainability of companies (Fig. 1.3). To a large extent, geopolitical changes come with a series of sanctions for the aggressor states, sanctions that have a boomerang effect, in the sense that in the current context when we talk about the globalisation of the world's economies characterised by powerful connections between states and companies, the sanctions imposed on the aggressor country also affect those who sanction, as the business environment is affected in both directions. For example, export and import restrictions have negative effects on the performance and sustainability of both supplier and customer companies. At the same time, restricting exports creates a surplus of goods for the supplier company, which may lead to additional costs for storage and maintenance or even destruction, and for the customer company, this could even lead to going out of business or insolvency. The reorientation of the supplier to another market is a lengthy process and the expected gains may not be sufficient to cover the costs, and for the customer company, the acquisition of the goods needed to do business in the new market could lead to increased production and supply costs.

Geopolitical changes have been ever-present in the international arena, but the latest changes are causing worries and fears for the international economic and political situation. As the scenarios are becoming increasingly uncertain, it is reasonable to expect that the political and economic balances will shift significantly, and the sustainable development of internationalised companies is a susceptible element due to their specific vulnerability, considering their exposure to external factors that cannot be managed and controlled. The latest events in the international arena represent the most significant changes in recent decades in the geopolitical framework intersecting with industrial, commercial and even monetary dynamics. In this context, geopolitical risks cause a situation of uncertainty in terms of the performance and sustainability of internationalised companies. At the same time, during periods of major geopolitical changes, companies in manufacturing-related

Dependence on funding from sanctioned financial institutions
Loss of a significant customer base/declining demand for products or services
Inability to sell products through already established channels
Possible restrictions on activities (including financing activity) that could be affected by sanctions
Long-term structural changes in the market, including supply chain disruptions
Inflation and price volatility
Significant changes in commodity prices or other market indicators

Fig. 1.3 The effects of geopolitical risks on company activity with implications for business performance and sustainability. *Source*: Developed by author

industries tend to save more money and protect themselves from risk contamination (Lee & Wang, 2021), as they tend to reduce activity during geopolitical crises, the supply chains being also affected. According to Lee and Tran (2021), geopolitical risk is a true macro-level shock that influences corporate investment with implications for company performance and sustainability. Therefore, if macroeconomic changes have a significant impact on managerial policies and especially on the firm's investment environment, geopolitical risk can represent a negative shock to the company's investments (Rashid & Saeed, 2017). Geopolitical risks are often underestimated by managers, who often lack the organisational managerial capacity to cope with the uncertainties induced by the business environment (Danneels, 2002) in the context of geopolitical changes.

The impact of geopolitical risk on the performance and sustainability of internationalised companies remains a largely unexplored topic, especially as geopolitical changes tend to play an increasingly important role in the global economy. Corporate performance and sustainability can be analysed in a more holistic view and through the prism of the implications of geopolitical risks on key economic and financial indicators.

1.3 International Financial Reporting Framework and the New Global Geopolitical Structure

The effectiveness of the international financial reporting system is influenced by geopolitical changes at both regional and global levels. The political factor is the technical instrument responsible for the process of regulating and implementing IFRS at the national level, and it can tip the balance for or against these standards at any time. In this respect, the IASB has to constantly assess the impact of geopolitical changes on the objectives of IFRS and reconfigure their structure according to economic realities. Because the IASB is a political rather than an apolitical organisation, the development of International Financial Reporting Standards is strongly affected by international and regional geopolitical shocks. However, the IASB does not recognise that geopolitical changes have some impact on IFRS. At a conference in London, in September 2019, where over 170 standard setters from 70 jurisdictions met, IASB Chairman Hans Hoogervorst noted that *"against the backdrop of heightened geopolitical frictions where the recent G7 meeting could not even agree on a common statement, our standard-setting community provides an excellent example of what can be achieved when people from all parts of the world work together towards a common goal"*(IFRS, 2019). Such conferences are held annually and discuss the main concerns of members responsible for standard setting and IFRS development. Given the escalation of geopolitical situations in recent times, no IASB summit has discussed the possible impact of these geopolitical changes on IFRS, with the latest topics debated at the September 2022 summit being: *"IASB update—update on the IASB's work plan and 22 active IASB projects; ISSB work—development of a global benchmark model for sustainability reporting; IFRS for*

SMEs—consultation on the update of the Standard; Primary Financial Statements—update on progress and details of key proposals; Feedback on IFRS standards for sustainability presentation" (IFRS, 2022). As we can see from the summary of this conference, the geopolitical changes are not a topical issue for the IASB, as they are not considered an impediment to further development of the international financial reporting framework.

In periods of major geopolitical changes, the quality of financial information is affected, amplifying information asymmetry. Domestic economic actors are always at an advantage when it comes to assessing geopolitical market risk compared to external stakeholders. Following Russia's invasion of Ukraine, as well as the sanctions imposed on Russian companies, there was a confirmed lack of disclosure by Russian companies on the direct and indirect impact of Russia's invasion of Ukraine and the imposed sanctions, financial performance, financial position and cash flow statements, measures taken to mitigate the impact and cyber security risks. Therefore, geopolitical changes determine an increased information asymmetry and information distortion, when one of the objectives of IFRS is to mitigate or even eliminate these elements. The promotion of IFRS around the world has slowed down as the global political situation has worsened, with many major economies becoming hesitant as they consider whether or not to commit further to IFRS implementation. According to Trajkovska (2013), *"significant organisational change at the IASB is needed, along with constructive engagement from all key stakeholders around the world"* to ensure the workability of IFRS. According to Trajkovska (2013), to further encourage the world's economies to adapt national accounting standards to IFRS, the IASB should:

- "minimise the unnecessary complexity of its standards and hold firm to the vision of principle-based standards that require a reasonable degree of reasonableness;
- establish workable models for impact assessments and post-implementation evaluations;
- be prepared to redesign the approach and scope of evaluations if initial results prove disappointing;
- make major changes in the scope and coverage of the Board's activities that will not be possible unless the IFRS Foundation's funding system is established on a secure and sustainable basis" (Gorgieva-Trajkovska et al., 2013);
- adopt IFRS in line with economic realities;
- assess the impact of geopolitical, social, and economic risks on the internationalisation of accounting.

Therefore, the further sustainable development of IFRS requires their harmonisation with geopolitical changes that affect the course of the economy from one period to another. The IASB needs to continuously provide further clarifications on the application of IFRS in times of crisis, especially for companies in regions directly affected by geopolitical changes. As the mechanism that connects with stakeholders and as a key element in economic and financial communication, IFRS must adapt to economic realities and respond to the needs of all stakeholders. Why are geopolitical changes dangerous for IFRS? Because, as Camfferman (2020) stated *"geopolitics is the opposite of globalisation, understood in terms of the increasing irrelevance of national borders for flows of economic resources and a general cooperative approach to managing international relations through common institutions"*. Thus, geopolitics being the opposite of globalisation is also a risk factor for the international financial reporting framework. The effort by the world's economies to converge national accounting standards to IFRS is closely linked to their desire to assert themselves and gain access to the international market. However, with recent geopolitical changes, major shifts could also occur in the international capital market, which may also rewrite the IFRS development path.

Achieving the IASB's goal of a single set of global standards is possible, but only if it takes a neutral stance on geopolitical changes while at the same time redesigning standards in line with economic realities.

1.4 Geo-Accounting: A New Concept or Paradigm for Investors and Other Stakeholders

Recent geopolitical changes could have repercussions for the international accounting system. Intensifying economic, political, and trade tensions between the West and the East could lead to a separation of the world's economies along political and economic power lines. Russia's energy monopoly, the expansion of China and India in the raw materials market and the strengthening of relations within the BRICS group could be important prerequisites for redesigning the international accounting system and developing regional accounting systems. This will require the introduction of a new concept in accounting science, such as geo-accounting, which would represent accounting systems in terms of geographical, social, and political factors, in the spirit of the expansionist theory. In practice, the accounting of a country or region is determined by its geographical location, as well as by its political and economic group membership. Geo-accounting can also be defined as an accounting doctrine that studies the impact of geographical, political, and social factors on the financial reporting framework.

Geo-accounting could be a new paradigm for investors and all stakeholders in general. It would increase information costs for stakeholders due to the inhomogeneity and lack of comparability of financial reporting data, which is only possible within companies applying the same standards for financial reporting. Regional reporting will limit the access of investors from outside the group and will contribute to increased economic and commercial relations within the group as well as to increased intra-group FDI flows. Paradigm shifts in the financial reporting system will be a real challenge for multinationals with a large number of subsidiaries in different regions, which will require them to adapt their subsidiary's financial reporting to the accounting policies and practices of the region. In practice, this will result in the multinational splitting into several structures, depending on the accounting practices and policies applied. This is not new for multinationals, as before

IFRS, companies' financial reporting was according to national GAAP and they had to apply accounting standards according to their geographical location.

As noted by other authors, accounting "is not only limited to technical issues but also to stakeholders' interests that have their roots embedded in the geopolitical framework" (Sandu et al., 2022). In other words, accounting has always been governed by the geopolitical factor, which holds the main regulatory and control mechanisms and has made significant contributions to the reform of accounting systems. Developed economies have been taken as examples of best practices in accounting standardisation by emerging and developing countries, the latter replicating the accounting policies and practices of developed economies in their national standards. Each economy is constructed differently, i.e. the functions of the economy are differentiated from country to country, just as the purpose of accounting and financial reporting is distinct depending on the objectives pursued by the policy framework, in particular the expansionist policy of the country. A key role in the development of accounting systems is attributed to the accounting profession, which has the role of reforming accounting in line with economic realities. However, the accounting profession is influenced by the political apparatus and is strongly affected by political vision and political stability or instability at national and international levels. As for the direction of accounting development, it will always be guided by political interest, especially in countries where accounting is strongly linked to taxation. The interest of the state will always be superior to other stakeholders, hence financial reporting will be more focused on maintaining the link between the state and the enterprise, and geopolitical changes will always project the course of accounting. Therefore, the differentiators of accounting systems are the result of geopolitical changes as well as other factors of social, religious, cultural, economic, or geographic nature.

The classification of accounting systems is not new to the accounting literature. Until the establishment of the IASB, this was the main preoccupation of researchers: the delineation of accounting systems according to political, economic, social, geographical, and so on factors. After the establishment of IFRS, research has focused on the study of international accounting harmonisation and convergence, i.e. the creation/development of the international accounting system. With considerable support from major political, economic, and commercial players such as the G20, G8, Financial Stability Board, and the World Bank, IFRS has spread across the globe as the set of standards that can bring transparency, accountability, and efficiency to financial markets worldwide. The political factor has been fully involved in the development of international financial reporting standards, without its involvement the implementation of IFRS at the international level would have been and is impossible.

The recent, new geopolitical changes are a real prerequisite for the return of regional accounting systems. Russia's exclusion from the UN and G8 following the invasion of Ukraine is leading to the formation of new international bodies. For example, Russia has declared the establishment of a new G8 made up of countries that do not apply sanctions to it: China, India, Russia, Indonesia, Brazil, Mexico, Iran, and Turkey (Pravda, 2022), which according to the source, has a GDP per capita 24.4% higher than the current G8. Thus, the expansionist policy of the BRICS group and the attraction of new allies are reshaping the international economy and paving the way for a new world order, which will implicitly have repercussions on the accounting and fiscal structure of these nations.

The strong link between accounting and taxation and the lack of an international tax code is also a geopolitical issue that affects the international accounting system and contributes to its diversification, depending on the tax policy of the nation or group. The lack of an international accounting and tax framework leads to increased economic crime and information asymmetry, which disadvantages the investment environment. We therefore believe that the establishment of regional accounting systems, as well as a regional or international tax framework, would help to reduce economic crime and tax evasion at regional, national, and international levels. Thus, regional accounting could be a mechanism for creating networks of accounting systems, interconnected but with distinctive elements that respond to the economic realities of the group as well as to other stakeholders outside the group. In practice, geo-accounting—depending on geographical location, economic, political, social, religious, cultural, and so on factors—would have a higher level of coverage and satisfaction of stakeholders' information needs and level of disclosure.

With this in mind, we believe that geopolitical changes need to be treated specially by accounting regulators, in particular the accounting profession, as they lead to significant changes in economic relations between companies, which implicitly affect the quality of financial reporting. At the same time, in periods of major geopolitical changes, the information needs of stakeholders are more pronounced, as these changes in the international political and economic arena generate several negative effects on the business environment, and assessing their impact on key economic and financial indicators provides more details about the dynamics of financial performance and soundness, and can thus act to reduce the risk of bankruptcy, business downsizing, or others.

1.5 Summary Conclusions

Being unpredictable and associated with a high degree of other risks, geopolitical risk is considered a threat to global economic stability. In this context, the business community together with regulatory institutions must adopt optimal strategies adapted to economic realities to cope with the effects of geopolitical risk on economic, financial, and social structures. These include building a customised framework of international financial reporting standards to cope with new paradigm shifts in financial reporting.

Geo-accounting can be considered as a possible scenario for the evolution of accounting standards and the functionality of multinationals in the context of the rewriting of the new world order, i.e. the shift of the centre of power. The current geopolitical context may also represent a major issue for the development of the IASB, which has to adapt to the geopolitical situation and adapt IFRS to economic realities, i.e. to support companies in applying accounting policies and practices in a crisis context. The development and sustainability of the International Financial Reporting Standards and their integration into the global system is possible if the IASB declares itself an apolitical institution and reviews its sponsors, which are mainly the USA and Europe, which are directly involved in the political changes of recent times.

In conclusion, the analysis of the effects of geopolitical changes on accounting systems is a perspective that should be considered and developed as we witness an increasing impact of geopolitical risk on accounting. At the same time, we believe that these reflections could be a prerequisite in the reconfiguration of national and/or regional accounting systems, that the accounting valences will develop in parallel with the geopolitical interests of the world's major powers, and that a new global economic reset will also decide a new accounting reset. Therefore, with the transition from US hegemony to a global political multipolarity in which BRICS will perhaps be the strongest pillar, we will also witness a paradigm shift in accounting, simultaneously influenced by the geopolitical factor and artificial intelligence where countries/groups of countries will impose their own rules according to national or group interest, moving from global accounting to geo-accounting.

References

Abdelal, R. (2015). The multinational firm and geopolitics: Europe, Russian energy, and power. *Business and Politics, 17*(3), 553–576.

Balcilar, M., Bonato, M., Demirer, R., & Gupta, R. (2018). Geopolitical risks and stock market dynamics of the BRICS. *Economic System, 42*(2), 295–306. https://doi.org/10.1016/j.ecosys.2017.05.008

Caldara, D., & Iacoviello, M. (2022). *Measuring geopolitical risk. International finance discussion papers 1222r1*. Board of Governors of the Federal Reserve System. https://doi.org/10.17016/IFDP.2022.1222r1

Callahan, W. A. (2016). China's 'Asia dream': The Belt Road initiative and the new regional order. *Asian Journal of Comparative Politics, 1*(3), 226–243. https://doi.org/10.1177/20578911166478

Camfferman, K. (2020). International accounting standard setting and geopolitics. *Accounting in Europe, 17*, 243–263. https://doi.org/10.1080/17449480.2020.1795214

Ceyhan, T., & Gulcan, N. (2022). Jeopolitik risk ile doğrudan yabancı yatırımlar ve finansal gelişmişlik arasındaki ilişki: Kónya panel nedensellik analizi. *Business and Economics Research Journal, 13*(4), 625–637.

Choi, S. Y. (2022). Evidence from a multiple and partial wavelet analysis on the impact of geopolitical concerns on stock markets in North-East Asian countries. *Finance Research Letters, 46*(B), 102465.

Danneels, E. (2002). The dynamics of product innovation and firm competences. *Strategic Management Journal, 23*, 1095–1121.

Depository Trust and Clearing Corporation. (2021, December 7). *Cyber risk seen as top threat to financial markets, with increasing concerns around inflation and climate change, according to new DTCC survey*. Dtcc.com. Retrieved from: https://www.dtcc.com/news/2021/december/07/inflation-and-climate-change-a-growing-threat-to-financial-markets

ESMA. (2022). ESMA report on trends, risks and vulnerabilities. *TRV Risk Monitor*, 2. Retrieved from: https://www.esma.europa.eu/sites/default/files/library/esma50-165-2229_trv_2-22.pdf

EY European Attractiveness Survey. (2022). Foreign direct investment in Europe, a game of two completely different halves: current volatility affects strategy, while long-term attractiveness induces confidence. [Investițiile străine directe în Europa, un joc cu două reprize complet diferite: actuala volatilitate afectează strategia, în timp ce atractivitatea pe termen lung induce încredere.] Retrieved from: https://www.ey.com/ro_ro/news/2022/5/investitiile-straine-directe-in-europa.

Gorgieva-Trajkovska, O., Georgieva Svrtinov, V., & Dimitrova, J. (2013). The future of IFRS (International Financial Reporting Standards). In *Јубилејна меѓународна научнопрактична конференција-Финансиите и финансиското сметководство-состојби, тенденции, перспективи, Стопанска академија Ценов, Свиштов, Бугарија, 2013.* ISBN 978-954-23-0910-9.

Ha, J., Lee, S., & So, I. (2021). The impact of uncertainty shocks: Evidence from geopolitical swings on the Korean Peninsula. *Oxford Bulletin of Economics and Statistics, 84*(1), 21–56. https://doi.org/10.1111/obes.12456

Hudson, R., & Urquhart, A. (2016). War and stock markets: The effect of World War II on the British stock market. *International Review of Financial Analysis, 40*, 166–177. https://doi.org/10.1016/j.irfa.2015.05.015

Huynh, L. D. T., Hoang, K., Hoang, K., & Ongena, S. R. G. (2023). *The impact of foreign sanctions on firm performance in Russia*. Swiss Finance Institute Research Paper No. 23-115. https://doi.org/10.2139/ssrn.4645442

IASB. (2022). *Conceptual framework for financial reporting*. IFRS Foundation.

IFRS. (2019). World Standard-setters Conference. Retrieved from: https://www.ifrs.org/news-and-events/news/2019/09/world-standard-setters-conference-2019

IFRS. (2022). IFRS Foundation's World Standard-setters Conference: A summary. Retrieved from: https://www.ifrs.org/news-and-events/news/2022/10/ifrs-foundations-world-standard-setters-conference-2022-a-summary

Kónya, L. (2006). Exports and growth: Granger causality analysis on OECD countries with a panel data approach. *Economic Modelling, 23*(6), 978–992.

Lee, A. T., & Tran, T. P. (2021). Does geopolitical risk matter for corporate investment? Evidence from emerging countries in Asia. *Journal of Multinational Financial Management, 62*, 100703. https://doi.org/10.1016/j.mulfin.2021.100703

Lee, C. C., & Wang, C. W. (2021). Firms' cash reserve, financial constraint, and geopolitical risk. *Pacific-Basin Finance Journal, 65*(C), 101480. https://doi.org/10.1016/j.pacfin.2020.101480

Nikkinen, J., & Vahamaa, S. (2010). Terrorism and stock market sentiment. *Financial Review, 45*(2), 263–275. https://doi.org/10.1111/j.1540-6288.2010.00246.x

Pástor, L., & Veronesi, P. (2013). Political uncertainty and risk premia. *Journal of Finance Economy, 110*(3), 520–545.

Pravda. (2022). Rusia a inventat un "nou Big Eight - cu Brazilia și Iran". Retrieved from https://www.pravda.com.ua/news/2022/06/11/7351902/

Rashid, A., & Saeed, M. (2017). Firms' investment decisions–explaining the role of uncertainty. *Journal Economic Studies, 44*, 833. https://doi.org/10.1108/JES-02-2016-0041

Russian Ministry of Finance. (2014). Press release: Minister of Finance Anton Siluanov to journalists. Retrieved from https://minfin.gov.ru/ru/document/?id_4=22285

Sandu, R., Zelinschi, D., & Ferry, L. (2022). Struggles in the accounting arena: A geopolitical reading of Romanian accounting reforms. *Accounting History, 28*(1), 143–169. https://doi.org/10.1177/10323732221109658

Smales, L. A. (2021). Geopolitical risk and volatility spillovers in oil and stock markets. *The Quarterly Review of Economics and Finance, 80*, 358–366. https://doi.org/10.1016/j.qref.2021.03.008

Smeets, M. (2018). Can economic sanctions be effective? In *WTO staff working paper, no. ERSD-2018-03*. World Trade Organization (WTO). https://doi.org/10.30875/0b967ac6-en

Sun, J., Makosa, L., Yang, J., Darlington, M., Yin, F., & Jachi, M. (2022). Economic sanctions and shared supply chains: A firm-level study of the contagion effects of smart sanctions on the performance of nontargeted firms. *The European Management Review, 19*(1), 92–106. https://doi.org/10.1111/emre.12497

Thi, T., Nguyen, T., Pham, B. T., & Sala, H. (2022). Being an emerging economy: To what extent do geopolitical risks hamper technology and ISD inflows? *Economic Analysis and Policy, 76*, 728–746.

Trajkovska, O. G., Svrtinov, V., & Dimitrova, J. (2013). *The future of IFRS*. UGD Academic Repository. Retrieved from https://eprints.ugd.edu.mk/8481/1/__ugd.edu.mk_private_UserFiles_olivera.trajkovska_Desktop_Trud-Svistov.pdf

UNCTAD. (2022). *Global foreign direct investment recovered to pre-pandemic levels in 2021 but uncertainty looms in 2022*. Retrieved from https://unctad.org/press-material/global-foreign-direct-investment-recovered-pre-pandemic-levels-2021-uncertainty

Whang, T. (2011). Playing to the home crowd? Symbolic use of economic sanctions in the United States. *International Studies Quarterly, 55*(3), 787–801. https://www.jstor.org/stable/23020066

Wolfers, J., & Zitzewitz, E. (2009). Using markets to inform policy: The case of the Iraq War. *Economica, 76*(302), 225–250. https://doi.org/10.1111/j.1468-0335.2008.00750.x

Yang, M., Zhang, Q., Yi, A., & Peng, P. (2021). Geopolitical risk and stock market volatility in emerging economies: Evidence from GARCH-MIDAS model. *Discrete Dynamics in Nature and Society, 2021*, 1–17. https://doi.org/10.1155/2021/1159358

Zhang, Y., & Hamori, S. (2022). A connectedness analysis among BRICS's geopolitical risks and the US macroeconomy. *Economic Analysis and Policy, 76*(C), 182–203. https://doi.org/10.1016/j.eap.2022.08.004

Chapter 2
Opportunities to Attract Foreign Direct Investments by Leveraging Financial Accounting Information

Financial accounting information is the main tool of communication between the company and its stakeholders, the effectiveness of which is determined by the quality of the reported financial accounting information and the way it is disseminated to stakeholders. The role of economic and financial communication is to strengthen the relationship between the company and its stakeholders through an appropriate presentation of management's ability to create value and raise its profile in the market in which it operates.

Financial reporting that complies with legislative requirements and specific accounting principles may be sufficient for users of financial accounting information, or additional details may be required to meet their needs. From the literature, as well as from the reporting practice of multinationals and larger companies in general, it can be observed that there is a growing interest among users of financial accounting information to integrate non-financial, qualitative, and quantitative information along with "accounting" information. It is believed that this would bring more transparency and efficiency to the financial reporting process, which also boosts the level of investor engagement (Saraite-Sariene et al., 2019). Although this type of information plays an increasingly significant role in the stakeholder communication process, there is a risk of "overburdening" companies with the need to report non-financial indicators or information that do not reflect their real interests or needs (Raucci & Tarquinio, 2020), thus constituting additional costs that cannot generate new added value.

While there is a need and demand to supplement financial and accounting disclosures with other disclosures of high interest to stakeholders, this process cannot be done haphazardly but requires the identification of benchmarks, rules, and principles to support and provide an appropriate framework for these forms of communication. Satisfying the information needs of users of financial information can also be optimised by striking a balance between the "mandatory" information reflected in financial statements and the "useful" information reflected in supplementary

A. Melega, *Geopolitical Risks in Financial Reporting and Transfer Pricing*, Contributions to Finance and Accounting,
https://doi.org/10.1007/978-3-031-76600-8_2

reports, indirectly also contributing to the efficiency of the financial market by attracting direct and socially responsible foreign direct investment. Thus, according to stakeholder theory, the enterprise must satisfy the needs or "create value" for all stakeholders. Increasing the efficiency of the financial market by attracting investment can only be done by creating strong links between the company and all its stakeholders, whether customers, suppliers, creditors, etc. The glue that binds the company and its stakeholders is economic and financial communication, which is mostly realised through financial reporting.

Another very important aspect that attracts the attention of users of financial accounting information is the quality of the information, reflected in its conformity with economic reality and international accounting standards, and this can also be correlated with management expertise and performance (Kaawaase et al., 2021) and/or the internal audit system (Namakavarani et al., 2021). Studies have shown that financial statements prepared under IFRS have higher credibility and recognition than those that comply only with national regulations, which in some cases are not harmonised with international regulations (Bassemir, 2018).

2.1 Stakeholder Theory and Other Users of Financial and Accounting Information

In modern financial systems that are characterised by a wide dispersion of ownership of productive capital, economic-financial communication plays a fundamental role in improving market efficiency, meeting the information needs of all categories of users and attracting financial and human resources for the development of companies (Kirvan, 2020). At the same time, effective economic-financial communication allows to create, develop, and maintain sustainable, qualitative, and professional relations with investors, thus strengthening the strategic and operational credibility of the company, in which sense we can state that information is the basis for the initiation and continuity of the market's operational mechanisms. In this process of financial communication between the company and its economic stakeholders, the company's ability to perform and create value for its stakeholders (Signori et al., 2021) is emphasised first and foremost, the benefits of which will be enjoyed first by investors and then by other categories of stakeholders. Practically, economic-financial communication strengthens these relationships by providing the necessary information support to inform decisions (Roychowdhury et al., 2019). At the same time, Roychowdhury et al. (2019) argue that there are two perspectives of influencing investment decisions that are not mutually exclusive, referring to those characteristics that reflect the quantity and accuracy of reported information, as well as those attributes that capture the nature and extent of communication about a particular transaction or economic event.

Communication theory is the scientific study of the phenomena of transmission or communication of different signals or information between two or more systems of the same or different nature. In the financial market context, the communication process is the set of strategies and tools used to make economic and financial information available to investors and all stakeholders. This process of transforming numerical data into meaningful information for the recipient requires, first and foremost, careful and accurate interpretation, in our context generally referring to the results of a company.

Financial communication is materialised by the totality of a company's initiatives and actions to provide timely information to shareholders as well as other categories of investors about the securities or any other projects or investment portfolios held, this information being also of interest to stock market regulators, supervisors and control authorities, financial analysts, specialised media and the general public (Prutianu, 2000).

Economic communication can be seen as a tool that a company's management uses to encourage the building of a transparent and trusting relationship in particular with investors, as well as to obtain their endorsement of the plan and strategies that the company intends to follow and implement (Coda, 1990). Therefore, financial communication does not only refer to a specific need, but it *"seeks to integrate different forms of communication to different degrees, according to their level of usefulness and contribution to the pursuit and achievement of the desired objective"* (Bertinetti, 1996).

Half-yearly, quarterly, and annual financial statements are the means by which an organisation's management conveys to the market information about its financial position and performance over a period. In other words, financial statements are a company's communication tool with internal or external users of financial information, which they have to subject to an extensive process of analysis that involves the application of methods of comparison, judgment, and evaluation on certain sections of the balance sheet or other components of financial reporting (Hasanaj & Kuqi, 2019). This analysis must be carried out with full attention and responsibility, as based on the obtained results, some of the most important investment, development, and planning decisions are made about the company's strategy and business, which will influence the business in the short, medium, or long term. The way these reports are prepared, as well as the accounting policies and practices applied in their preparation, has a significant impact on the quality level of information provided to the general public.

According to Avram et al. (2017), the role of annual financial statements in financial communication is reflected in the following aspects:

- is a means of knowledge, control, and analysis of the activity of organisations for boards of directors, general meetings of shareholders or associates, as well as for tax institutions, thus enabling the communication of relevant accounting and financial information correctly and clearly
- ensures the dynamics analysis and the communication of the evolution of economic and financial indicators for two consecutive years, through their structure and content
- informs the issuance and implementation of decisions for current and prospective activity
- is an important factor in communicating the information needed to organise and manage accounting

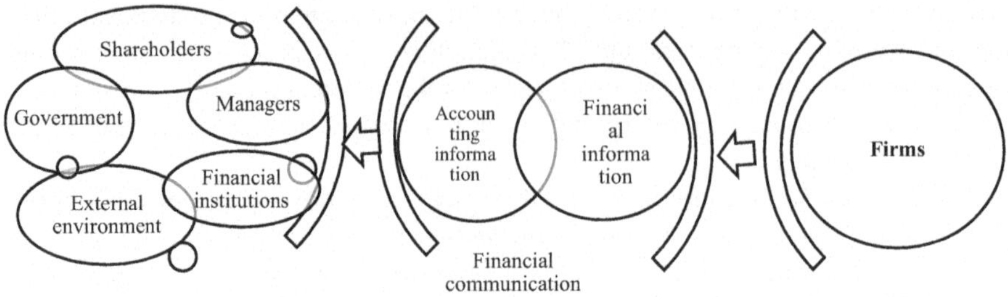

Fig. 2.1 Graphical representation of financial communication. *Source*: Adapted from Lezeu (2004)

Summarising the above, it can be said that financial communication provides financial accounting information on the performance of the enterprise to both the internal and external environment of the enterprise (Fig. 2.1).

Issues such as corporate governance, business ethics, stakeholder relations, transparency, and effective communication are currently the subject of extensive and informed scientific and technical debate. Most studies conducted on this topic tend to confirm that annual financial statements should no longer be a mere purely accounting report, but a forward-looking information package that encompasses areas other than financial, thus providing a much broader perspective on the company's strategies and development directions, not only from an economic point of view, but also from the perspective of corporate governance, environment, and social responsibility, thus increasing the company's competitiveness and value (Li et al., 2018). This also substantiates the need to practice integrated reporting that links financial and strategic performance information in a single report (Navarrete-Oyarce et al., 2021), thus supporting policies that are oriented towards sustainable business development (Avesani, 2020).

The effectiveness of corporate disclosure is of particular importance for listed companies and companies with large-scale shareholdings, the convergence of strong and differentiated interests and information asymmetry generating the need to regulate the relationship between companies and investors—who are the main providers of capital in the context of stock markets—so that stakeholders are protected from the negative manifestation of any conflicts of interest, although both parties promote sustainable value creation (Dallas, 2018). Currently, the provisions contained in IFRS standards aim to provide the most useful and factual information to all stakeholders.

Effective economic-financial communication fosters a correct perception of the returns and results obtained and expected, as well as the related risks, including a full and true appreciation of the company in terms of its economic value. Therefore, if the analysis carried out—taking these aspects into account—shows that the expected return exceeds the cost of capital, then the investment is economically viable and creates value for the investor.

The need for timely disclosure of performance and qualitative reporting of financial statement data requires the involvement of different categories of stakeholders or professional personalities according to the relevant regulatory framework in the preparation, supervision, approval, review, analysis, and use of reports that communicate information and data about a particular company.

Business communication that focuses on the current and future economic, financial, and capital aspects of a company can be:

- basic, which meets legislative regulatory requirements (mandatory reporting)
- voluntary or additional, which represents the shift from a culture of compliance to one of transparency.

Mandatory disclosures derive from legislative constraints aimed at protecting third parties and providing a certain level of security for the company's stakeholders. The IASB's Board of Directors believes that the annual financial statements prepared under International Accounting Standards effectively meet the common and basic information needs of most users.

Voluntary disclosure, on the other hand, is that part of the information provided that is not subject to reporting and certification obligations, regardless of its quantitative (expressed in value or non-value terms) or qualitative nature or the channel through which it is transmitted, which can take different forms such as financial statements, press releases, websites, and others. Voluntary disclosure of economic and financial information therefore aims at meeting stakeholders' expectations by triggering a feedback process on the information received by them.

Considering all the aspects mentioned above, we can appreciate that the process of economic-financial communication has a fundamental role in creating, optimising, and maintaining the relationships between companies and their investors, as well as with other categories of users of financial information. As mentioned above, in the context of the economic-financial communication process, the annual financial reports play a key role in facilitating and building a transparent and efficient relationship between a company and its stakeholders, as they present the company's financial position and performance. Practically, economic-financial communication is the main tool in maintaining sustainable relationships with stakeholders, which according to stakeholder theory is the key to business sustainability (Freeman et al., 2021). Satisfying the needs of all stakeholders is the main objective of stakeholder theory, which promotes equal treatment of all stakeholders, which is opposed to the ideology promoted by investor theory that *"the main purpose of the enterprise is to promote the interests of investors"*, i.e. *"to make a profit at any cost"*. Certainly, the information needs of investors are superior to those of other stakeholders. Their role is central to the sustainability of the business, but the enterprise must provide information that equally satisfies the needs of all stakeholders in such a way as to create interconnected relationships between them. According to Jones (1995), satisfying the legitimate, legal, and moral claims of all stakeholders can be a means for the firm to maximise its total asset value. However, studies in the literature argue that the stakeholder theory should be readapted to the current economic context (Klettner, 2021) characterised by an escalation of investment power, which places investors as the central power in business sustainability. Thus, a hierarchy of stakeholders is created according to their influence on the firm's activity and vice versa—according to the impact of the firm's activity on them. The stakeholder hierarchy has been constructed by many researchers according to the level of influence of different economic, social, or regulatory factors on the firm's activity (Table 2.1).

In this vein, we can observe that all researchers attribute to investors the fundamental role in the sustainability of the business, as they are the category of stakeholders without whom the activity of the enterprise would be impossible since the investment activity of the enterprise is the engine that generates value. Therefore, we argue that the stakeholder theory should be redesigned according to the level of importance of stakeholders for the activity of the investor-centred enterprise, and a direct communication channel with investors would be optimal, as it would strengthen the relationship with them. In the current geopolitical context, investors are strongly affected by the political, economic, social, and military strategies of governments and by the intensification of investment risks and fluctuations in international financial markets. The increase in investment risks generated by the overlapping crises of recent times (health, energy, military, economic, political, social, economic, political) increases the role of economic and financial communication in the investor–business relationship. The need for information of the investors is not limited to the results obtained by the enterprise, but also to the economic, political, social, and military context in which the enterprise operates, as well as its response to the main national and international events. This raises the question of whether current corporate reporting fully meets the information needs of investors and, of course, other parties directly or indirectly involved in the organisation's activities. Being more focused on gross economic, social, and environmental results, economic and financial reporting does not provide concrete data on the impact of political, social, military, macro and microeconomic factors on the obtained results. In practice, taken in isolation, economic and financial reporting is not sufficient for a meaningful analysis of investment risks without taking into account information on the national performance of the economy or industry to which the company belongs.

2.1.1 Objectives of Financial Statements in Relation to the Information Transparency

The purpose of the financial statements is to present as truthfully and fairly as possible a company's assets and liabilities, economic and financial situation. Depending on the fulfilment of the criteria for classification into different categories of companies in terms of size, different sets of financial statements have to be prepared, which consist of a balance sheet, profit and loss account, notes, statement of changes in equity and cash flow statement. The information contained in these reports is of major interest to several subjects such as shareholders, creditors, and credit institutions for whom regular information on the financial position and performance achieved by a company over a given period must be provided. However, the objectives of financial statements are not only limited to these aspects, as these reports are also of particular interest to the company's internal management (Cote, 2020), being

Table 2.1 Classification of stakeholders according to the literature

Authors	Stakeholder categories	Explanations	Examples of stakeholders
Freeman et al. (2018)	Primary	Are involved in value creation and their continued participation is necessary for the firm's survival.	Employees and external stakeholders such as customers, suppliers and financiers, investors, etc.
	Secondary	They do not contribute directly to a firm's value-creation processes and are therefore unnecessary for its survival. However, they have a legitimate interest in the firm's actions and can influence the interests of primary stakeholder groups.	NGOs, trade unions, media, special interest groups, competitors, regulators, and government.
Navarro (2008)	Internal	Directly linked to the business activity.	Investors/shareholders, partners, trade unions, workers, and strategic partners
	External	Linked indirectly to the activity of the enterprise.	Authorities, lobby groups, NGOs, competitors, consumers, etc.
Institute for Higher Business Studies (IESE) (2002)	Consubstantial	Stakeholders without whom the existence of a company would be impossible.	Shareholders and investors
	Contractual	Contractual stakeholders correspond to those with whom the company has some kind of formal contract.	Employees, customers, suppliers, financial institutions, etc.
	Contextual	The contextual ones are those that play a role in achieving the credibility of the organisation and acceptance of its activities.	Society, local and national public administrations, local community, etc.
Kerzner (2013)	Financial	Directly linked to the investment activity of the enterprise.	Investors/shareholders, financial institutions or providers of capital, and creditors.
	Organisational	Directly linked to management activity and strategic business planning.	Executive directors, board, directors, general employees, and administrators
	Product-market	Related to the economic, financial, and social activity of the enterprise.	Customers, suppliers, competitors, trade unions, government agencies, and local government committees.

Source: Adapted from Uribe Macías (2017) and Eisenreich et al. (2021)

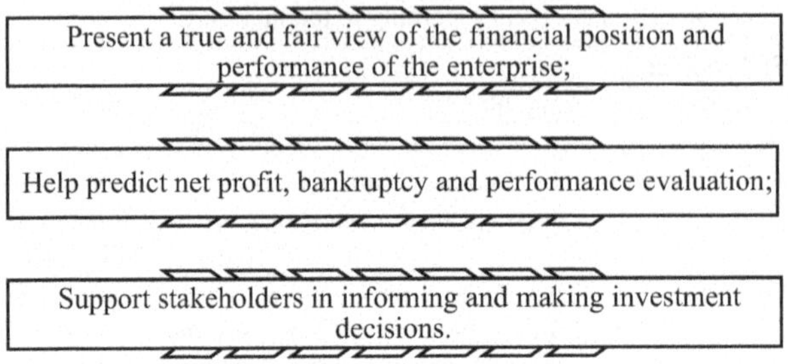

Fig. 2.2 Objectives of Financial Statements under the IASB's General Conceptual Framework. *Source*: Prepared by the author according to the IASB General Conceptual Framework

used as a useful tool for organising and planning internal activities and development strategies.

To meet the needs of information users and to ensure a high level of credibility and originality of the financial statements, it is essential to know the objectives and purpose of the financial statements, which are highlighted in the figure below (Fig. 2.2):

The objectives of financial statements are set primarily according to the needs of external users who do not have the authority to prescribe the desired information and as a result must rely on the information communicated by the information management department (Accounting Standards Board, 1995). This information is formulated and structured to satisfy the common needs and interests of multiple users about the enterprise's ability to generate cash flows, using investment and lending decisions as a guide. Informing both external and internal users about the financial performance and position of the enterprise is also the main objective of financial accounting. For external users of accounting information, financial reports prepared and published regularly are frequently the only source of data collected about an organisation. In the view of Needles et al. (2013), the financial statements represent the current financial position, analysed in terms of liquidity, efficiency, going concern and capital maintenance, as this information is essential for stakeholders such as investors, business partners, and others.

Information contained in financial statements can have a dual function, such as:

- a set of indications and data collected annually which show in a structured, summarised, and simple way the results of the enterprise; therefore, a primary objective of financial statements is to inform particular customers and creditors about the way the business is organised and managed
- not analysed as a set of data but as a collection of monetary and financial values that are used to evaluate the company's management and its evolution over time.

The overall objective of financial reporting is to provide *"financial information about the reporting entity that is useful to existing and potential investors, as well as lenders of credit or loans, in the decisions they have to make about providing resources to the entity"* (CECCAR, 2015). According to Sorter and Gans (1974), the objectives of financial statements can be summarised in the following order (Fig. 2.3):

Objective 1

- *Provide lenders and investors with data they can use to forecast, contrast and assess potential cash flows in terms of uncertainty, timing and associated value.*

Objective 2

- *Primarily for the benefit of those users who regard them as the primary source of information about the economic activities of an enterprise and who have limited access to other sources of information..*

Objective 3

- *Providing data to users to forecast, contrast and assess the earning power of businesses.*

Objective 4

- *Providing data that can be used to assess the enterprise ability to efficiently allocate resources to achieve its main objective.*

Objective 5

- *Providing interpretive and factual transaction and other data that are useful in forecasting, contrasting, and evaluating the firm's earnings power. With respect to the interpretation, evaluation, prediction or estimation, the fundamental assumptions underlying them should be publicly disclosed.*

Fig. 2.3 Objectives of the Financial Statements. *Source*: Adapted from Sorter & Gans, 1974

Financial statements are therefore a corporate communication tool designed to keep stakeholders informed about the financial and economic situation of the company. As these reports are the main communication tool used by a company to illustrate its current financial situation and the forecasts for its activities in the short term, these documents must be accessible to all users of financial information. As mentioned earlier, the objectives of financial statements focus on the informational interests of the users, being the main means of providing reliable, certain, and credible information (Lennard, 2007). According to Hampton (1977), the objective of financial statements is *"to convey understandable information about certain financial aspects of the business, and they may reflect the financial position at a point in time as presented in the balance sheet or a series of activities over a period of time, a role fulfilled by the income statement"*. FASB (2008) argues that financial reporting does not have a purpose in itself, but is intended to provide information that is useful in making economic and business decisions: *"The objectives of financial reporting are not immutable, but are affected by factors specific to the economic, legal, political, and social environment in which economic activity is conducted and in which financial reporting takes place"*. Summarising the above, we can state that the primary objective of financial statements is to provide credible and reliable information to meet the information needs of all stakeholders. The fundamental objective or role of the financial statements is to provide information of a superior quality to facilitate decision-making and the formulation of opinions on the activity of the enterprise and its impact on the social, economic, and environmental environments. However, we can subscribe to the fact that the objectives of financial statements can take different connotations depending on the environment in which a company operates or the strategic planning of its management. Therefore, the objectives of financial statements may sometimes not be in line with national or international regulations on financial reporting, and they are often tailored to the overall objectives of the company, sometimes even subject to fraud. The literature refers more to the general objectives of financial statements in line with international standards and principles, ignoring the fact that they can be adapted to the company's development directions. Achieving the fundamental objectives of financial statements can only be done by increasing the level of disclosure and transparency of information which is one of the main prerogatives of international financial reporting principles and standards in meeting the information needs of stakeholders.

2.1.2 Limits and Obstacles in Meeting Stakeholders' Information Needs with a Focus on Investors

As already mentioned, financial statements are the main information tool used by a company and they are considered *"a means by which the company communicates information about its economic activity both to external users (such as financiers, suppliers, business partners, etc.) and to the company's management"* (Bencini & Mancaruso, 2016). Salvioni (1992) argues that *"financial statements are the most widespread instrument of global economic communication aimed at periodically conveying potentially satisfactory information about the basic guidelines and related methods of maintaining economic and management conditions"*. Rees (1990) states that *"the annual financial statements of a group of enterprises or an individual company constitute the basic tool used in forecasting and analysing accounting data by financial analysts"*. Therefore, the primary role or objective of financial statements is to provide information on the state of the position and performance of the enterprise for all categories of stakeholders. Because of the large number of users of these types of information and the different economic, legislative, political, and social contexts in which companies operate, financial statements cannot fully and timely meet the needs of all stakeholders (Roy et al., 2017), as each stakeholder is interested in certain information that may not be reflected in the financial statements at all or in some contexts, it is addressed in a rather abstract manner, making it difficult to meet the information needs of all stakeholders. Often, accounting professionals prepare financial statements to meet the needs of particular users of financial information, in line with business purposes. The main limitation of financial statements is therefore their neutrality which, after several legislative interventions, has been regulated as a qualitative characteristic of financial statements, but which cannot be absolute despite all the existing rules.

Financial statements are documents which reflect in a summarised and simplified way the economic and financial realities of the enterprise and are prepared by accounting professionals. The personnel responsible for preparing financial statements must present, interpret, and evaluate the activities of the enterprise in a limited way, depending on the possessed expertise, acquired knowledge, and gained experience and skills, influenced by the professional judgment developed during work (Prayoga & Afrizal, 2021). The limitations associated with the interpretation and analytical skills of accounting professionals can lead to incorrect valuations that do not reflect the reality of the economic and financial situation of the enterprise, as they must provide information in a clear, truthful, and accurate manner. However, ensuring these attributes depends on the professional's competence and attitude. Melis (2008) argues that *"the discretion inherent in the valuation process should not be used by those who prepare financial statements to manage the information for their own or the company's governing purposes"*. This side of judgment and interpretability of financial information can generate a certain level of mistrust in the relationships specific to such a context, thus highlighting a negative aspect of the disclosure function of financial statements.

Based on our literature review, accounting regulations, and conceptual framework, we have identified the following limitations of financial statements (Fig. 2.4).

The financial statements present information at historical cost (Sihna, 2009). Transactions are initially recorded at cost, and the values of assets and liabilities may change over time. Some items such as marketable securities are modified to match changes in market values, but other items such as fixed assets may remain unchanged. Thus, the balance sheet could give an incorrect picture if a large part of the values presented are based on historical costs.

The financial statements are not adjusted for inflation (Pleşco, 2013). When preparing the financial statements, the inflation rate is not considered, so if inflation is relatively high, the amounts associated with the assets and liabilities on the balance sheet will appear extremely low, because they are not adjusted for inflation.

The financial statements do not include some intangible assets. Many intangible assets are not recorded as assets; instead, any subsequent expenditures related to an intangible asset are immediately recorded as current expenses. This policy can drastically understate the value of a business, particularly when large investments are made to build a brand or develop new products.

Financial statements only cover a certain period. A user of financial statements may get an incorrect view of a company's financial results or cash flows by analysing only a particular reporting period. The results of any period may vary with

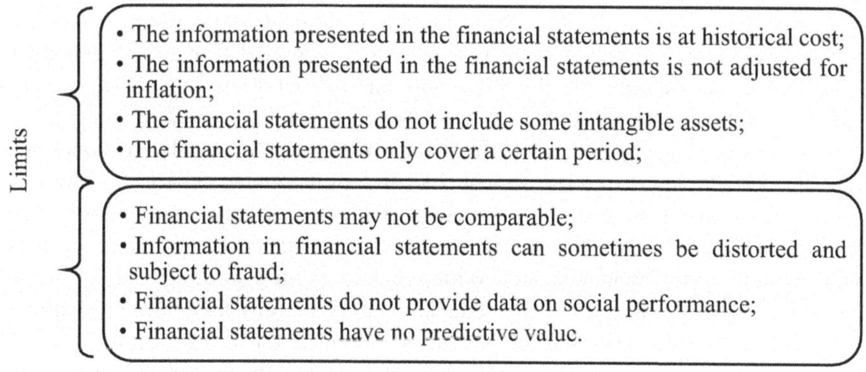

Fig. 2.4 Limitations of Financial Statements. *Source*: Developed by author

positive or negative fluctuations, depending on various internal or external factors such as an increase or decrease in sales volume due to an increase or decrease in demand for the offered products or services, employee performance, seasonality of business, macroeconomic equilibrium, political and legislative stability, and the level of social security.

Financial statements may not be comparable. If a user wants to compare the results of different companies, their financial statements are not always comparable because entities use different accounting reporting practices, depending also on the applied legal framework.

The information in financial statements can sometimes be distorted and subject to fraud. A company's management team may deliberately distort the reported results, which can occur when there is more or less justified pressure to report excellent results.

Financial statements do not provide data on the social (Feleagă, 1996) and environmental *problems/outcomes* as a result of the activities carried out by the enterprise.

Financial statements have no predictive value. The information in a set of financial statements provides information about the historical results or financial condition of an enterprise at a particular date but does not provide any information about future events.

The literature points out that the main limitations and obstacles to financial accounting disclosures are attributed to the process of convergence of national accounting standards (GAAP) to the international accounting framework (Table 2.2). The implementation of IFRS is a laborious and lengthy process, and during the transition period, due to the lack of infrastructure, skills, and competencies required by IFRS, the information presented by companies that have adopted IFRS may be distorted and of poor quality.

Thus, we can appreciate that financial statements are a set of documents with a high level of usefulness, but before any investment decision, it is very important to perform a detailed analysis of them to identify the limits that could distort their content and level of reliability. If initially the question of the limits and obstacles arising from the level of disclosure and transparency of information was raised, a very important aspect is the linguistic and textual elements of economic and financial communication. Even if there is a general conceptual framework issued by IASB that aims to standardise the micro and macrostructure of financial communication, there are divergences in the interpretation of standards or of certain balance sheet items due to the limitations of financial reporting professionals. Informational limitations lead to increased investment risks and limit companies' access to foreign direct and socially responsible investments, which are currently a lifeline for some economies in the context of overlapping crises. In this respect, regulators, together with accounting professionals, need to intervene to identify solutions that minimise the limitations and obstacles of financial statements, thereby facilitating stakeholders' access to truthful information that can be the basis for fair decisions. Some of the limitations of financial statements are detrimental to the accounting profession as they are strictly related to the level of training of accountants, which can be

Table 2.2 Limits and obstacles to financial statement disclosures

Obstacles and limits	Explanations according to the literature
Accounting professionals' limited judgment	The limited judgment of accounting professionals in applying IFRS, driven by the lack of the unique skills and abilities required by International Financial Reporting Standards, leads to distorted financial reporting. Depending on the chosen strategy, nations that have implemented IFRS face various problems related to the ability to verify its correct application. According to Herbert et al. (2014), the lack of qualified auditors and accountants who are technically capable of implementing IFRS is one of the biggest obstacles encountered during the implementation process, leading to errors in financial reporting, especially the use of old practices under national standards. The challenges related to limited professional judgment are intrinsic to human behaviour. Inadequate incentive mechanisms, insufficient support from board members and management, inadequate training and professional development, problems in managing accounting changes, and poor allocation of resources and internal staff are just some of the list of limitations and obstacles that can be encountered in quality financial reporting. When these issues are combined with business models, their uncertainties and complexities, limited accounting judgment is further threatened, leading to inappropriate application of IFRS, which ultimately affects the quality of financial accounting information presented in financial reports.
Technical and process barriers	Poor business performance will inevitably make IFRS implementation prolonged or completely unsuccessful (Herbert et al., 2014). Technical and process barriers are associated with both process management and limited professional judgment. The existence of limited resources, inadequate skills functionality and management below the application level imply transactional handicaps. The lack of IT specialists with technical knowledge of IFRS who can interpret and translate IFRS into IT changes, the level of information technology (IT) infrastructure required in a company, the conversion needs across business entities and nations, the overlap of global and national regulatory considerations, and the complexity of IFRS technical accounting standards are just a few examples of technical and process impediments that translate to the quality of financial reporting.
Knowledge of international accounting practices	Prepared following Generally Accepted Accounting Principles (GAAP) for different nations, financial statements will be viewed from different angles by a user, even if some nations have adopted IFRS partially or fully. Thus, there is an issue of informing users of financial statements (Ikpefan & Akande, 2012).
Vocational training	The lack of training facilities and university curricula is one of the barriers to the full implementation of IFRS. According to Ikpefan and Akande (2012), stakeholders should train IFRS practitioners and integrate IFRS into university accounting curricula.
Taxation	Accounting professionals face issues related to taxation and the convergence of national legislation with IFRS. How are tax liabilities resulting from GAAP and IFRS convergence handled under current tax law? If this issue is not managed, the organisation will have to undertake additional administrative work (Ikpefan & Akande, 2012).

(continued)

Table 2.2 (continued)

Obstacles and limits	Explanations according to the literature
Fair value	In the IFRS format, fair value is used to measure most items in the financial statements, which leads to subjectivity and volatility in determining fair value. Ikpefan and Akande (2012) consider that it is debatable whether this adjustment should be used when calculating distributable profit when it appears in the income statement as a gain or loss.
Reporting system	IFRS reporting and disclosure requirements need to be adapted by companies by modifying their current business reporting models. To correct this anomaly, information systems must be created to incorporate the new requirements on related party transactions, segment reporting, fixed assets, etc. Reducing the risk of business interruption would be possible through effective internal control (Ikpefan & Akande, 2012).
Changing the law	IFRS will lead to inconsistencies with existing legislation. Different regulators are currently dealing with the reporting requirements and their rules take precedence over other laws. Although IFRS does not recognise such overriding laws, steps should be taken to amend them so that they are updated promptly (Ikpefan & Akande, 2012).

Source: Adapted from Ikpefan and Akande (2012) and Herbert et al. (2014)

removed by organising refresher courses. However, other limitations are legislative, requiring the intervention of national and international regulatory bodies, with the process sometimes delayed by political factors and government priorities. At the same time, the limitations and obstacles of financial statements lead to a failure to achieve their purpose and objectives in the process of communicating with stakeholders. In this line of ideas, it is circumscribed that informational limitations practically contribute to the increase in the level of information asymmetry which is in antithesis with the stakeholder theory.

2.1.3 Prospects for Developing Stakeholder Theory in the Current Global Geopolitical Context

The recent social, political, military, and health disruptions have reshaped the entire international business environment by redirecting investment flows towards business environments that offer higher security of invested capital at the expense of access to rich and cheap resources. In the context of the military and social crisis at the European Union's borders, the main concern of stakeholders is "security", whether we are talking about investors who want "investment security" or civil society who wants "security of a stable livelihood in conditions of peace and equity". Basically, in these times, stakeholders are seeking to fulfil survival, security, and social needs, and the need for information circumscribes these needs. Thus, the enterprise must provide information to stakeholders that underpins this safety, connecting all stakeholders around this need. By providing stakeholders with a guarantee of security, the company credits its security. According to the stakeholder theory that was developed by Freeman (1984), the enterprise must respond to the needs of all individuals and groups of people directly involved in the enterprise's activities or whose interests are affected by its activities. Therefore, the management of the enterprise must identify the needs of all stakeholders and respond to them equally, thereby achieving a balance between their interests. Integrating stakeholder theory—which is a norm of business ethics—into management strategies ensures the sustainable development of the business and increases the overall value of the enterprise. Aligning organisational interests with the interests of all stakeholders (Shah & Guild, 2022) is a successful model for charting a sustainable business path. The same idea is sustained by Bundy et al. (2018) who argue that "management can benefit more from cooperative behaviour by effectively sharing values and strategies and aligning their interests with stakeholders". However, management prioritises stakeholders according to their level of importance in the organisational framework, giving priority to those that are essential to the business. This is especially accentuated in times of crisis when the main goal of the firm is to minimise the effects of the crisis on its investment activity, which is proven also by Gonzalez-Perez et al. (2021) who argue that in times of crisis, "organisations prioritise stakeholders that provide resources essential for survival".

According to Zech (2013), stakeholders are affected and involved to different extents in times of crisis and therefore "their needs and requirements need to be balanced and prioritised wherever appropriate, and professional crisis management and crisis communication can help build support and trust in companies from all stakeholders". In practice, meeting stakeholders' needs is influenced by communication management in times of crisis and beyond. For effective communication with stakeholders and to satisfy their information needs, the company needs to prioritise them according to their relationship with the company and at the same time classify their needs into: primary, secondary, and tertiary. Maslow's pyramid can be used as an example of how to categorise these needs, as the model can be adapted to the needs of stakeholders. For example, the common and primary need for all stakeholders is survivability or safety: employees want a safe working environment and optimal working conditions, while investors want security of investment or the creation of trustful links with the company. Crane (2020) argues that focusing on trust as a fundamental need of all stakeholders empowers mutually beneficial and productive relationships that facilitate value creation. In other words, the enterprise must create value for all stakeholders, thereby creating interconnections between them. Also, according to Bonnafous-Boucher and Rendtorff (2016), the firm must continuously monitor "how such interconnections impact key stakeholders and the organisation and how the views of these stakeholders directly impact the success of the firm's strategic measures". However, stakeholder theory becomes touchy for the enterprise, considering that personal needs always prevail over the needs of others and thus there will always be stakeholders who are kept close to the enterprise, stakeholders who are aligned with the needs and strategies of the enterprise, and stakeholders who are somewhat isolated or left in the shadows. As long as the main goal of enterprise management is profit generation or profit maximisation, there will be priority and non-priority stakeholders. According to Narbel and Muff (2017), stakeholder theory cannot produce its full effects as long as it "is anchored in the traditional view of the firm, defining it as an entity whose legitimate purpose is to generate economic value for itself and its owners, relying on regulation as a compensatory mechanism for the externalities it generates". These aspects can be considered the main limitations of the stakeholder theory, as it is too generalist, in the sense that the needs of some stakeholders will always be prioritised over others: "stakeholder theory cannot be a theory for everyone" as Freeman et al. (2020) stated.

Stakeholder theory adapted to the current needs and context can become a perspective for strategic management in managing stakeholder relations, and to truly become a "theory" for the enterprise, it is necessary to realise a general epistemology of it and to eliminate contextual overlaps between ideas. At the same time, we believe that stakeholder theory should be superimposed on shareholder theory, in the sense that "yes", the enterprise should create value for all stakeholders but in the order of their participation in the enterprise, with the centrality given to investors. Through investment, value can also be created for other stakeholders. For example, investing in a new production unit generates new jobs (social need), contributes to reducing unemployment, and increases the revenues of local public budgets through taxes. Therefore, we can say that investors/shareholders are the main actors in creating value for enterprises and other stakeholders.

2.2 Quality of Financial Statement Information and Attracting Foreign Direct Investment

The integrity of financial reporting and accounting standards are considered essential components of an economy's financial regulatory framework. It has generally been argued that financial accounting information prepared under generally recognised principles or standards will ensure or contribute to transparency and accountability, optimal corporate governance, stability of the financial system, efficient functioning of financial markets, and appropriate allocation of capital and resource flows. The quality of financial statement disclosures about a nation's level of development has been a topic of debate for researchers, with a focus on the implications of adopting or implementing IFRS as financial statement disclosure quality standards and on the attraction of socially responsible foreign direct investments by emerging and developing economies (Table 2.3). The competition of the world's economies to attract foreign investments has accelerated the process of convergence of national accounting standards to the international accounting benchmark, with a focus on the quality of financial reporting and economic and financial communication with stakeholders, especially investors. Therefore, the quality of financial statement disclosures is a determining factor in attracting foreign direct and socially responsible foreign investments, as this information is the fundamental tool for decision-making and investment risk assessment. At the same time, companies that prioritise high-quality disclosures in their financial statements and sound environmental, social, and governance (ESG) practices are more likely to attract socially

Table 2.3 Meta-analysis of works on IFRS adoption, quality of financial statement disclosures, and FDI attraction

Author	Research aim/purpose/question	Results
Cieslik and Hamza (2022)	This paper is based on the proposed eclectic paradigm as an analytical framework to investigate the effects of IFRS adoption on FDI inflows.	Findings indicate that FDI inflows are positively associated with IFRS, and countries that implement accounting standards receive a higher increase in FDI inflows. Furthermore, the results show that institutional quality plays an important role in attracting FDI.
Oberholzer et al. (2022)	The study aims to determine the success rate of African countries that have adopted IFRS in attracting FDI.	The authors conclude that with the adoption of IFRS as a similarity between the sample countries, they experienced different degrees of success in attracting foreign investments. At the same time, the authors argue that we need to understand that IFRS adoption cannot and does not guarantee an equal degree of success in attracting foreign investments.
Omotoso et al. (2021)	The adoption and implementation of IFRS is expected to enhance the quality and credibility of financial statements in terms of reliability, transparency, and comparability. As a consequence, it implies improving the functioning of the capital market and influencing the flow of foreign investment to IFRS adopters.	Consistent with decision utility theory, the findings indicate that foreign portfolio investment is attracted to companies whose financial statements are prepared under IFRS. The adoption of IFRS is a change in the information environment that removes information barriers faced by users of financial statements. The development of IFRS contributes to improving the usefulness of financial reporting by facilitating comparability and reliability of financial information. This influences foreign investors to move their capital to such an economy, consequently increasing the flow of foreign investment.
Nurunnabi (2006)	The objective of this study is to summarise the literature on the economic impact of the implementation of International Financial Reporting Standards (IFRS).	There is significant evidence that adopting a set of high-quality harmonised accounting standards (e.g. IFRS) fosters trade and foreign direct investment (FDI), financial transparency and comparability and reduces information asymmetries.

(continued)

Table 2.3 (continued)

Author	Research aim/purpose/question	Results
Mameche and Masood (2021)	The paper aims to analyse the association between IFRS adoption and FDI in the Gulf Cooperation Council (GCC) countries from 1980 to 2017, using the autoregressive distributed lag autoregressive model.	Their results showed that IFRS in the GCC countries had a positive effect of about 3% in the short run, while in the long run, it led to a 10.4% decrease in FDI. They argue that the negative association can be explained by the fact that foreign investors may see the increased quality of IFRS financial reporting as an important cost.
Apriana and Irawan (2019)	This study analyses the effect of tax incentives and IFRS adoption on foreign direct investments in ASEAN countries using panel data regression.	The results indicate that IFRS adoption in the ASEAN region has a positive effect on FDI inflows. The results support that harmonisation of local standards with IFRS leads to increased FDI inflows. Uniform accounting standards make it easier for investors to compare information. At the same time, the authors argue that companies can improve the efficiency of the financial reporting process beyond standardisation.
Yousefinejad et al. (2018)	The paper aims to examine the quality of financial reporting and its effect on attracting FDI.	According to the study, IFRS and FDI are linked through information asymmetry. Overall, the authors concluded and confirmed the strong positive relationship between IFRS and FDI inflows, providing sufficient evidence and arguing that IFRS is a significant factor in improving FDI inflows, thus contributing to economic growth.
Beneish et al. (2015)	The study investigates whether the mandatory adoption of IFRS is associated with increased foreign portfolio investment in financial markets.	IFRS adoption has a significantly larger effect on external debt than on foreign equity flows. This result is consistent with the idea that debt investors are larger consumers of financial statement information. At the same time, the authors argue that IFRS is more likely to reflect an improved quality of financial reporting than greater comparability of financial statements.

Source: Adapted by the author according to the literature

responsible investors (SRI). This is because investors are interested in investing in companies that are transparent and accountable and offer high-quality disclosures in financial statements. Therefore, these qualities can help companies improve their reputation and gain the trust of stakeholders, leading to increased access to capital and lower cost of capital.

According to the above meta-analysis, we can observe that most studies attribute the quality of financial statement disclosures to a positive role in attracting foreign direct investments. The information costs generated by the poor quality of financial information, amplified by information asymmetries reflected in the institutional, linguistic, political, geographical, and historical barriers that persist between nations, impact economic actors operating within these borders and lead to reduced FDI inflows and socially responsible foreign direct investments. At the same time, they represent an obstacle to the current trend towards globalisation of capital flows that allows the free flow of capital to those economies that have the best reward system according to current risk-reward attributes. The implementation of IFRS does not ensure that the quality of disclosures in financial statements will improve and lead to higher levels of foreign direct and socially responsible investments as long as the other institutional components do not match the level of quality that investors want. For example, some researchers argue that there is a negative association between the adoption of International Standards and the level of FDI inflows (Efobi et al., 2014; Nnadi & Soobaroyen, 2015), while other empirical studies argue that there is no association between IFRS and FDI (Owusu et al., 2017). This demonstrates that investors' interests are not only about the quality of financial statement disclosures, but a broad spectrum of opportunities that the investee country could offer.

Investors are the main consumers of financial accounting information, and the quality of this information and the way a company communicates with them can have some influence on their attractiveness for investment projects, especially in times of crisis, when the predictability of return and risk of invested capital is one of the main concerns. At the same time, high-quality financial statements increase not only the trust of investors but also that of lenders and other stakeholders, thus contributing to a favourable investment climate. To enhance the quality of financial statement disclosures, a key role is assigned to the harmonisation of accounting policies and treatments that facilitate financial accounting communication among stakeholders worldwide, thereby removing information barriers to the flow of socially responsible foreign direct investment flows.

Therefore, the quality of information presented in financial statements plays a key role in promoting economic stability at the global level. In an economy characterised by large and rapid international capital flows, transparency and accuracy in the timely provision of economic data can reduce uncertainty and improve the ability of the market and investors to assess risks.

For financial statements to achieve their objective of *"providing financial information about the reporting entity that is useful to existing and potential investors, as well as to different classes of creditors in the decisions they make about providing resources to the entity"* (CECCAR, 2015), they must provide comparable, qualitative, and verifiable data. The IASB's General Conceptual Framework for Financial Reporting sets out some qualitative characteristics that financial statements should meet, and these are also taken up in the national accounting regulations of different countries in the form of principles.

According to ESMA guidance (2014), *"Qualitative characteristics are the attributes that determine the usefulness of the information provided in financial statements. The four most important qualitative characteristics are understandability, relevance, credibility and comparability"*. Qualitative characteristics apply equally to financial information in general-purpose financial statements as to financial information provided in other ways.

The general conceptual framework of financial reporting classifies the qualitative characteristics of financial information into (Fig. 2.5):

- Fundamental quality characteristics
- Amplifying quality characteristics

According to Van Beest and Boelens (2009), fundamental qualitative characteristics are the most important and determine the content of financial statement disclosures, and amplifying qualitative characteristics are the characteristics that amplify the usefulness of accounting information.

Relevance and faithful representation (reliability as it is referred to in the literature) are important qualities of financial reporting that both the Financial Accounting Standards Board (FASB) and the International Accounting Standards Board (IASB) use in standard setting (IASB, 2018a, 2018b, 2018c). Relevance refers to the presentation of information on the subject matter that can help users of financial information make the right decisions in a given context. In other words, relevance addresses the appropriateness of accounting methods/policies, practices, and information (e.g. fair value, historical cost) in a financial information user's decision-making, and for it to be recognised as relevant, it must have a confirmatory value of past events and predictive value that provides predictive power of possible future events (CFI Team, 2022).

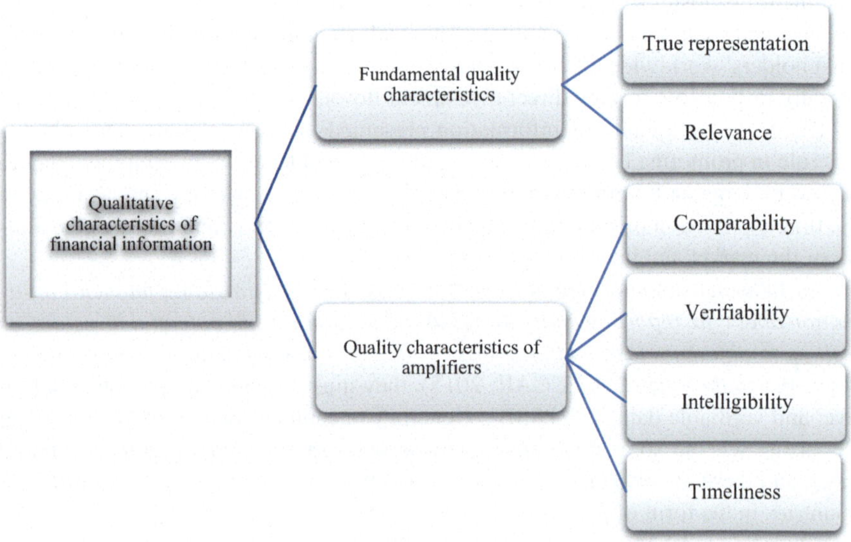

Fig. 2.5 Qualitative characteristics of information presented in the financial statements. *Source*: IASB (2018a, 2018b, 2018c)

In terms of faithful representation, it is concerned with the presentation of complete information without errors or omissions (Abdel-Khalik, 2019) about the phenomena occurring in the enterprise. Presenting information in financial statements without errors does not mean "perfect in all respects", because no matter how much effort accounting professionals put into preparing financial statements, they will not be able to accurately present all the transactions taking place in the enterprise. In the transactions that occur every day, some estimates of prices are made that cannot be determined to be accurate or inaccurate. The conceptual framework states that *"a representation of this estimate can be faithful if the amount is clearly and accurately described as an estimate and the nature and limitations of the estimation process are explained"* (CECCAR, 2015). While relevance and faithful representation are necessary for information to be useful in decision-making, information can be relevant without being reliable and can be reliable without being relevant (FASB, 2010).

The conceptual framework informs the process of applying the fundamental characteristics, which consists of three steps. The first step is to identify the economic phenomenon whose information may be useful to users of financial information, followed by a process of assessing and analysing that phenomenon, which concludes by determining the type of information that the phenomenon generates. The information shall be accurately analysed and evaluated to determine whether it provides an accurate representation of the economic phenomenon.

Comparability, verifiability, timeliness, and understandability are qualitative characteristics that enhance the usefulness of information that is relevant and faithfully represents the economic phenomena occurring in the enterprise. Information in financial statements cannot be relevant and reliable if it is not timely and cannot be compared, verified and, of course, understood by all users of financial information.

The comparability of financial information enables users of financial information to make comparisons between data presented by different companies in different business environments, which is only possible when the same accounting principles are used in the preparation of financial statements. Comparability of information is not only about comparing the financial data of different companies but also about comparing data from the same company but from different financial years. Thus, a high level of comparability of financial statements leads to more accurate forecasts of profits and performance in general, resulting in lower costs of acquiring information and more financial information with a higher level of quality (Endrawes et al., 2020).

Verifiability implies that different independent and informed observers can reach a not necessarily complete consensus or agreement that a given representation is faithful.

Intelligibility. To facilitate economic decision-making, one of the characteristics that accounting information must possess is that it is readily understandable by a reader of financial statements who has at least a reasonable understanding of the dynamics of the business, accounting, and economic activity, and the willingness to examine the information with normal diligence. If this knowledge is not possessed by the reader, the specific accounting language of financial statements could be a communication barrier that disrupts the transfer of this information (Zadorozhnyi et al., 2021). Therefore, as much as possible, financial statements should be presented in a way that allows them to be understood by different categories of users of financial information.

Timeliness means "providing timely information to decision-makers so that they can base their decisions on current and substantiated information specific to the relevant economic context. In general, the older the information, the less useful it is. However, some information may continue to be timely long after the end of the reporting period because, for example, some users may need to identify and assess changes in the financial performance and financial position of the enterprise" (IASB, 2018a, 2018b, 2018c).

Several studies can be found in the literature on the qualitative characteristics of financial information and their impact on the profitability of the firm's business. Most studies focus on the study of qualitative characteristics based on a relationship between earnings and returns or value relevance. Most common studies discuss value relevance, analysing or relating two fundamental characteristics, namely relevance and faithful representation (Barth et al., 2001). Kadous et al. (2011) argue that in the context of fair value measurement, users of financial information do not consider relevance and faithful representation as independent characteristics. Power (2010) argues that faithful representation was developed by the FASB and IASB to better suit the use of fair value which was perceived to be more relevant (useful for decision-making) (Table 2.4).

Therefore, qualitative characteristics, considered either individually or as a group, cannot make information useful if that information is irrelevant, or does not provide an accurate representation of the economic phenomena occurring in the enterprise over a period. Therefore, fundamental and enhancer quality characteristics are closely interrelated, with one characteristic maximising the value and importance of another. The quality of financial accounting information plays an essential role in investment decisions, mitigating risks and also helping to reduce information asymmetry, which is a major impediment for investors in the correct and efficient allocation of investments.

2.2.1 Impact of Accounting Policies on the Quality of Financial Statements and Attracting FDI

The overlapping crises of the last 3 years have shown us that financial statements should provide users with financial information with a higher level of usefulness in management decision-making. The challenge is therefore to redesign IFRS standardised accounting policies and treatments to enhance the transparency and efficiency of global capital markets. Today's financial markets are not fully transparent and prices do not reflect all the information held by management and often do not directly correlate with their fundamental value. There is a growing need for tools to measure the performance of companies, as it is clear that valuations based on cost

Table 2.4 Findings from the literature on the qualitative characteristics of financial accounting information

Characteristics			Findings from the literature	Author
Qualitative characteristics of financial information	Fundamentals	Faithful representation	Accounting theory does not guide at all the definition of a faithful representation of the economic phenomena it intends to represent. The lack of specified conditions for recognising reliable financial information affects the purpose of financial reporting. The confirmatory and predictive value of financial information that is currently demanded by stakeholders shows the need to redefine the concept of faithful representation to ensure its conformity with the conceptual accounting framework and at the same time, to take into account modern information content.	Strojek-Filus et al. (2015)
			It is difficult to measure faithful representation directly by providing only an assessment of the annual report, as information about actual economic events is needed to ensure faithful representation.	Botosan (2004)
			Accurate representation of the investment climate and financial reporting information has a significant role to play in attracting foreign direct investment and ensuring predictability of earnings.	Shollapur et al. (2010)
		Relevance	Relevant financial information can influence a decision by helping consumers to make predictions about past, current, and future outcomes, confirming or correcting previous assumptions.	Shaikh et al. (2022)
			Accurate representation and relevance have greater potential to improve the quality of financial reporting.	Mbobo and Ekpo (2016)
	Amplifiers	Comparability	Comparability of financial statements decreases the cost of acquiring information and increases the overall quantity and quality of information available to stakeholders.	de Franco et al. (2011)
			Comparability is the qualitative characteristic that enables users to identify and understand the similarities and differences between items. It helps investors, creditors, and other third parties to make informed capital allocation decisions. The achievement of comparability depends on the application of a common set of financial reporting standards and their requirements, particularly those relating to the measurement and recognition of assets and liabilities. Greater comparability can reduce the costs of comparing investment opportunities and improving the quality of financial reporting information.	Barth (2013)
			Comparability of financial information contributes to a more efficient allocation of capital and effective analysis of investment risk.	Chauhan and Kumar (2019)
		Verifiability	Verifiability is "a quality that can be demonstrated by achieving a high level of agreement between different measures using the same method; it is the extent to which information is reproducible given the same data and assumptions".	DeLone and McLean (2003)
			Verifiability is used to assure users that the information faithfully represents economic reality. However, some cases and items cannot be verified in financial information because they may require necessary disclosure of the underlying assumption. The verifiability of financial statements has a significant positive effect on the return on equity.	Amahalu and Obi (2020)
			Increased verifiability allows financially constrained firms to finance projects by pledging more assets to lenders, making contract renegotiation in times of distress more difficult and increasing the likelihood of bankruptcy. Reforms that improve asset verifiability have a substantial impact on access to sources of credit.	Giambona et al. (2022)
		Intelligibility	Financial statements can be somewhat difficult for the uninitiated to understand, so they should be prepared in such a way that users can understand their content. Intelligibility will increase when information is categorised and presented clearly and concisely.	Zayol et al. (2017)
			A positive relationship was found between understanding financial statements and investment decisions.	Agaregh and Eneji (2017)
		Timeliness	Timeliness is measured by using the natural logarithm of the number of days between the end of the financial year and the signature on the auditor's report or the date on which the financial statements were made public.	Vestine et al. (2016)
			Financial reports are used by investors and lenders to decide where to invest or not to invest their scarce resources in a particular organisation. The timeliness of financial information has a significant influence on investment decisions.	Minnis and Shroff (2017)

Source: Adapted by the author from literature

alone are a significant limitation in the presence of volatile values to ensure the quality and transparency of financial information.

Therefore, in the current market scenario that requires companies to provide timely financial information, directly linked to their fundamental value, it is essential to show a high level of adaptability to the varying information requirements of stakeholders, aiming to satisfy them by using a language that is as accessible as possible, but professional at the same time. This need is particularly acute in companies listed on regulated markets or large international groups. These new information requirements are putting pressure on management and accounting professionals in small and medium-sized enterprises, which are at the core of the business environment in terms of economic contribution and local social support, given the predominance of this category in the structure of national economies.

According to the National Action Plans on Business and Human Rights (2022), there are an estimated 400 million SMEs at the global level, which constitute *"the backbone of economies worldwide, being the main source of job creation worldwide, accounting for over 95% of enterprises and between 60% - 70% of jobs"*.

In recent years, there has been a significant number of such companies that have decided to prepare their financial statements under the International Financial Reporting Standards issued by the IASB (IAS/IFRS), even though they are not, in substance, required to do so, suggesting that certain benefits of this practice have been identified, among which we can mention the following (Këri & Jupe, 2018; Mohamed et al., 2020; Zahid & Simga-Mugan, 2019):

- The possibility of attracting more investments
- The possibility to perform comparability analysis
- Increased reliability of financial statements
- IFRS reporting is more comprehensive and addresses issues not covered in the national accounting standards
- Increased efficiency of audit missions and SME assessment processes
- In some contexts, IFRS reporting is more simplistic than that under national accounting standards, with detailed information available on how to implement them.

The fact that SMEs are increasingly interested in preparing their financial reports following IFRS requirements confirms the growing need for improved economic and financial information communicated outside the corporate context, as well as for better readability on an international scale and a common accounting language that can provide the basis for developing comparative analysis.

The need for a single set of global financial reporting standards is associated with the phenomenon of globalisation of the world economy, with the degree of integration and globalisation of financial markets having increased significantly in recent decades. A materialisation of this statement can be seen in the fact that 495 companies from 47 countries are currently listed on the New York Stock Exchange, representing 20% of all listed companies and 33% of total market capitalisation. Recognising the interdependence of international capital markets, IFRS is the set of global standards needed to underpin and enhance the sustainability of the global economy.

In this regard, more and more countries are beginning to use the IFRS framework as a reference point in developing regulations on the preparation of financial statements by companies, as it has been found that their application contributes to increased transparency and quality of the reporting process (Key & Kim, 2020), reducing the cost of capital (Saha & Bose, 2021) and initiating the investment flows. To ensure a certain level of transparency and credibility in stock markets, most legislative forums in countries around the world have made it mandatory for companies operating in such financial markets to prepare and report financial statements under the International Financial Reporting Standards. At present, these standards are the only ones that ensure a relatively optimal level of transparency, quality, and comparability of financial statements, which simplifies the process of cross-border financial communication so specific to a highly globalised economy such as the one we live in.

The adoption of International Financial Reporting Standards at the level of listed entities has enormously influenced the quality of financial and accounting information and has strengthened the communication relationship between all stakeholders. With the adoption of IFRS by listed entities, a decrease in the frequency of financial scandals has also been noticed, which are caused by intentional misinterpretations of various rules, principles, and regulations or even their willful omission in the development of financial strategies, planning, and forecasts. Abata (2015) argues that the global adoption of IFRS is an essential tool in reducing or mitigating financial reporting offences, as the quality of financial reporting is significantly and positively influenced by its proper application (Benyasrisawat, 2011).

The impact of IFRS adoption on the quality of financial reporting has been discussed in several studies such as the one of Morais and Curto (2008) who, by comparing the accounting data of 34 Portuguese-listed firms, analysed whether IFRS adoption can be associated with an increase in revenues and high-value relevance of financial accounting information. The results of the research showed that IFRS adoption was associated with an increase in revenue, while the value relevance of financial accounting information decreased. Chen et al. (2008) compared the quality of financial accounting disclosures of listed companies in 15 EU member states before and after the adoption of International Financial Reporting Standards and found that most of the financial accounting disclosure quality indicators improved after the adoption of IFRS by the companies in the analysed EU member countries.

Qu et al. (2012) analysed investors' reactions to financial disclosures published both pre- and post-IFRS convergence in China. Considering sample data from 309 listed Chinese companies and using multiple regression analysis, they observed that IFRS adoption increased the quality of financial accounting disclosures for investors in the Chinese A-share market. They also found that earnings per share relative to the book value of equity is a key determinant of market returns both before and after IFRS adoption. The adoption of International Financial Reporting Standards by listed companies in China has led to increased shareholder credibility of earnings reported by listed companies in the collateral pricing. The post-IFRS convergence period has seen increased investor trust in financial statement disclosures.

With the adoption of International Financial Reporting Standards by listed companies, higher profitability has been observed on both domestic and foreign exchanges, as well as fewer transactions at undervalued prices. The benefits of adopting IFRS are also reflected in a visible increase in investments, facilitated by the increased quality of the information presented in the financial statements and their high level of comparability.

Preparing financial statements under IFRS enables decision-makers in different capital markets to have access to the same high-quality information at an affordable cost. Tweedie and Seidenstein (2005) argue that the establishment of global accounting standards that are consistent, comprehensive, and based on clear principles would contribute to the smooth and efficient functioning of international capital markets and the growth and consolidation of corporate financing sources.

The structure of sources of corporate finance is important, as the raising of capital from different internal and external sources of finance requires an increasing level of public accountability, transparency, and communication. This is particularly true in countries such as the United States of America (USA) and the United Kingdom (UK), where stock markets are highly developed and where a significant number of corporations are owned by a wide range of shareholders. Here, managers attach significant importance to the requirements of investors, whose interests have come to dominate the structure and content of financial statements.

In contrast to these countries, in Germany, Japan, and Switzerland, banks are a much more important source of funding, so their interests tend to influence the preparation of financial statements more than those of investors.

From the above examples, we can conclude that financial statements are prepared to cater more to a particular category of users of financial information, namely those who have a higher contribution to capital funding. The application of IFRS by listed companies stimulates investors' interest and willingness to trade because, firstly, they replace country-specific national standards and therefore reduce the costs of information processing and, secondly, IFRS are of higher quality than many other national standards, increasing the visibility of investments and ensuring equal accessibility for all information users.

2.2.2 Opportunities to Reduce Information Asymmetries

The accounting information reflected in financial statements is particularly important as it is on this basis that investors construct their investment decisions and initiatives in a stock market. Global financial markets therefore attach great importance to the preparation and regular dissemination of this information to investors. According to Al-Shabib and Al-Jabouri (2005), any defect in this information leads to information asymmetry, which contributes to low financial market efficiency and is directly reflected in stock prices.

Disclosure of financial statements should provide similar information to all parties and reduce or eliminate any information discrepancy among investors.

Information asymmetry is generally defined as the difference and divergence in information available to users of financial information. It is also defined as *"incomplete or inadequate information characterised by variation in the amount of information available to different parties involved in transactions, which therefore does not place them on an equal footing in transaction processing"* (Wang et al., 2011). Brown and Hillegeist (2007) highlighted that *"information asymmetry arises when some investors obtain private information while other investors have only publicly available information"*.

To create a satisfactory image that facilitates benefits (e.g. obtaining loans), in financial statements that are made public, companies sometimes present a financial performance that does not correspond to reality, precisely to meet their financial reporting objectives by exploiting their internal information advantage (Roychowdhury et al., 2019). This raises issues of asymmetry and credibility of information presented in the financial statements. For example, in some transactions taking place in the securities market, investors who only had access to public information that was misrepresented are subject to higher investment risk than other investors who had access to the correct information. Information asymmetry should be viewed through the prism of the usefulness of the information presented in the financial statements. Useful can be defined as information presented in a reliable, credible, and timely manner to all stakeholders.

Asymmetry of information leads to a lack of credibility of the information presented in the financial statements. The information shows signs of asymmetry in market exchange conditions due to the behaviour of trading entities. The lack of ability to accept it as it is, as well as the desire to convey to the public a deliberately erroneous situation or only a certain part of the reality of an enterprise, causes "some individuals to act in such a way as to convey only certain information (which is in their interest), others to conceal it, partially disclose it or present it in such a way as to improve their image or at least not to worsen the existing one" (Yasinskiy, n.d.).

The credibility or reliability of information in financial statements is considered to be one of the most important characteristics of financial accounting information for their users. Reliability of information is a qualitative characteristic acquired by financial accounting information, under the condition that national and international accounting principles and regulations are considered in the preparation of the financial statements. Inaccurate or distorted information is the result of the influence of political, economic, and cognitive factors.

Today, users of financial information are concerned about the veracity of the information presented in financial statements, a concern that has been heightened by the numerous financial scandals (the Enron scandal in the US, the Wirecard scandal in Germany, the Xerox scandal, the Parmalat scandal, etc.) that have resulted in distorted, false or even fraudulent information being presented to the public. Economic crime "typically involves complex methods of misusing or misdirecting funds, overstating revenues, understating expenses, overstating the value of corporate assets, or under-reporting the existence of liabilities (this can be done either manually or through deep learning). All of these actions or schemes may involve one or more employees or even individuals in management, bank accounts or a company itself, and are misleading to both investors and shareholders" (Financial Scandals, 2003).

As a result of the financial scandals and thus the misrepresentation of financial accounting information, West (2003) posed the question, *"Is there still credibility in the current accounting system?"* This doubt about the credibility of the information that financial statements provide has arisen because accountants or accounting professionals who prepare financial statements must make *"independent judgments about the truth and accuracy of the information in annual financial statements, a privilege granted by accounting rules"* (Bayou et al., 2011). Misrepresentation of financial information only amplifies its asymmetry, thereby diminishing the credibility or relevance of the information presented in the financial statements, putting their users in a difficult position.

The extent to which investors rely on the information reported in financial statements depends on the credibility of those financial statements, i.e. the trust or belief that investors have in the financial statements under review. Companies usually confirm the credibility of financial statements with the help of an independent auditor who is responsible for verifying the accuracy of this information. However, the effect of the audit on the credibility of the financial statements depends on the independence of the auditor and the thoroughness with which the audit engagement is carried out. An increase in the credibility of reporting can also positively influence the extent to which investors rely on financial statement information both for entering into loan agreements that govern the terms under which capital is exchanged and for general information about the operations and performance achieved by companies. As a result, an increase in reporting credibility can increase a company's access to external financing, which can enhance its ability to invest in new projects.

Financial accounting information is highly relevant to all users of financial information, and how it is presented and the accounting principles and practices underlying the financial statements are essential in determining their credibility and quality. The presentation of distorted information, which is sometimes subject to fraud, amplifies the asymmetry of information which is a limitation of the financial market faced by users of information.

The integration of capital markets, the internationalisation of business and, in general, the globalisation of the economy has highlighted the need to create a universal accounting language to provide users of financial information with comparable and easily understandable information. The process of preparing financial statements is influenced by the accounting system of the country in which the entity operates, which in turn is influenced by the social, political, and cultural factors of the country. Therefore, different environments generate different accounting rules and consequently make financial statements not easily comparable.

To overcome these critical issues, international organisations have started a process of worldwide harmonisation, standardisation, and accounting convergence since the last century, by developing standards and principles that can be globally applied, namely those mentioned so far throughout this paper: the IAS/IFRS.

International accounting convergence is expressed both in eliminating differences between national accounting standards and in improving the quality of national accounting standards, thus allowing greater comparability. The process of international accounting convergence is driven by the need to reduce the risk associated with the free movement of capital and the cost of acquiring it, by enhancing the comparability of data and information. The premise of accounting convergence is the internationalisation of accounting, a process that will facilitate a global collaboration between companies, the best-known example of international convergence being between US GAAP and IFRS.

In 2002, the IASB and the FASB signed a joint agreement, the so-called Norwalk Agreement, in which they committed themselves to develop a set of accounting principles that could be used both nationally and internationally (Memorandum of Understanding, 2002). The convergence process continues for the time being with the elimination of differences between IAS-IFRS and US GAAP. The main problem of convergence is that IAS/IFRS and US GAAP are two fundamentally different accounting systems: the US GAAP is based on detailed rules that emphasise legal form rather than economic substance as is the case with IAS-IFRS. This difference in turn implies other differences in the recognition and measurement of revenue and extraordinary items, the practice of inventory valuation methods, and the presentation of income statements and balance sheets (Saleha et al., 2020).

Convergence promotes harmonisation and represents the integration requirements of international economies. Any organisation that wants to remain in the international market cannot ignore the trend of international convergence of accounting regulations that differ from one country to another depending on the peculiarities of the economic environment, legal system, cultural philosophies, regulatory structures, and users of accounting information. Without considering national circumstances, level of audit development, or environmental performance, not all countries may be able to achieve real convergence. Convergence is driven by several factors, including the belief that the existence of a single set of standards (IFRS) will increase the comparability of accounting data of different entities and thus reduce information asymmetry, facilitating investment flows.

Information asymmetry is one of the biggest problems faced by users of financial information and the quality of accounting information suffers as a result. However, the process of convergence to IFRS could mitigate the negative effect of information asymmetry, thereby improving the quality of financial statements. Disclosure asymmetry may be reduced after the adoption of international standards, as the main objective of accounting harmonisation is to improve the relevance and comparability of disclosures.Information asymmetry is a condition in which information is not fully shared between individuals who are part of the economic process; therefore, some of the users of financial information have access to more information than the rest of the participants and can take advantage of this configuration. This creates an imbalance of power in transactions, which can sometimes cause transactions to fail, leading in the worst case to some kind of market failure or deadlock. The reliability and relevance of financial information depend on the accounting principles applied. In addition, for better comparability of results, it is necessary to provide a regulatory framework at the international level for the disclosure of financial information so that the decisions to be taken are fair and well-informed (Turki et al., 2017). Standard-setting bodies assume that by applying the conceptual framework developed by the IASB, a reduction in information asymmetry is generated, which reduces the risk perceived by investors and consequently the cost of capital. However, contrary to the expectations of standard setters, Cuijpers and Buijink (2005) and Daske (2006) find an insignificant relationship between the voluntary adoption of IFRS and the cost of capital.Foreign investors prefer markets with fewer information asymmetries and high-quality financial information that allows them to evaluate investment prospects at a lower cost (Nejad et al., 2017). Therefore, International Financial Reporting Standards are used as one of the critical elements to increase transparency and reduce information asymmetries. Many proponents believe that "IFRS reporting is of higher quality than GAAP-compliant reporting and that their adoption improves financial transparency, decreases information asymmetry in capital markets, promotes cross-border comparability, attracts foreign capital inflows, and consequently lowers the cost of capital" (Levitt, 1998).In the hope of decreasing information asymmetry and providing users of financial information with accurate and relevant information, a large number of the world's countries have embarked on a process of convergence to International Financial Reporting Standards. The IASB supports countries that intend to adopt IFRS by providing them with a conceptual framework and guidance on the necessary steps they need to take in adopting IFRS.International Financial Reporting Standards are the main language of communication for users of financial information and are widely used worldwide. According to data from the IFRS Foundation, International Financial Reporting Standards are currently mandatory in 144 jurisdictions for companies listed on a regulated market, with another 12 jurisdictions allowing their use (IASB, 2018a, 2018b, 2018c) (Fig. 2.6).The adoption of the international accounting framework at a global level will considerably reduce information asymmetry, providing users of financial information with an appropriate framework for conducting transactions and reducing investment risks. Information asymmetry,

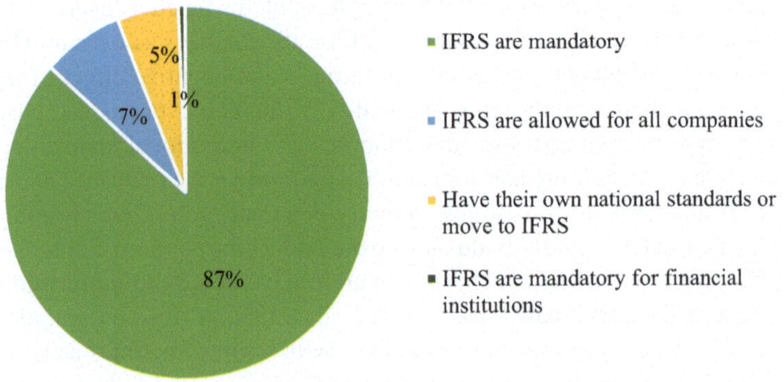

Fig. 2.6 Using International Financial Reporting Standards internationally. *Source*: IASB (2018a, 2018b, 2018c)

however, can arise when entering a new market. Known as the "North-South" model, it presents a situation where private capital typically flows from developed to emerging countries. The "South-South" model, whereby firms in emerging markets invest in other emerging markets, and the "South-North" model, whereby emerging economy nations invest in developed economies, are the results of changes in FDI flows. The challenges faced by foreign investors are largely the same as those faced by domestic investors, but they also face additional challenges that expose them to a higher cost of capital. By improving external monitoring, the adoption of IFRS is anticipated to help reduce information asymmetry. According to Barth et al. (2008), IFRS adoption can reduce the cost of capital by increasing comparability and transparency. Due to lower risk premiums, they facilitate company valuation for potential foreign investors and increase the value of firms. A nation can adopt IFRS in one of three way: endorsement, wholesale adoption, or convergence. A nation can completely abandon its national accounting standard in favour of IFRS without making any changes for several reasons, including lack of manpower, practical reasons, or economic considerations. In a converged adoption, national regulations are gradually adapted to IFRS requirements. This strategy is preferred by nations such as the US, China, and India, where IFRS were not immediately incorporated into their accounting system. Comparable areas are identified and divergent areas are gradually brought closer to IFRS. Using this method, the regional or national body scrutinises IFRS before adopting them into law. This strategy will result in the country or region having a particular version of IFRS that allows flexibility in dealing with country or region-specific accounting issues with a consistently tailored solution (Nnadi, 2011). The literature has provided strong evidence on the benefits of IFRS adoption on FDI flows. According to Marquez-Ramos (2008), the process of accounting convergence in the EU has helped to reduce unfamiliarity and information asymmetries between firms in different countries. This led to a decrease in information costs, which in turn encouraged international trade and FDI flows.

According to the study of Portes and Rey (2005), market investors have been shown to have variable and unequal access to the information needed to value financial assets. It draws attention to the mismatch in the international capital market, which has been exacerbated by information asymmetries and familiarity effects. Studies suggest that the lack of information available as a result of information asymmetries is of much greater importance compared to the investment diversification opportunities offered by foreign markets. Therefore, understanding accounting principles can improve access to the information needed to value assets in different markets and help reduce or eliminate information asymmetries. Therefore, improving the comparability, transparency, and ease of understanding of financial reporting will contribute to increasing the amount of capital raised through FDI. Accounting can be the method of describing or presenting the location and performance of an enterprise. The information asymmetries resulting from disparities in accounting standards have a significant impact on the flow of foreign direct and socially responsible investments, as they play a key role in how investors allocate their resources when investing in another country.

2.3 Adopting IFRS and Attracting Foreign Direct Investment in BRICS Economies

In the context of globalisation and the development of international relations between the countries of the world, more and more attention is being paid to foreign direct investments, and more recently to socially responsible investments. Investment cooperation plays an important role in the economies of many countries and contributes to economic growth. Thanks to foreign investments, recipient countries have the possibility and the resources to modernise roads and information infrastructure, invest in research and development activities supporting the production of new technologies, invest in education or support various social projects that increase the quality of life, all of which contribute to stabilisation and stimulation of the national economy, leading to increased international competitiveness.

In the literature, a country's economic growth is also correlated with the level of efficiency, transparency, and performance of the national accounting system, as accounting is an important component of a country's overall contribution to economic development, and its improper or erroneous application can be a significant impediment to the recording of economic progress (Gray & Roberts, 1991). According to Hope et al. (2006), the adoption of IFRS in accounting reporting practice is a tool through which countries can improve their legislative regulations to provide greater protection for investors and their interests and make their capital markets more accessible to foreign investors by increasing the transparency and comparability of financial accounting information. Efficient allocation of resources is essential for an economy to stimulate the most productive sectors and thus generate growth. Therefore, in an environment where accounting information is not perceived to be viable and reliable, inefficient allocation of resources is very likely, but as mentioned earlier in this paper, the adoption of IFRS can improve the quality of financial accounting information, thereby also leading to an increase in the efficiency of capital allocation (Owusu et al., 2022). Since these aspects of interest to investors are improved by the adoption of the IFRS reporting framework, we can appreciate that it also leads to an increase in their trust in the information received, which will allow a correct substantiation of investment decisions with a positive impact on the flow of foreign direct and socially responsible investments.

Recently, the focus has shifted from attracting foreign direct investments as a simple source of financing for the economy to a socially sustainable source focused not only on generating profits but also on contributing to the social and economic development of the host country. This approach recognises that investments can have both positive and negative impacts on local communities and emphasises the importance of investing in a responsible, sustainable, and mutually beneficial way. To this end, investors should have a long-term perspective that considers the social and environmental impacts of their investments. They should engage with other stakeholders and local communities to understand the needs, concerns, and priorities of the community and strive to build relationships that enable them to contribute to social and economic development in a way that respects local culture, values, and traditions. In general, socially sustainable foreign direct investments are a holistic investment approach that prioritises social and economic development while being accountable, transparent, and inclusive. In practice, investments have the potential to bring positive change and encourage investors to adopt a long-term vision that prioritises social, environmental, and economic sustainability.

In today's global context, various economic cooperation initiatives provide benefits to all participating countries that pursue and actively engage in achieving common goals. From the multitude of such economic cooperations existing at the global level, we will focus our attention on an association of emerging economies—these having the main potential for global economic growth (Dolgikh, 2017)—namely, 5 of the largest, represented by Brazil, Russia, India, China, and South Africa, known by the acronym BRICS. The foundations for this cooperation were laid in 2001 (Chen, 2022) and this grouping of states has continued to develop to this day by seeking various opportunities for cooperation in areas such as trade, investment, infrastructure development and other areas of interest to them that would strengthen their position and competitiveness on the international stage.

Although the topic of the impact of IFRS adoption on foreign direct investment flows is a current and interesting topic, we can note that the literature is not abundant with papers related to this topic, especially regarding the BRICS countries. Dolgikh (2017) conducted a study that analysed the evolution of the accounting system and legislation of Russia, India, and Brazil, as well as their progress in the process of alignment with international standards and principles stipulated in IFRS, taking as analysis period the years 2001–2014 and highlighting the evolution of foreign direct investment flows for the same period. Out of all the three countries, Brazil shows the highest increase in FDI inflows, with the value obtained in 2014 being almost 7 times higher than in 2005, having adopted the IFRS framework since 2007. India has also recorded increases in FDI inflows, but only adopted IFRS in 2016, so this increase—which is not as sharp as in Brazil—cannot be attributed to the benefits of IFRS adoption. As for Russian FDI inflows, they are almost half the amount in 2014 compared to 2010, as Russian companies have been able to apply IFRS since 2011. Therefore, in the same analysed period, it can be observed that different results can be obtained for the considered countries, which means that the implementation of IFRS at the national level is not the only factor able to influence the trend of the FDI inflows. The manifestation of the economic effects of IFRS implementation is likely to depend on the functionality of the institutional infrastructure, as well as the strength and capacity of national institutions to implement the regulations and programmes of the reference field (Henock & Oktay, 2012), as well as other internal or external factors.

A concrete example of this is reflected in the results of DeFond et al. (2018) which show that after the adoption of the IFRS framework by China, FDI inflows have not increased, finding evidence of declining volumes in some contexts. They find that the returns of foreign institutional investors have also declined, especially among investors from countries with weak legal systems and weak institutions in terms of the implementation of investment mechanisms that have also adopted the IFRS framework. Therefore, the paper concluded that China's weak institutional infrastructure hinders the IFRS adoption objective of attracting institutional investments by improving the quality of reported financial information. Regarding the FDI inflows in South Africa, Nnadi and Soobaroyen (2015) find that legal and socio-economic factors, including the rule of law, the legal system, and the level of corruption, play a much more important role in attracting FDI to African countries than the mere adoption of the IFRS framework. However, IFRS adoption is nevertheless found to significantly increase the value of South African companies as the country has a relatively more developed capital market than many other African countries, thus being a potential for the country to benefit from the implementation of market-oriented accounting legislation such as the IFRS framework (Agyei-Boapeah et al., 2020).

Therefore, although the adoption of IFRS in accounting reporting practice simplifies the process of international financial reporting thus stimulating cross-border capital transfers, there are other risks than those related to the quality of financial information for FDI flows and these can refer to: political environment (Rafat & Farahani, 2019) that involves the international diplomatic status and image, as well as the domestic status reflected in the existence or non-existence of civil or ethnic conflicts and in the centralised or decentralised economic policies practiced by authorities; fluctuating behaviour of regulatory authorities (Zhang, 2022) which may not provide the optimal level of regulatory stability and predictability, so necessary in business planning processes; governance infrastructure (Ross, 2019) which refers to the inability of some states to absorb socially responsible foreign direct investments due to the lack of infrastructure to implement an effective investment mechanism; other issues that fall outside the ability of companies to control or influence in order to attract foreign direct investments.

We can observe that the impact of IFRS framework adoption on the flow of foreign direct investment is different in the five countries that form the BRICS economic cooperation. This phenomenon is caused by fundamental differences between these countries related to the political and cultural environment, the type of economy (centralised or decentralised), the stability, balance, and predictability of the legislative system, the institutional infrastructure, the degree of openness to foreign markets, and so on. Therefore, although there is evidence that the adoption of IFRS increases the quality of financial and accounting reporting and thus of communication with stakeholders, in some countries, this effect is not always translated into a positive influence on the flow of foreign direct investments, as other influencing factors significantly reduce this advantage of IFRS adoption.

2.4 Summary Conclusions

The value or importance of the information reflected in financial reports is determined by the quality of the information. Based on this premise, to satisfy the information needs of stakeholders, companies should design financial reports following accounting rules, principles, and standards, as financial communication plays an important role in the company's relationship with its stakeholders.

In the context of economic and financial communication, financial statements are considered the main information tool for stakeholders, playing a fundamental role in determining the level of corporate transparency. However, financial statements cannot fully satisfy the information needs of stakeholders, which is why other information on various non-financial indicators (social, environmental, and governance) are reported alongside the core financial statements, highlighting the level of corporate responsibility of the reporting company, while having the potential to enhance the value of the company. Stakeholders have different information needs, and of these, it is certainly that the shareholders are most in need of a clear overview of the company's strategies, path, and business development directions, but also of a more in-depth view focused on the achieved performance indicators and the practical results in reaching the performance targets set by different development strategies. From another perspective, we can analyse the creditors who are interested in the company being well managed by the management so that the uncertainty and risks related to the credit granted are brought and kept as low as possible, while suppliers are more interested in understanding the company's expansion prospects that could influence the existing contractual relationships and of course whether it is solvent, thus ensuring business continuity. On the other hand, each of the customers in the company's portfolio has different interests depending on the product or service purchased from it. Therefore, meeting the information needs of all stakeholders is not a simplistic process, but one that requires effort, study, involvement, and initiative on the part of the people responsible, who of course need to have the knowledge and skills to carry out this work effectively.

Another very important aspect for stakeholders is the quality of the information reflected in the financial reports, the level of which is determined by the extent to which the qualitative characteristics discussed above, namely relevance, comparability, reliability, and understandability, are reflected in the content of the financial reports. It is possible to make decisions that have a real contribution to increasing the competitiveness of economic entities if they are based on qualitative financial accounting information.

Analysing the information presented in financial statements is an important step in the decision-making process. From the analysis of the financial statements, it is possible to determine the financial position of a company, how it has performed over a certain period and what future trends might materialise. Such reports can be used to inform shareholders about how profitable their investments are, as their main aim is to make a return on their capital allocation. The BRICS countries have seen an increase in foreign direct investment inflows since 2000, despite having poor infrastructure, technological gaps, and unskilled labour compared to those of developed nations. Trade openness, macroeconomic stability, and infrastructure are the main drivers of FDI in BRICS nations. However, it has also been shown that market size, labour costs, financial crisis, and good governance are not important factors for FDI. To remain competitive in global trade, BRICS nations need to advance infrastructure development and maintain macroeconomic stability. In addition, the BRICS need to increase trade openness by removing trade barriers through policies such as trade goods deductions and tax exemptions. Implementing liberal trade policies and improving the quality of institutional governance to attract more

FDI agents in the future are the biggest challenges for the BRICS countries to maintain their performance in FDI inflows. The stability and economic growth of the BRICS countries lead to optimistic prospects for FDI inflows; therefore, trade openness and good infrastructure will continue to be the main determinants in the future.

Finally, we would like to add that making informed decisions that are in line with reality and contribute to solving the problems arising in the company's activity depends on the quality of the information provided in the financial reports. At the same time, investment performance is directly influenced by the quality of the information, faithful representation, and correct application of accounting practices and policies, so that they do not distort the information, but correctly reflect the position and performance of the enterprise, which is the main concern for users of financial information, being a tool for assessing risks and determining the effectiveness and efficiency of the economic activities.

References

Abata, M. A. (2015). The impact of International Financial Reporting Standard (IFRS) adoption on financial reporting practice in the Nigerian banking sector. *Journal of Policy and Development Studies, 9*(2), 169–184.

Abdel-Khalik, A. R. (2019). Failing faithful representations of financial statements: Issues in reporting financial instruments. *Abacus, 55*(4), 676–708. https://doi.org/10.1111/abac.12176

Accounting Standards Board. (1995). *Exposure draft statement of principles for financial reporting*. ASB.

Agaregh, B. A., & Eneji, I. G. (2017). The impact of financial information on investment decisions: A review of literature. *International Journal of Accounting Research, 5*(2), 91–96.

Agyei-Boapeah, H., Machokoto, M., Amankwah-Amoah, J., Tunyi, A., & Fosu, S. (2020). IFRS adoption and firm value: African evidence. *Accounting Forum, 44*(3), 238–261. https://doi.org/10.1080/01559982.2020.1766755

Al-Shabib, D., & Al-Jabouri, A. R. (2005). The importance of the development of the securities control authority to raise the efficiency of the financial market. In *The fourth scientific conference*. Philadelphia University.

Amahalu, N. N., & Obi, J. C. (2020). Effect of financial statement quality on investment decisions of quoted deposit money banks in Nigeria. *International Journal of Management Studies and Social Science Research, 2*(4), 99.

Apriana, Y., & Irawan, T. (2019). The impact of tax incentives and IFRS adoption on foreign direct investment in ASEAN countries. *International Journal of Innovation, Creativity and Change, 5*(2), 1195.

Avesani, M. (2020). Sustainability, sustainable development and business sustainability. In *Life cycle sustainability assessment for decision-making* (pp. 21–38). Elsevier. https://doi.org/10.1016/B978-0-12-818355-7.00002-6

Avram, C. D., Avram, M., & Drgomir, I. (2017). Annual financial statements as a financial communication support. *Ovidius University Annals, Economics Sciences Series, 17*(1), 406.

Barth, M. E. (2013). Global comparability in financial reporting: What, why, how, and when? *China Journal of Accounting Studies, 1*(1), 2–12. https://doi.org/10.1080/21697221.2013.781765

Barth, M. E., Beaver, W. H., & Landsman, W. R. (2001). The relevance of the value relevance literature for financial accounting standard setting: Another view. *Journal of Accounting and Economics, 31*(1–3), 77–104. https://doi.org/10.1016/S0165-4101(01)00019-2

Barth, M. E., Landsman, W. R., & Lang, M. H. (2008). International accounting standards and accounting quality. *Journal of Accounting Research, 46*(3), 467–498. https://doi.org/10.1111/j.1475-679X.2008.00287.x

Bassemir, M. (2018). Why do private firms adopt IFRS? *Accounting and Business Research, 48*(3), 237–263. https://doi.org/10.1080/00014788.2017.1357459

Bayou, M. E., Reinstein, A., & Williams, P. F. (2011). To tell the truth: A discussion of issues concerning truth and ethics in accounting. *Accounting, Organizations and Society, 36*(2), 109–124. https://doi.org/10.1016/j.aos.2011.02.001

Bencini, F., & Mancaruso, M. (2016). Le analisi di bilancio alla luce di Basilea 2. *Contabilità, Finanza e Controllo, il Gruppo 24 Ore, 1*, 20.

Beneish, M. D., Miller, B. P., & Yohn, T. L. (2015). Macroeconomic evidence on the impact of mandatory IFRS adoption on equity and debt markets. *Journal of Accounting and Public Policy, 34*(1), 1–27. https://doi.org/10.1016/j.jaccpubpol.2014.10.002

Benyasrisawat, P. (2011). *Earnings persistence, value relevance, and earnings timeliness: The case of Thailand*. Doctoral Thesis, Durham University.

Bertinetti, G. (1996). *Comunicazione finanziaria aziendale e teoria della finanza*. Egea.

Bonnafous-Boucher, M., & Rendtorff, D. J. (2016). *Stakeholder theory: A model for strategic management*. Springer.

Botosan, C. (2004). Discussion of a framework for the analysis of risk communication. *The International Journal of Accounting, 39*(3), 289–295. https://doi.org/10.1016/j.intacc.2004.06.007

Brown, S., & Hillegeist, S. (2007). How disclosure quality affects the level of information asymmetry. *Review of Accounting Studies, 12*(2–3), 443–477. https://doi.org/10.1007/s11142-007-9032-5

Bundy, J., Vogel, R. M., & Zachary, M. A. (2018). Organization–stakeholder fit: A dynamic theory of cooperation, compromise, and conflict between an organization and its stakeholders. *Strategic Management Journal, 39*(2), 476–501. https://doi.org/10.1002/smj.2736

CECCAR. (2015). *Cadrul general conceptual, paragraful OB2, în lucrarea Standardele Internaţionale de Raportare Financiară (IFRSs). Norme oficiale emise la 1 ianuarie 2015* (p. A25). Partea A, CECCAR.

CFI Team. (2022). Qualitative characteristics of accounting information. Retrieved from: https://corporatefinanceinstitute.com/resources/knowledge/accounting/qualitative-characteristics-of-accounting-information/

Chauhan, Y., & Kumar, S. B. (2019). Does accounting comparability alleviate the informational disadvantage of foreign investors? *International Review of Economics & Finance, 60*, 114–129. https://doi.org/10.1016/j.iref.2018.12.018

Chen, J. (2022). *Brazil, Russia, India, China and South Africa (BRICS)*. Investopedia. Retrieved from: https://www.investopedia.com/terms/b/brics.asp

Chen, H., Tang, Q., Jiang, Y., & Lin, Z. (2008). The role of International Financial Reporting Standards in accounting quality: Evidence from the European Union. *Journal of International Financial Management & Accounting, 21*(3), 220–278.

Cieslik, A., & Hamza, S. (2022). Inward ISD, IFRS adoption, and institutional quality: Insights from the MENA countries. *International Journal of Financial Studies, 10*(3), 47. https://doi.org/10.3390/ijfs10030047

Coda, V. (1990). Strategie d'impresa e comunicazione: il legame mancate. *Finanza, Marketing e Produzione, 1*, 10.

Cote, C. (2020). *How & why managers use financial statements?* Harvard Business School Online.

Crane, B. (2020). Revisiting who, when, and why stakeholders matter: Trust and stakeholder connectedness. *Business & Society, 59*(2), 263–286. https://doi.org/10.1177/0007650318756983

Cuijpers, R., & Buijink, W. (2005). Voluntary adoption of non-local GAAP in the European Union: A study of determinants and consequences. *European Accounting Review, 14*(3), 487–524. https://doi.org/10.1080/0963818042000337132

Dallas, S. G. (2018). *Stock exchanges and shareholder rights: A race to the top, not the bottom?* Harvard Law School Forum on Corporate Governance. Retrieved from: https://corpgov.law.harvard.edu/2018/12/28/stock-exchanges-and-shareholder-rights-a-race-to-the-top-not-the-bottom/

Daske, H. (2006). Economic benefits of adopting IFRS or US-GAAP—Have the expected cost of equity capital really decreased? *Journal of Business Finance and Accounting, 33*(3), 329–373.

De Franco, G., Kothari, S. P., & Verdi, R. S. (2011). The benefits of financial statement comparability. *Journal of Accounting Research, 49*(4), 895–931. https://doi.org/10.5923/j.ijfa.20160504.03

DeFond, M., Gao, X., Li, O. Z., & Xia, L. (2018). IFRS adoption in China and foreign institutional investments. *China Journal of Accounting Research, 12*(1), 1–32. https://doi.org/10.1016/j.cjar.2018.07.006

DeLone, W. H., & McLean, E. R. (2003). The DeLone and McLean model of information systems success: A ten-year update. *Journal of Management Information Systems, 19*(4), 9–30.

Dolgikh, T. (2017). The IFRS adoption by BRICS countries: A comparative analysis. In D. Procházka (Ed.), *New trends in finance and accounting* (pp. 373–383). https://doi.org/10.1007/978-3-319-49559-0_35

Efobi, U., Matthias, N., Odebiyi, J., & Beecroft, I. (2014). Do the rules attract the money? Implication of IFRS adoption on foreign direct investment. *SSRN*. https://doi.org/10.2139/ssrn.2460967

Eisenreich, A., Füller, J., & Stuchtey, M. (2021). Open circular innovation: How companies can develop circular innovations in collaboration with stakeholders. *Sustainability, 13*(23), 13456. https://doi.org/10.3390/su132313456

Endrawes, M., Feng, Z., Lu, M., & Shan, Y. (2020). Audit committee characteristics and financial statement comparability. *Accounting & Finance, 60*(3), 2361–2395. https://doi.org/10.1111/acfi.12354

ESMA. (2014). Ghid ESMA pentru aplicarea standardelor referitoare la informații financiare. Retrieved from: https://www.esma.europa.eu/sites/default/files/library/2015/11/2014-esma-1293ro.pdf

Feleagă, N. (1996). Controverse contabile. *Economica*.

Financial Accounting Standards Board (FASB). (2008). Original pronouncements as amended. Statement of Financial Accounting Concepts No. 1. Retrieved from: https://www.fasb.org/resources/ccurl/816/894/aop_CON1.pdf

Financial Accounting Standards Board (FASB). (2010). *Statement of financial accounting concepts no.8: Conceptual framework for financial reporting*. Financial Accounting Standards Board. Retrieved from: https://prd-live-faf-sites-binary.s3.us-east-1.amazonaws.com/Concepts_Statement_No_8_Chapter_1_As_Issued.pdf

Freeman, R. E. (1984). *Strategic management: A stakeholder approach*. Pitman.

Freeman, R. E., Dmytriyev, S. D., & Phillips, R. A. (2021). Stakeholder theory and the resource-based view of the firm. *Journal of Management, 47*(7), 1757–1770. https://doi.org/10.1177/0149206321993576

Freeman, R. E., Harrison, J. S., & Zyglidopoulos, S. (2018). *Stakeholder theory: Concepts and strategies*. Cambridge University Press.

Freeman, R. E., Phillips, R., & Sisodia, R. (2020). Tensions in stakeholder theory. *Business & Society, 59*(2), 213–231. https://doi.org/10.1177/0007650318773750

Giambona, E., Lopez-de-Silanes, F., & Matta, R. (2022). Stiffing the creditor: Asset verifiability and bankruptcy. *Journal of Financial Intermediation, 52*, 100962. https://doi.org/10.1016/j.jfi.2022.100962

Gonzalez-Perez, M. A., Cordova, M., Hermans, M., Nava-Aguirre, K. M., Monje-Cueto, F., Mingo, S., Tobon, S., Rodriguez, C. A., & Salvaj, E. H. (2021). Crises conducting stakeholder salience: Shifts in the evolution of private universities' governance in Latin America. *Corporate Governance, 21*(6), 1194–1214. https://doi.org/10.1108/CG-09-2020-0397

Gray, S. J., & Roberts, C. B. (1991). East-west accounting issues: A new agenda. *Accounting Horizons, 5*(1), 42–50.

Hampton, J. (1977). *Financial decision making: Concept, problems and cases*. Prentice Hall.

Hasanaj, P., & Kuqi, B. (2019). Analysis of financial statements. *Humanities and Social Science Research, 2*, 17–27. https://doi.org/10.30560/hssr.v2n2p17

Henock, L., & Oktay, U. (2012). The effect of IFRS on foreign direct investments: Evidence from cross-border acquisitions. Retrieved from: https://www.fox.temple.edu/wp-content/uploads/2012/08/IFRS_4_2012.pdf

Herbert, W. E., Ene, E., & Tsegba, I. N. (2014). Globalization of financial reporting: Obstacles to international financial reporting standards (IFRS) adoption in Nigeria. *Asian Journal of Business and Management Sciences, 3*(12), 25–41.

Hope, O. K., Jin, J. Y., & Kang, T. (2006). Empirical evidence on jurisdictions that adopt IFRS. *SSRN Electronic Journal*. https://doi.org/10.2139/ssrn.751264

IASB. (2018a). *Conceptual framework for financial reporting*. IFRS Foundation. Retrieved from: http://eifrs.ifrs.org/eifrs/PdfAlone?id=24380&sidebarOption=UnaccompaniedConceptual

IASB. (2018b). Pag. A26, punctul 2.33.

IASB. (2018c). *Use of IFRS standards around the world*. IFRS Foundation. Retrieved from: https://cdn.ifrs.org/-/media/feature/around-the-world/adoption/use-of-ifrs-around-the-world-overview-sept-2018.pdf?la=en

Ikpefan, O. A., & Akande, A. O. (2012). International financial reporting standard (IFRS): Benefits, obstacles and intrigues for implementation in Nigeria. *Research Journal of Finance and Accounting, 3*(10), 143.

Instituto de Estudios Superiores de la Empresa. (2002). *Código de gobierno para la empresa sostenible*. Universidad de Navarra. Retrieved from: https://www.iese.edu/media/research/pdfs/ESTUDIO-94.pdf

Jones, T. M. (1995). Instrumental stakeholder theory: A synthesis of ethics and economics. *Academy of Management Review, 20*(2), 404–437. https://doi.org/10.2307/258852

Kaawaase, T. K., Nairuba, C., Akankunda, B., & Bananuka, J. (2021). Corporate governance, internal audit quality and financial reporting quality of financial institutions. *Asian Journal of Accounting Research, 6*(3), 348–366. https://doi.org/10.1108/AJAR-11-2020-0117

Kadous, K., Koonce, L. L., & Thayer, J. M. (2011). Do financial statement users judge relevance based on properties of reliability? Emory Public Law Research Paper No. 10-114, Emory Law and Economics Research Paper No. 10-73. https://doi.org/10.2139/ssrn.1639132.

Këri, L., & Jupe, A. (2018). Implementing IFRS for SME-a challenge for Albania. *Albanian Journal of Agricultural Sciences, 17*(4), 203–210.

Kerzner, H. (2013). *Project management: A systems approach to planning, scheduling, and controlling* (11th ed.). John Wiley & Sons.

Key, K. G., & Kim, J. Y. (2020). IFRS and accounting quality: Additional evidence from Korea. *Journal of International Accounting, Auditing and Taxation, 39*, 100306. https://doi.org/10.1016/j.intaccaudtax.2020.100306

Kirvan, P. (2020). *How compliance provides stakeholders evidence of success*. TechTarget, Network. Retrieved from: https://www.techtarget.com/searchcio/tip/How-compliance-provides-stakeholders-evidence-of-success

Klettner, A. (2021). Stewardship codes and the role of institutional investors in corporate governance: An international comparison and typology. *British Journal of Management, 32*(4), 988–1006. https://doi.org/10.1111/1467-8551.12466

Lennard, A. (2007). Stewardship and the objectives of financial statements: A comment on IASB's preliminary views on an improved conceptual framework for financial reporting: The objective of financial reporting and qualitative characteristics of decision-useful financial reporting information. *Accounting in Europe, 4*(1), 51–66.

Levitt, A. (1998). The importance of high-quality accounting standards. *Accounting Horizons, 12*(2), 79–82.

Lezeu, D. N. (2004). *Analysis of the financial statements of the company*. Economic Publishing House.

Li, Y., Gong, M., Zhang, X.-Y., & Koh, L. (2018). The impact of environmental, social and governance disclosure on firm value: The role of CEO power. *The British Accounting Review, 50*(1), 60–75. https://doi.org/10.1016/j.bar.2017.09.007

Mameche, Y., & Masood, A. (2021). Macroeconomic evidence on the impact of mandatory IFRS adoption on ISD in the IFA (GCC) countries. *Journal of Accounting in Emerging Economies, 11*(4), 610–631. https://doi.org/10.1108/JAEE-04-2020-0084

Marquez-Ramos, L. (2008). The effect of IFRS adoption on trade and foreign direct investments. In *International trade and finance association conference papers* (Vol. 19).

Mbobo, E. M., & Ekpo, N. B. (2016). Operationalising the qualitative characteristics of financial reporting. *International Journal of Finance and Accounting, 5*(4), 184–192.

Melis, A. (2008). *La qualità dell'informazione esterna. Principi contabili ed evidenze empiriche*. Giuffrè Editore.

Memorandum of Understanding. (2002). The Norwalk Agreement—Sottoscritto a Norwalk, Connecticut, USA il 18 Settembre. Retrieved from: https://www.ifrs.org/content/dam/ifrs/around-the-world/mous/norwalk-agreement-2002.pdf

Minnis, M., & Shroff, N. (2017). Why regulate private firm disclosure and auditing? *Accounting and Business Research, 47*(5), 473–502.

Mohamed, W., Yasseen, Y., & Nkhi, N. (2020). International financial reporting standards for small and medium-sized entities: A survey showing insights of South African accounting practitioners. *Journal of Economic and Financial Sciences, 13*(1), 9. https://doi.org/10.4102/jef.v13i1.489

Morais, A. I., & Curto, J. D. (2008). Accounting quality and the adoption of IASB standards: Portuguese evidence. *Revista Contabilidade & Finanças, 19*(48), 103–111. https://doi.org/10.1590/S1519-70772008000300009

Namakavarani, O. M., Daryaei, A. A., Askarany, D., & Askary, S. (2021). Audit committee characteristics and quality of financial information: The role of the internal information environment and political connections. *Journal of Risk and Financial Management, 14*(6), 273. https://doi.org/10.3390/jrfm14060273

Narbel, F., & Muff, K. (2017). Should the evolution of stakeholder theory be discontinued given its limitations? *Theoretical Economics Letters, 7*, 1357–1381. https://doi.org/10.4236/tel.2017.75092

National Action Plans on Business and Human Rights. (2022). Small & medium-sized enterprises. Retrieved from: https://globalnaps.org/issue/small-medium-enterprises

Navarrete-Oyarce, J., Gallegos, J. A., Moraga-Flores, H., & Gallizo, J. L. (2021). Integrated reporting as an academic research concept in the area of business. *Sustainability, 13*(14), 7741. https://doi.org/10.3390/su13147741

Navarro, F. (2008). *Responsabilidad social corporativa: Teoría y práctica*. ESIC editorial.

Needles, B. E., Powers, M., & Crosson, S. V. (2013). *Principles of accounting* (12th ed.). Cengage Learning.

Nejad, M. Y., Ahmad, A., Salleh, F., & Rhaim, R. A. (2017). IFRS adoption, information asymmetry and ISD. In *International conference on accounting studies (ICAS), Putrajaya, Malaysia*.

Nnadi, M. (2011). IFRS adoption and financial results of EU companies: The challenge of nomenclature-evidence from the UK, France, and Germany. *SSRN Electronic Journal*. Retrieved from: https://ssrn.com/abstract=1779506

Nnadi, M., & Soobaroyen, T. (2015). International financial reporting standards and foreign direct investment: The case of Africa. *Advances in Accounting, 31*(2), 228–238. https://doi.org/10.1016/j.adiac.2015.09.007

Nurunnabi, H. (2006). *Transfer pricing of intrafirm sales as a profit shifting channel-Evidence from German firm data*. ZEW-Centre for European Economic Research Discussion Paper, 06-084. https://doi.org/10.2139/ssrn.955758

Oberholzer, M., Omotoso, M., Schutte, D., & Buys, P. (2022). The relative success of IFRS adopted African countries to attract foreign investment. *Studia Universitatis Babes-Bolyai Oeconomica, 67*(1), 44–62. https://doi.org/10.2478/subboec-2022-0004

Omotoso, M. O., Schutte, D. P., & Oberholzer, M. (2021). The effect of the adoption of International Financial Reporting Standards on foreign portfolio investment in Africa. *Journal of Economic and Financial Sciences, 36*(1), 57–79. https://doi.org/10.1080/10291954.2021.1909940

Owusu, G. M., Nur, A. M. S., Suppiah, S. D. K., & Siong, H. L. (2017). IFRS adoption, institutional quality and foreign direct investment inflows: A dynamic panel analysis. *Asian Journal of Business and Accounting, 10*(2), 43–75.

Owusu, G. M. Y., Suppiah, S. D. K., Saat, N. A. M., & Law, S. H. (2022). IFRS adoption and economic growth in developing economies. *International Journal of Economics and Accounting, 11*(1), 73–98.

Pleşco, O. (2013). Limitele informaţionale ale situaţiilor financiare în România. *Management Intercultural, 15*(1/27), 67.

Portes, R., & Rey, H. (2005). The determinants of cross-border equity flows. *Journal of International Economics, 65*(2), 269–296.

Power, M. (2010). Fair value accounting, financial economics and the transformation of reliability. *Accounting and Business Research, International Accounting Policy Forum, 40*(3), 197–210. https://doi.org/10.1080/00014788.2010.9663394

Prayoga, I., & Afrizal, T. (2021). Perceptions of educators, accounting students and accountants public accountant against ethics of financial statement preparation. *Budapest International Research and Critics Institute-Journal, 4*(1), 89–101. https://doi.org/10.33258/birci.v4i1.1539

Prutianu, Ş. (2000). *Manual de comunicare şi negociere în afaceri*. Editura Polirom.

Qu, W., Fong, M., & Oliver, J. (2012). Does IFRS convergence improve quality of accounting information? Evidence from the Chinese stock market. *Corporate Ownership and Control, 9*(4), 187–196. https://doi.org/10.22495/cocv9i4c1art5

Rafat, M., & Farahani, M. (2019). The country risks and foreign direct investment (ISD). *Iranian Economic Review, 23*(1), 235–260. https://doi.org/10.22059/ier.2018.69107

Raucci, D., & Tarquinio, L. (2020). Sustainability performance indicators and non-financial information reporting: Evidence from the Italian case. *Administrative Sciences, 10*(1), 13. https://doi.org/10.3390/admsci10010013

Rees, B. (1990). *Financial analysis*. Prentice Hall.

Ross, A. G. (2019). Governance infrastructure and ISD flows in developing countries. *Transnational Corporations Review, 11*(2), 109–119. https://doi.org/10.1080/19186444.2019.1640572

Roy, A., Weijden Trudy, V. D., & Vries, N. D. (2017). Challenges of satisfaction of key stakeholders of the district health system of Bangladesh and ways to improve: A qualitative study. *Health Systems and Policy Research, 4*(2), 2. https://doi.org/10.21767/2254-9137.100074

Roychowdhury, S., Shroff, N., & Verdi, R. S. (2019). The effects of financial reporting and disclosure on corporate investment: A review. *Journal of Accounting and Economics, 68*(2–3), 101246. https://doi.org/10.1016/j.jacceco.2019.101246

Saha, A., & Bose, S. (2021). Do IFRS disclosure requirements reduce the cost of capital? Evidence from Australia. *Accounting & Finance, 61*(3), 4669–4701. https://doi.org/10.1111/acfi.12744

Saleha, A. F., Rashidb, A. M., & Suwaidc, M. A. (2020). The transition from US GAAP to IFRS: Fundamental differences and their implications on financial statements that Walmart should know. *International Journal of Innovation, Creativity and Change, 11*(5), 314.

Salvioni, D. M. (1992). *Il bilancio d'esercizio nella comunicazione integrata d'impresa*. Giappichelli.

Saraite-Sariene, L., Alonso-Cañadas, J., Galán-Valdivieso, F., & Caba-Pérez, C. (2019). Non-financial information versus financial as a key to stakeholder engagement: A higher education perspective. *Sustainability, 12*(1), 331. https://doi.org/10.3390/su12010331

Scandaluri financiare. (2003). Retrieved from: https://ro.qaz.wiki/wiki/Accounting_scandals#The_fraud_triangle

Shah, M. U., & Guild, P. D. (2022). Stakeholder engagement strategy of technology firms: A review and applied view of stakeholder theory. *Technovation, 114*, 102460. https://doi.org/10.1016/j.technovation.2022.102460

Shaikh, M. H., Mustafa, F., Bishop, B. G., & Zeb, M. A. (2022). Qualitative characteristics of an accounting information system inside a financial corporation: A case study on multi-method information at Haines Watts Corporation. *International Journal of Innovative Science and Research Technology, 7*(3), 69. https://doi.org/10.5281/zenodo.6366729

Shollapur, M. R., Maheshwari, S. K., & Tate, U. S. (2010). FDI accounting in India and China: A need for harmonization. *DIAS Technology Review, 6*(2), 8–14.
Signori, S., San-Jose, L., Retolaza, J. L., & Rusconi, G. (2021). Stakeholder value creation: Comparing ESG and value added in European companies. *Sustainability, 13*(3), 1392. https://doi.org/10.3390/su13031392
Sihna, G. (2009). *Financial statement analysis*. PHI Learning Private Limited.
Sorter, F. E., & Gans, S. (1974). *Foundations of accounting theory*. Wiley.
Strojek-Filus, M., Szewieczek, A., & Maruszewska, E. W. (2015). Reliability and faithful representation in the accounting theory—A literature review. In *2nd international scientific conference on social sciences and arts SGEM2015, SGEM2015 conference proceedings, political, sciences, low, finance, economics & tourism, Aug 26-Sept 01, 2015 Book 2* (Vol. 2, pp. 291–298). https://doi.org/10.5593/sgemsocial2015D22
Turki, H., Wali, S., & Boujelbene, Y. (2017). IFRS mandatory adoption effect on the information asymmetry: Immediate or delayed? *Australasian Accounting, Business and Finance Journal, 11*(1), 55–77. https://doi.org/10.14453/aabfj.v11i1.5
Tweedie, D., & Seidenstein, T. R. (2005). Setting a global standard: The case for accounting convergence. *Northwestern Journal of International Law & Business, 25*, 589.
Uribe Macías, M. E. (2017). Analysis of construction projects stakeholders from corporate social responsibility. *Cuadernos De Administración, 33*(58), 58–76. https://doi.org/10.25100/cdea.v33i58.4517
Van Beest, B. G., & Boelens, S. (2009). Quality of financial reporting: Measuring qualitative characteristics. In *NiCE working paper 09–108, Nijmegen, The Netherlands*.
Vestine, M., Kule, J. W., & Mbabazi, M. (2016). Effect of financial analysis on investment decision making in Bank of Kigali. *European Journal of Business and Social Sciences, 5*(6), 279–303.
Wang, J. Y., Probst, J., Stoskopf, C., Sanders, J., & McTigue, J. (2011). Information asymmetry and performance tilting in hospitals: A national empirical study. *Health Economics, 20*(12), 1487–1506. https://doi.org/10.1002/hec.1689
West, B. (2003). *Professionalism and accounting rules*. Routledge.
Yasinskiy, Y. A. (n.d.). Novaya informatsionno-povedencheskaya paradigma: konets ravnovesnoy teorii ili yeye vtoroye dykhaniye. Retrieved from: https://institutiones.com/general/640-informacionno-povedenceskaya-paradigma.html
Yousefinejad, M., Ahmad, A., Salleh, F. M., Rahim, R. A., & Azam, H. M. (2018). The mediating effect of information asymmetry on IFRS and foreign direct investment. *International Journal of Economics and Management, 12*(2), 641–656. Retrieved from: http://www.ijem.upm.edu.my
Zadorozhnyi, Z.-M., Ometsinska, I., & Muravskiy, V. (2021). Determinants of firm's innovation: Increasing the transparency of financial statements. *Marketing and Management of Innovations, 2*, 74–86. https://doi.org/10.21272/mmi.2021.2-0674
Zahid, R. A., & Simga-Mugan, C. (2019). An analysis of IFRS and SME-IFRS adoption determinants: A worldwide study. *Emerging Markets Finance and Trade, 55*(2), 391–408. https://doi.org/10.1080/1540496X.2018.1500890
Zayol, P. I., Agaregh, T., & Eneji, B. E. (2017). Effect of financial information on investment decision making by shareholders of banks in Nigeria. *IOSR International Journal of Economics and Finance, 8*(3), 20–31.
Zech, N. (2013). Stakeholder relationship management in the context of crisis management. In *New challenges of economic and business development*. University of Latvia.
Zhang, X. (2022). Research and strategies on the risks of foreign direct investment in different countries. In *5th international conference on economy development and social sciences research (EDSSR)*. Retrieved from: https://webofproceedings.org/proceedings_series/ECOM/EDSSR%202022/WHCP22060.pdf

Chapter 3
Financial Reporting Framework in Emerging Economies: BRICS

The purpose of this chapter is to analyse the financial reporting framework of companies in the emerging BRICS economies (Brazil, Russia, India, China, and South Africa). To this end, a three-dimensional framework based on political, economic, and cultural components has been developed to analyse the accounting systems in these countries. Currently, only China, India, and South Africa are revising and translating IAS/IFRS (known as "informed divergence"), while Brazil and Russia are only copying them. This section of the paper aims to highlight the accounting practices of the five nations, drawing a parallel in terms of their contrasts with the International Financial Reporting Standards. The BRICS countries are actively involved in the convergence of national GAAP to IAS/IFRS; however, there are still significant differences between national accounting practices in emerging countries and international standards. This is due to both the unique economic conditions of developing countries and a general "resistance" to adopting IAS/IFRS in their entirety.

Comparative international accounting research has grown significantly due to the increasing emphasis on efforts to unify national accounting standards with international ones. However, many ramifications of accounting harmonisation have not yet been fully explored by researchers, as most existing research has focused on identifying similarities and variations between the accounting systems of different nations, directing the research path towards the transition from national GAAP to the international accounting benchmark.

In analysing accounting systems, it is important to consider the intrinsic values of nations and how these influence national accounting customs and practices. For example, we find numerous studies in the literature that explain international accounting disparities through the lenses of culture, politics, economics, and religion (Choi & Meek, 2011; Gray, 1988). According to Puxty et al. (1987), the factors that influence a nation's accounting regulations and practices are market, state, and

A. Melega, *Geopolitical Risks in Financial Reporting and Transfer Pricing*, Contributions to Finance and Accounting,
https://doi.org/10.1007/978-3-031-76600-8_3

society. These factors have a major influence on the convergence process of national accounting standards with international standards.

In recent years, the assessment criteria of accounting systems have come under scrutiny and analysis by researchers and practitioners as more and more countries decide to adopt International Financial Reporting Standards (IAS/IFRS). In most studies, researchers continue to study the same developed countries, ignoring the fact that things are changing in developing countries such as the emerging BRICS economies. Research on accounting harmonisation and convergence has so far fallen into two distinct groups. The first group of research highlights the characteristics of the convergence process by examining the relationship between the costs and benefits of implementing a single set of accounting standards, while the second group of researchers typically investigates single countries or homogeneous areas to determine the extent to which national standards conform to international accounting standards. Research clusters based on geographical proximity are the subject of comparative regional investigations. However, there are only a few studies that also look at nations that have similar characteristics or affinities to a particular cluster (Zeghal & Mhedhbi, 2006). Studies that have focused on the analysis of accounting systems in the BRICS countries tend to focus mainly on the evolution of accounting regulations and practices that have occurred following the introduction of IAS/IFRS. Borker (2012b) analysed the influence of cultural dimensions on the dimension of accounting value in Russia and Brazil and observed that there are significant parallels between the disclosure procedures in these countries, identifying several cultural distinctions. Walton (2004) argues that a single accounting model is not viable to define, partly because of the survival of national cultural components in accounting. An effective bridge between accounting procedures and economics can be built by studying political economy in conjunction with "cultural explanations". According to a large number of experts, accounting is not just about certain principles of accounting technique but is also a cultural and sociological issue.

To better understand the co-evolution of the process of accounting harmonisation and convergence, further research on the relationships between national and international accounting standards is needed. For emerging countries, there is a clear lack of research on how accounting systems in these countries have evolved. In light of the recent trend of convergence towards IFRS/IAS and the inter-linkages between countries, the effectiveness of most research is questionable since it is only seen from one perspective. More research is needed to understand how accounting could be used to assess local community responses to global stimuli such as economic, political, environmental, and social pressures (Lehman, 1995). For the same reasons as Stephen (2014), Lehman (1995) questions the current status of the BRICS states in the global capitalist system. Globalisation leads countries to standardise their accounting practices, which has the potential to reshape local cultural norms. IAS/IFRS are an example of this, given the difficulty that developing nations may have in adopting accounting standards based on different frameworks than those currently used by industrialised countries (Irvine, 2008; Rodrigues & Craig, 2007).

In this vein, the main concerns have been raised about discrepancies in financial reporting between nations, as they do not have the same characteristics and principles when it comes to international accounting.

3.1 Particular Features of Accounting Policies and Practices Applied by BRICS Economies

National and international accounting regulations are the legal basis for conducting business. Accounting policies and practices are essential tools for ensuring that the economic process is well conducted and that financial statements contain relevant information for all stakeholders. BRICS economies have joined the international effort to improve accounting policies and practices to ensure that they provide relevant and reliable information. Most BRICS countries have fully adopted the International Financial Reporting Standards or only for a specific category of enterprises or have aligned national standards with international ones.

To ensure the understanding and practical application of national and international accounting standards, the bodies responsible for them in the BRICS economies have issued various practical guidelines, rules, and laws to guide their application. The practical guides are voluntary as compared to accounting regulations and their purpose is to facilitate the understanding of the concepts, principles, accounting policies, and general issues of national and international accounting standards and to provide solutions on their application to obtain relevant and comparable information for all categories of information users.

The BRICS economic and political bloc is formed from the most powerful emerging economies, playing a key role in the global market. International organisations are paying close attention to the evolution of the BRICS economies, following their development path. Although the BRICS economies are a unitary bloc, accounting policies and practices differ from country to country. One rather important aspect that I have noticed is that the BRICS economies have not addressed the issue of convergence of national standards to the international benchmark at any summit. I believe that a cooperative agreement among the BRICS members to adopt the international accounting benchmark would be welcomed, leading to a smooth flow of foreign direct and socially responsible investments.

The process of converging national accounting standards to the international accounting benchmark (IAS/IFRS) has formally ended in Brazil. It obliges all categories of enterprises to prepare financial statements following international accounting policies and practices (IAS/IFRS), being one of the first countries to formally adopt IFRS for SMEs in November 2009. IFRS are now mandatory for non-regulated enterprises (i.e. non-regulated companies, banks, insurance companies, etc.) below the threshold of annual gross revenues of USD 120 million or total assets of USD 100 million. Therefore, since 2010, SMEs have adapted their accounting policies to fit the new framework, but it can still be observed that some old practices from national accounting standards for SMEs are still widely used.

According to an analysis of the application of IFRS by SMEs in Brazil, IFAC found that SMEs in practice still use accounting policies from the old standards. For example, when implementing accounting policies for fixed assets we can observe that *"future costs of restoration or dismantling are not accrued at all, and the residual value is consistently ignored, resulting in the amortisation of the total cost, thus not reflecting the actual value used" (IASB, n.d.)*. The vast majority of companies use the maximum annual depreciation rates allowed as deductible for local corporate income tax purposes. Under the international accounting benchmark, the general principles appear to be simple: cost means "cost plus any refund of properly accrued estimated payments". The depreciable amount is "cost less residual value" (also an estimate). Allocating periods on a reasonable basis means that the best estimate of useful economic life should be made at the beginning of the period. This is a fairly simple procedure, but we know that for some industries in particular, the practical adoption of such simple rules can lead to complicated technical calculations. Estimates are a key feature of today's financial reporting. As a consequence, various negative effects on reported financial information automatically follow: "the value of assets on the balance sheet is not necessarily correct or approximates fair value; costs or expenses allocated to the periods in which the assets are used are wrong; and gains or losses from the disposal of the asset are equally wrong, closing the vicious circle of potentially misleading financial information" (Rodi, 2015).

From the above, we can conclude that the convergence process in Brazil continues even after the adoption of IFRS because the use of the new accounting policies requires an imperative study on the part of those who apply them. These discrepancies resulting from the use of international accounting policies are the result of their misunderstanding by accounting professionals; therefore, standard-setting bodies should focus on assessing these discrepancies and developing IFRS application guidelines that facilitate the use of international accounting policies.

In Russia, the national accounting referential is composed of 24 federal standards (PBUs) that cover accounting policies for economic transactions. For example, PBU standard 1 *"Accounting policy of the enterprise"*, approved by Order of the Ministry of Finance of Russia dated October 6, 2008, is the basis for the formation and disclosure of the accounting policies for the enterprises. To ensure compliance with international accounting principles, the standard has undergone numerous amendments and additions, the last amendment being in April 2017 when several articles of the standard were revised, some of which were supplemented or even deleted.

This standard is a guide for the development of the enterprise's accounting policies manual which is mandatory under the legislation of Russia. The standard provides explanations on selecting accounting policies so that they ensure (Ministry of Finance of the Russian Federation, 2008):

- The completeness of all economic activities reflected in the accounts (completeness)
- Timely reflection of all events arising from the enterprise's activity (topicality)
- Recognition of expenses and income on a prudent basis

- The reflection in the accounts of economic events that result not so much from their legal form as from their economic content (economic over legal)
- Reconciliation of the analytical accounting data with the turnover and balances of the summary accounting accounts on the last calendar day of each month (consistency requirement)
- Rational accounting based on management conditions and the size of the enterprise, as well as on the relationship between the costs of generating information and its value (the rationality requirement)

Under PBU 1, entities that prepare consolidated financial statements under IFRS may be guided—in developing their accounting policy manual—by Federal Accounting Standards, taking into account the requirements of International Financial Reporting Standards. In particular, such an organisation has the right not to apply the accounting policies and practices established by the federal accounting standards when they lead to inconsistency of the enterprise's accounting policies with the requirements of International Financial Reporting Standards.

Under the standard, an enterprise's accounting policies are applied consistently from one fiscal year to the next. Changes in accounting policies can be made only in certain circumstances, such as changes in legislation or significant changes in the conditions of operation of the enterprise (reorganisation or change in the profile of activity). Change in accounting policies requires obtaining more relevant information. Entities are required to disclose accounting policies and practices to ensure that users of financial information can reliably assess the financial position of the enterprise, the financial results of its activities, and the cash flow statement.

The accounting policies and practices in Russia aim to achieve high-quality information that provides reliable information on the financial position and performance of the enterprise. Compared to International Financial Reporting Standards, accounting policies and practices reflected in national standards are more restrictive, with less flexibility. This can be explained by the fact that the accounting system in Russia is connected to taxation, the accounting information being strongly influenced by the legal form of events and transactions, tax regulations having a significant impact on the accounting practices.

Accounting policies and practices in India converge with the International Accounting Standards of Accounting IAS/IFRS. The Indian Accounting Standards (Ind AS), as notified under Section 133 of the Companies Act, 2013, have been formulated keeping in view the Indian economic and legal environment and the aim to converge with IFRS. Hence, Ind-AS are in line with International Financial Reporting Standards and represent a single set of accounting policies. Indian Accounting Standards Ind-AS are mandatory. For the proper application of accounting policies and practices, the accounting profession in India, represented by the Institute of Chartered Accountants of India (ICAI), has developed a Framework for the Preparation and Presentation of Financial Statements, the contents of which are taken from the IASB's Conceptual Framework and adapted to the Indian business environment. The Indian accounting standard setters are continuously analysing Indian and international standards to narrow down any differences so that the Indian standards eventually fully meet the international requirements. The new Ind AS accounting standards provide greater flexibility than the old ones by providing scope for modifications, which is very important for the Indian business environment. In any inflationary economic circumstance, the Ind-AS principles provide room for modifications, with the Ind AS 29 "Financial Reporting in Hyperinflationary Economies" standard helping to deal with any escalated economic situation.

China's accounting policies and practices are unique because they come from a socialist period when the state was the sole owner of industry. In socialist economies, the main concern of managers is to maximise profit "not just on paper" but also in reality. This is why financial statements are not given much attention, especially the quality of the information they contain. As a result, financial statements are prepared to meet the information needs of the state, not of other stakeholders. The old Chinese accounting standards are an inventory tool for enterprise assets.

For further integration into the capital markets, China has adopted a significant number of international IAS/IFRS, with the old Chinese Accounting Standards (CAS) largely replaced by International Financial Reporting Standards (IFRS) to bring China in line with the requirements of the international environment. The similarity between Chinese accounting policies and practices and IFRS is about 90–95%.

Before the adoption of IFRS, Chinese companies trading shares in the United States had to prepare three sets of financial statements, one using Chinese accounting standards (China GAAP), one using international standards (IFRS), and one using North American GAAP (US GAAP). However, since 2008, the US Securities and Exchange Commission (SEC) has allowed foreign private issuers to use IFRS financial statements. China's adoption of IFRS has led to a smooth flow of foreign investment and reduced some of the costs that Chinese companies face in preparing financial statements. China's accounting policies and practices are contained in 38 accounting standards converging with IFRS. The main purpose of developing CAS standards was to reduce financial fraud and optimise the country's tax strategy.

With the adoption of new accounting policies and practices, Chinese accounting standard setters are paying particular attention to the quality of disclosures in financial statements to meet the needs of all stakeholders. However, the government remains the main user of financial information, with enterprises focusing more on meeting government information needs.

Under regulations adopted under South African legislation enacted in 2011, South African entities are permitted to use either International Financial Reporting Standards, IFRS for SMEs, or South African standards (SA GAAP), depending on the public interest of the entity. The South African Accounting Standards are effectively the same as IFRS except for IFRS 1 "First-time Adoption of International Financial Reporting Standards" and the new IFRS and IFRIC that were issued after May 2011. As of 2012, the Accounting Practices Board (APB) and the Financial Reporting Standards Council (FRSC) decided to withdraw the South African Accounting Standards (SA GAAP) in their entirety. Accounting standard setters in South Africa are concerned with developing accounting policies and practices that are fully consistent with the proposed objectives of "providing relevant and reliable information".

From the above, it can be concluded that South Africa and Brazil have made considerable progress in adopting international accounting policies and practices, with China, India, and Russia being more reluctant to adopt IFRS, this reluctance being influenced by government policy.

3.2 Objectives and Structure of Financial Reporting by Companies in the BRICS Economies

Most emerging markets have become more integrated in recent years by liberalising and regulating stock markets, improving their institutional infrastructure and developing more efficient communication technologies. BRICS economies play a central and crucial role in global flows of goods and services. For example, BRICS countries have more comprehensive stock exchanges compared to other newly industrialised markets such as Indonesia, Mexico, or Turkey (Nnadi & Tanna, 2019). At the same time, these countries have proven to be quite resilient to global macroeconomic shocks (Makin & Arora, 2014). Another common feature of these countries is their institutional gaps, sometimes culminating in a total absence of accounting regulations (Doh et al., 2017) or their mismatch with the needs of accounting information users.

BRICS countries have also aligned themselves to some extent with the process of international accounting convergence. Thus, they have adopted the International Financial Reporting Standards and have adapted their national GAAPs to conform to international accounting regulations (Ghio & Verona, 2015). In recent years, all BRICS countries have started the process of convergence to IAS/IFRS. Unlike other countries, Russia and Brazil have decided on full convergence of national GAAPs by directly adopting IAS/IFRS in their legislation. On the other hand, China and India have issued or intend to issue new national accounting standards based on IAS/IFRS.

In Brazil, International Financial Reporting Standards are mandatory for the consolidated financial statements of listed companies for financial years ending on or after December 31, 2010 (Carneiro et al., 2017). The Consolidated Accounts Act (LoCA), signed in 2010, introduced requirements for the use of IFRS for consolidated financial statements in Russia beginning in 2012. In January 2015, the Indian Ministry of Corporate Affairs (MCA) released a revised roadmap reflecting that companies with a net worth of Rs 500 million (approximately US$ 71 million) or more will be required to comply mandatorily with Indian Accounting Standards (Ind AS), which are largely converged with IFRS, from April 1, 2016 (MCA, 2015).

According to Sokolov and Pyatov (2009), the adoption of IFRS in Russia has led to a review of accounting methodology. International standards influence local accounting mainly in two ways: by embedding its parts into local legislative requirements and standards, as well as through direct IFRS financial reporting by a significant number of Russian enterprises.

The idea of implementing IFRS in Russia first emerged in the early 1990s when the government was about to fully move to financial reporting under International Financial Reporting Standards. By the start of accounting reform in the late 1990s, Russia had inherited from the Soviet Union the economic relations established under the planned economy system. This period was marked by certain particularities, such as the state regulation of accounting by issuing binding normative documents for enforcement, standardisation, and complete unification of accounting procedures and records, as well as the implementation of the unified accounting system. Subsequently, the main purpose of accounting was to ensure the security and rational use of public property. Despite the obvious advantages of the Soviet accounting system, it failed to meet the challenges presented by the new management conditions of the market economy.

The course for transition to international standards was mapped out in the Program for Accounting Reform in Compliance with International Financial Reporting Standards approved by RF Government Resolution No. 283 of March 6, 1998, which states that "the purpose of the accounting system reform is to adjust the national accounting system to the requirements of the market economy and IFRS" (Government of the Russian Federation, 1998).

In China, the accounting harmonisation process was somewhat different. The Ministry of Finance in China, by directly taking over standards from IFRS has moved Chinese GAAP towards convergence with IFRS (Peng & van der Laan Smith, 2010). In South Africa, the option to use SA GAAP or IFRS existed from 1995 to 2012 (Prather-Kinsey, 2006). Since 2012, only International Financial Reporting Standards have been allowed to be used (Table 3.1).

Even though the five countries have progressively liberalised their markets in recent decades, the restrictions imposed by political market regulation ("statism") prevalent in China, India and Russia represent a clear pattern that seeks to resist a pervasive and dominant stance on international financial reporting practices. Some scholars have linked IFRS adoption to institutional commitment, but have also coined the term "label adoption" (Daske et al., 2008). The phenomenon of label adoption arises when countries use internationally accepted regulations for reputational purposes only and do not fully commit and engage, a cause that hinders the process of developing and adopting a single global set of standards (Guerreiro et al., 2012). At the same time, however, we have to take into account that India and China have been slower adopters of IAS/IFRS. Brazil is at the most advanced level, as it has already introduced IFRS for SMEs, which means that small and medium-sized firms usually considered "watchdogs" of local values also have to adopt this set of standards based on a different framework from national accounting standards.

The main objective of the adoption of International Financial Reporting Standards by the BRICS economies is to facilitate companies' access to the international market. The adoption of IFRS does not also imply an increase in the quality of information in the financial reports of companies in these countries. For example, Li et al. (2014) analysed the reliability of financial reporting in emerging BRICS

Table 3.1 Status of adoption of International Financial Reporting Standards in BRICS Economies

Areas of application of IFRS	Brazil	Russia	India	China	South Africa
IFRS mandatory for national public companies	Mandatory	IFRS standards are mandatory for listed companies, financial institutions, and some government-owned companies.	Indian Accounting Standards (Ind AS) are largely based on and aligned with IFRS. However, India has not adopted IFRS for domestic company reporting and has not formally committed to its adoption.	China's national standards are substantially converged with IFRS, and China is committed to adopting IFRS for reporting by at least some domestic companies, although there is no timetable for finalising the process. Chinese companies, accounting for more than 30% of total domestic market capitalisation produce IFRS-compliant financial statements as a result of their dual listing in Hong Kong and other international markets.	Mandatory
IFRS standards are mandatory or permitted for listings by foreign companies	Mandatory	Mandatory for some, allowed for others.	–	Foreign companies do not currently trade in the Chinese securities markets. Therefore, there is no relevant regulation on whether these companies are allowed to use IFRS.	IFRS is mandatory for some foreign companies: Primary listing is on the Johannesburg Stock Exchange (JSE). Home country GAAP or IFRS is permitted if a company's primary listing is outside South Africa and the JSE listing is secondary.

(continued)

Table 3.1 (continued)

Areas of application of IFRS	Brazil	Russia	India	China	South Africa
IFRS for SMEs is mandatory or permitted	Mandatory	–	–	–	Permitted
IFRS standard for SMEs under review	–	Under review	–	–	–

Source: International Financial Reporting Standards Worldwide: www.ifrs.org

economies, finding that financial statement disclosures contain significant and systemic signs of misreporting, particularly in China and Russia. Errors in financial reporting can be caused by the low level of training of accounting professionals in the application of international financial reporting standards or the uneven convergence of national standards to IFRS. The lack of openness of the BRICS economies and the strong linkage of accounting to taxation, as well as the cosmetic adoption of IFRS, lead to inefficiencies. In practice, the main objective of financial reporting in the BRICS economies is to meet the information needs first of all at the government level, then of tax bodies and then of other stakeholders.

3.3 Strengths and Weaknesses of Financial Reporting by Companies in BRICS Economies

The competitiveness and globalisation of capital markets have focused investors' attention on world economies that can offer some degree of political, economic, and social stability—important factors in ensuring and assessing investment risk. With this in mind, the world's governments are constantly assessing their economic, social, and political indicators, as well as the quality of financial reporting, to provide investors with a secure investment environment. The quality of financial information is a key determinant in attracting foreign direct investments, as financial reporting provides factual data for the assessment and predictability of investment risks. To strengthen their image on the international market and to increase the level of foreign direct investments, BRICS economies have adopted, some partially, some fully, the International Financial Reporting Standards, which are considered the benchmark of quality in financial reporting. However, the adoption of IFRS by the BRICS economies has not also led to a significant increase in the quality of financial reporting, with considerable discrepancies between IFRS and the new converged standards, with some complex concepts and topics being omitted.

The limitations or weaknesses of the financial reporting of companies in the BRICS countries are in terms of disclosure of information, as well as the characteristics of the accounting systems, such as high statutory control, uniformity, conservatism and even secrecy, which is the opposite of the International Financial Reporting Standards that advocate characteristics such as professionalism, flexibility, and transparency. In practice, the accounting systems in the BRICS economies have a value profile more distant from IFRS, which affects the quality of information in financial reporting, as well as the effectiveness of convergence of national GAAPs to the international accounting benchmark. A similar finding was also made by Borker (2012a) who analysed Gray's (1988) hypotheses, arguing that Russia and Brazil have accounting values that are at odds with IFRS, while India and China have derivative accounting values that are to a greater extent consistent with the values associated with IFRS. He also states that India appears to be somewhat closer to IFRS values than China, but both are significantly different from Russia and Brazil. The conceptual basis, international accounting policies and practices are partly different from the accounting and financial reporting systems in the emerging BRICS economies. The differential application of accounting policies and practices undermines the comparability of information in the financial reports of BRICS companies and increases the cost of disclosure for investors. The informational disparities caused by the incorrect application of IFRS lead to increased information asymmetry, which is considered one of the main limitations of financial reporting. Findings in the literature emphasise that BRICS countries are lagging far behind in the qualitative and quantitative results on IFRS adoption, which once again demonstrates that the statement of these countries on IFRS adoption is a political one, aimed at facilitating the access of these economies to the international market. Some researchers argue that although financial reporting is opaque in BRICS countries, it remains attractive to investors (Bao, 2009), managing to remain the main contender in attracting foreign direct investments. Thus, the limitations of financial reporting by companies in BRICS countries are differences in the application or transcription of International Financial Reporting Standards into domestic accounting regulations (Table 3.2).

According to the data in the Table above, we can observe that the BRICS economies operate a dualistic accounting system, which on the one hand requires companies to comply with national accounting regulations and practices, and on the other hand, requires them to prepare their financial statements under International Financial Reporting Standards, this being more emphasised in Russia. At the same time, we can observe that China and South Africa have the highest level of integration of IFRS into national rules and regulations compared to the other BRICS countries. However, despite the substantial convergence of Chinese and South African GAAP to IFRS, foreign-invested enterprises in China and South Africa need to be aware that key differences still exist and these will have consequences for the finances of Chinese and South African subsidiaries compared to the group as a whole. South African accounting standards have been the closest to IFRS; therefore,

Table 3.2 The limitations of financial reporting by companies in emerging BRICS economies conditional on IFRS application impairments

Brazil	Russia	India	China	South Africa
Research and development expenditure should be capitalised as an asset and amortised over the estimated future period.	National Financial Reporting Standards (FRS) do not apply the fair value concept.	In the Financial Statements, it is not possible to forecast the flows related to interest payments or receipts.	Under Chinese accounting standards, companies can only use the historical cost method to value fixed and intangible assets.	GAAP is based on rules and IFRS is based on principles.
Brazilian standards allow revaluation including negative revaluation of assets. The proposed amendment to the corporate law provides for revaluation only in cases of corporate reorganisation.	Intangible assets are not impaired.	Exchange rate differences related to foreign currencies are to be capitalised, rather than accounting for them in the profit or loss for the year.	Chinese accounting standards stipulate that expenses are classified by their function, while IFRS classifies expenses by their nature.	
Goodwill, treated as a premium, should be reported as an asset and amortised over its useful life, not to exceed 10 years.	Most financial instruments are carried at acquisition cost.		The Chinese standards (ASBs) have not been revised since their issuance in 2006, where only interpretations of IFRS amendments were issued to provide authoritative guidance. As a result, we can conclude that Chinese accounting standards are characterised by delayed implementation of IFRS. Therefore, foreign-invested enterprises in China can expect some divergence between their Chinese subsidiary and other international subsidiaries.	
Legislation requires accounting for the effects of temporary differences, such as tax credits, deferred tax assets, and provisions for deferred income tax.	Lease financing may be redeemed or repaid in accordance with the parties to the contract.			

Source: Prepared by the author according to national accounting regulations of the BRICS economies

the differences are insignificant, the only difference is that South African GAAP is based on strict rules, while IFRS is based on principles. Evidence from the literature shows that the use of IFRS, per se, does not translate into increased value relevance of accounting figures, as numerous country-specific factors such as the level of enforcement, legal mechanisms, and incentives of those preparing accounting information are likely to affect the outcome of IFRS adoption (Callao et al., 2007).

However, the financial reporting of companies in BRICS countries has improved considerably compared to the pre-IFRS periods, with considerably fewer inconsistencies in company financial statements and inadequate financial information for proper risk assessment and decision-making by investors. The adoption of IFRS by BRICS companies has contributed to increased transparency and a higher quality of information in IFRS-compliant financial statements, which can be observed because they are oriented to the needs of investors, not tax authorities (Bagaeva, 2010). Increasing the quality of financial reporting of BRICS companies facilitates their access to external financing. The attractiveness or strengths of BRICS companies' financial reporting are primarily emphasised by the economic performance of these companies, which provides investors with certainty about the return on invested capital.

3.4 Comparative Analysis of the Financial Reporting Structure of BRICS Economies

The structure and content of financial reports are essential elements in ensuring effective economic-financial communication that provides users of financial accounting information with comparable, real, relevant, current, and accurately represented data. Financial reports demonstrate the financial health or state of the enterprise and are the tool used by management and investors in decision-making. The quality of decisions made by management is influenced by the information presented in financial reports, as well as the accuracy and clarity of the data. Companies in BRICS countries are trying to keep pace with globalisation trends and adjust their financial reporting to international standards, thereby facilitating stakeholders' access to quality financial and non-financial information to facilitate their decision-making. Thus, the financial reports of BRICS companies are primarily aimed at meeting the information needs of stakeholders, in particular investors and regulators, and are structured in such a way as to faithfully present the position and performance of the company. The structure of financial reporting in the BRICS business environment is similar, with companies required to prepare the following set of financial reports: balance sheet, income statement, cash flow statement, and notes to the financial statements (Table 3.3).

The application of IFRS standards by companies in BRICS countries makes them more competitive, increases the trust of foreign partners, and also makes it possible to make better management decisions. IFRS reporting of financial position

Table 3.3 Financial reporting structure of companies in emerging BRICS economies

IFRS	Brazil	Russia	India	China	South Africa
Accounting standards governing the structure and presentation of financial statements					
IAS 1—presentation of financial statements	BR GAAP—CPC 26 (R1) presentation of financial statements	PBU standard 4—Enterprise financial statements	Indian accounting standard 1—presentation of financial statements	Chinese accounting standards for business enterprises no.37—presentation of financial statements (CAS37).	GRAP standard 1—presentation of financial statements
Objectives of financial reporting					
The objective of financial statements is to provide information about the financial position, financial performance, and cash flows of an entity that are useful to a wide range of users in making economic decisions. Financial statements also show the results of management's stewardship of the resources entrusted to it.	The objective of financial statements is to provide information about the equity and financial position, performance and cash flows of an entity that are useful to a wide range of users in evaluating and making economic decisions. The financial statements are also intended to present the results of management's performance in discharging its duties and responsibilities in managing the resources entrusted.	The financial statements should give a true and fair view of the financial position of the organisation, the financial results of its activities, and the changes in its financial position. The accounting statements made under the rules laid down in the accounting regulatory acts are considered reliable and complete.	The objective of financial statements is to provide information about the financial position, financial performance, and cash flows of an entity that is useful to a wide range of users in making economic decisions.	Disclosure of financial instruments includes the presentation and disclosure of financial instruments. When an entity presents financial reports, it shall classify financial instruments based on their characteristics and the nature of the relevant disclosures.	Financial statements are a structured representation of the financial position and financial performance of an entity. The objective of financial statements is to provide information about the financial position, financial performance, and cash flows of an entity that is useful to a wide range of users in making and evaluating decisions about the allocation of resources.

Reporting period					
A reporting period is the period covered by a set of financial statements. It is usually for a month, a quarter, or a year.	January 1–December 31	January 1–December 31	April 1–April 31	January 1–December 31	January 1–December 31
Composition of financial statements					
Balance sheet					
Profit and loss account					
Statement of changes in equity					
Cash flow statement					

Source: Developed by author

and financial performance helps companies in BRICS countries simplify economic decision-making and attract investments. The main source of useful information for external and internal users is financial reporting. Financial statements are a group of reporting forms that reflect a company's financial situation and financial results for a given period. The reporting should contain basic information about assets, liabilities, capital, expenses, and income. When studied carefully, financial statements can help to find ways to improve the performance of a business, revealing the reasons for its success as well as its shortcomings. The reporting system of companies in Brazil, India, China, and South Africa is largely in line with International Financial Reporting Standards since these countries have fully adopted IAS 1—Presentation of Financial Statements. Within the BRICS group, the Russian accounting system has the most differences between national standards and IFRS. For example, Russian standards call financial reporting—accounting reporting, which means that it is necessary only to fulfil the requirements of the law and meet the demands of tax authorities, therefore it cannot meet the needs of a wide range of users, as IFRS standards require.

The most important source of information about the assets and liabilities of BRICS companies is the balance sheet. According to national IFRS-compliant standards, Brazil, India, China, and South Africa recommend but do not require companies to classify assets and liabilities into long term and short term, while companies in Russia are required to arrange balance sheet items in ascending or descending order of liquidity. Another difference between the financial reporting of Brazilian, Indian, Chinese, South African, and Russian companies is the composition of profit and loss statement indicators. The reports of the companies from these countries, except for Russia, do not present income and expense items as extraordinary, while Russian companies recognise them as extraordinary. At the same time, all BRICS companies also disclose additional financial information if it is useful to stakeholders to reflect the actual financial position and performance of the company. The statement of changes in equity is broadly similar across the five countries, forming part of the explanatory notes provided for each reporting period. Based on this form of reporting, it is possible to determine the state of equity, its structure and the changes during the reporting period. In the cash flow statement, users can find information on expenses and cash equivalents from various activities, and it is used by companies in Brazil, India, China, and South Africa, but less by Russian companies, which treat it as an appendix to the balance sheet. The big discrepancy in cash flow reporting among the five countries is that Russian companies treat cash as cash on hand, in foreign currency, and other settlement accounts in the context of current activities, while companies in the other countries define cash flows in operating, investing, and financial activities, also mentioning cash equivalents.

Increasing the efficiency of BRICS business activities is determined by the quality of financial reporting, which ensures an optimal relationship with stakeholders. The quality of financial reporting of BRICS companies is also influenced by the level of IFRS adoption. The preparation of financial statements under international standards ensures the presentation of true, complete, and reliable information about the company's financial position and performance. Thus, financial reporting standards within the BRICS group are close in many aspects, but preparing the financial statements under IFRS prioritises the needs of investors over other groups of users of financial statements. The rigidity of accounting regulations in the BRICS economies is taking its toll on the efficiency of companies' financial reporting. National standards that are partially converged (some of them) to IFRS enable BRICS companies to formally comply with legislative requirements, to meet the information needs of government bodies and at the same time to provide objective and reliable information to other stakeholders, thus facilitating international market entry.

Financial reporting within the BRICS group is mainly oriented towards attracting foreign direct investment. In this respect, in addition to the aforementioned reports, companies also disclose information on other indicators that are not included in the balance sheet, income statement, or cash flow statement. They have oriented their reporting towards international requirements, taking up the concept of integrated reporting, reporting information on economic, social, and environmental performance. The extent of internationalisation (Kang & Gray, 2014) contributes to the increasing financial and non-financial disclosure of companies in BRICS countries. However, financial reporting within this group remains quite opaque due to geographical, economic, political, and social factors. The strongest role in the opaqueness of financial reporting of companies in BRICS countries belongs to geopolitical factors and implicitly to the interests of these countries in global economic and social policy. Therefore, the application of IFRS by companies in the BRICS countries is susceptible in terms of the quality of disclosures, especially as state holdings in the economies of these countries are very high, especially in key areas that are directly targeted by foreign direct investments.

3.5 IFRS Financial Reporting and Attracting Foreign Direct Investment in BRICS Economies

In an environment characterised by high inflation and strong economic growth, the performance of companies in emerging BRICS economies tends to be positive, even as bond yields rise and developed market economies are doing better. The positive growth trend of BRICS companies is primarily driven by the major inflow of foreign direct investments, which is an important factor in their economic and social development. FDI is an element of internationalisation of companies through the creation of subsidiaries in other countries, and the high quality of financial reporting of BRICS companies will further contribute to their accessibility to socially responsible FDI flows. Financial reporting is the glue that binds the company to its stakeholders, providing them with the information they need to analyse and assess the firm's performance. Companies listed on a regulated market in the BRICS countries have implemented international rules on financial reporting, thus succeeding in increasing foreign ownership in the company.

Skilled labour force, natural resources, and permissive legislation are some of the most important factors in attracting foreign direct investments by companies in BRICS emerging economies. According to researchers, the level of foreign investment inflows is conditioned by several factors such as market size (Shatz & Venables, 2000), GDP (Zhang & Daly, 2011), industrial growth (Hryckiewicz & Kowalewski, 2010), political and legal systems (Naudé & Krugell, 2007), level of information and communication technology (Addison & Heshmati, 2003), and others. Cross-border cooperation and the creation of political and economic blocs can increase the volume of foreign direct and socially responsible investment flows (Asiedu, 2006). The creation of political and economic blocs directly contributes to the enlargement of markets, trade routes, and free movement of goods and people. At the same time, in times of crisis, the countries that form a bloc can support each other and encourage intra-bloc investment flows through various policies developed jointly by all Member States. One example is the BRICS economies which have set up their bank—the New Development Bank, an alternative to the World Bank and the International Monetary Fund. The main purpose of establishing this bank is "to finance infrastructure and sustainable development projects in the BRICS and developing countries" (Agreement on the New Development Bank of July 15, 2014, ratified by Federal Law No. 29-FZ of March 8, 2015). To support the BRICS economies in combating the effects of COVID-19, the New Development Bank issued four loans to India, China, Brazil, and South Africa.

The literature has provided strong evidence of the link between investment inflows and economic growth, which is seen as a stimulus for sustainable development and productivity growth (Gunby et al., 2017). FDI inflows play a significant role in economic growth (Nair-Reichert & Weinhold, 2001). At the same time, Pradhan (2002) and Agrawal (2005) have shown the opposite. They analysed the effects of FDI inflows in India on economic growth using the production function and concluded that economic growth is not positively influenced by FDI. According to Teodorescu (2013), FDI has both positive and negative effects from the perspective of the sustainable development process. Among the first ones, we can mention the creation of new jobs, transfer of technology as well as know-how, export competitiveness, and increased competition, and among the negative ones, we can list the exclusion of domestic investment when the FDI inflows increase, the monopolistic nature of FDI, and the fluctuations of the exchange rates as the FDI increases. A very important aspect in the analysis of FDI inflows is the relationship between the rate of FDI and the social and environmental performance of emerging economies. We know very well that in terms of living standards and pollution, most emerging economies face major problems. Due to environmental policies that are either non-existent or not enforced, some multinationals exceed the level of emissions of gases and pollutants permitted in their home countries, where the state keeps a close eye on how companies comply with environmental protection legislation. However, the effect can also be the reverse, as the experiences of management and investors from developed countries with strict environmental protection policies can bring in better solutions and technologies to reduce the level of pollution from the company's operations. The Global Trade Alert report warns that foreign direct investment flows to emerging markets have a limited contribution to promoting sustainable development (Evenett & Fritz, 2021). This limitation is caused by the negligence of governments that favour foreign investment and fail to develop clear and strict legislative rules on environmental and social protection. I believe that the government—as one of the most important stakeholders—must constantly assess the environmental and social performance of multinationals operating in their jurisdiction and encourage socially responsible investments. Although emerging economies are the largest recipients of foreign direct investment inflows, the standard of living of their populations is very low compared to developed countries. This is due to poor access to education and low awareness of the policies concerning the system of setting the minimum wage in the economy—a factor that multinationals take advantage of, inflation, etc. A study by Grosu et al. (2021) showed that the economic growth and sustainable development of a country have a strong relationship with the level of education of the population, because as they state, the educational process "ensures the generation, transfer and dissemination of sustainable knowledge in society and business, and the synergy between higher education (universities), business (industry), government and the public (civil society) can create a basis for the sustainable development of the national economy, increase the level of environmental protection, reduce CO_2 emissions, ensure the rational use of exhaustive resources, create new environmentally friendly products and raise the living standards of the population".

According to Spar and Yoffie (1999), the competition for foreign investment inflows generates a decline in labour and environmental standards, calling this competition a "race to the bottom". One of the key factors for foreign investment flows in emerging economies is the cost of human resources. Low standards of living, high illiteracy, and unskilled labour are key determinants in multinationals' wage-setting. To retain their skilled staff, multinationals have a more motivating wage system, offering their employees better working standards compared to domestic firms. Unskilled workers, who make up the bulk of the population in emerging economies, are neglected in terms of pay and labour standards. This is where the state must intervene by establishing labour laws and codes that protect employees and provide them with equal working conditions.

Firm performance is conditioned by foreign investment inflows. According to research by Gorodnichenko et al. (2014), it is noted that firms with foreign capital perform much better than firms with domestic capital. This is mainly due to the transfer of technology and knowledge from the parent firm to the subsidiaries. The productivity and high performance of foreign-owned companies are also determined by their much more attractive wage offer than that of domestic-owned companies, which makes skilled workers and specialists choose to work for foreign-owned ones.

Currently, the performance of enterprises in emerging BRICS economies is being evaluated by stakeholders from the perspective of business sustainability, environmental protection, and energy regeneration measures. Li ct al. (2020) analysed the performance of businesses in the BRICS economies in relation to energy, economic, and environmental sustainability in these countries, concluding that out of the group of five, China and Brazil outperform the others, achieving a sustainability index score of 0.96. To achieve long-term environmental sustainability, the researchers argue that the BRICS economies need to implement a policy that encourages cross-border trade in renewable energy. Bhattarai and Negi (2020) analysed the relationship between firm performance and foreign direct investment inflows in India during the period of 2004–2018 and their results showed that the level of foreign direct investment inflows positively influences profit, sales, and employment.

Business performance in the BRICS emerging economies is conditioned by factors such as tax, environmental, and social policies, economic growth, size and type of market in which they operate, the connectivity of economic relations with other countries, and the country's ability to attract foreign direct investment inflows. Due to human resource and raw material costs, the cost of production in emerging economies is substantially lower compared to developed economies, which contributes to the economic performance of the enterprises. Comparing two subsidiaries, one operating in an emerging country and the other in a developed country, with the same characteristics (number of employees, raw materials used) and disregarding tax policies, we observe that the cost of production is much lower in the emerging country subsidiary, which makes companies in BRICS countries much more attractive to investors, the quality of financial reporting being a factor with little implication on attracting FDI. Therefore, companies from BRICS countries are managing to be competitive in attracting FDI, which has been growing significantly in recent times. The level of FDI inflows to the BRICS economies started to increase significantly since 2005, a period characterised by a boom in cross-border investment flows. This growth lasted until 2008–2009 when the world economies were hit by the economic crisis. However, companies in BRICS countries have held up compared to developed economies, falling 40% compared to 54% in developed economies. Thus, companies in BRICS countries are more resilient to economic downturns, mainly due to their abundance of raw materials and low cost of production. In times of crisis, investors are more cautious and reluctant to invest, focusing more on analysing investment risks and refusing to invest in high-risk projects and uncertain and unstable markets. At the same time, during the recession, there is also a liquidity constraint which negatively influences the investment process and mainly the level of investment flows. After the recession in 2009, foreign investment flows continued to increase, thus, according to UNCTAD (2013), the share of foreign investment to BRICS economies in 2012 reached a level of 20% of the global share. Companies from the BRICS countries play a key role in the global investment pattern, as they are a power that tilts the balance of foreign investment flows in favour of emerging economies. To further encourage investors to invest in BRICS companies, BRICS governments have committed to adopt the International Accounting Reporting Framework to improve financial reporting and meet investors' information needs.

Before the adoption of IFRS by BRICS companies, the FDI flows fluctuated (Table 3.4), mainly due to the economic crisis of 2008–2009. However, the BRICS economies experienced high FDI inflows. After the recession in 2009, FDI inflows continued to increase, so that the share of FDI to the BRICS economies reached

Table 3.4 Evolution of foreign investment flows (million USD) in the period before the adoption of International Financial Reporting Standards

	Year						
Country	2005	2006	2007	2008	2009	2010	2011
Brazil	15,066	18,822	34,585	45,058	25,949		
China	104,109	124,082					
India	7606	20,336	25,483	47,472	35,582	27,397	
Russia	14,375	37,442	54,922	75,856	27,752	31,668	36,868
South Africa	6683	303	6764	8172	8614	4015	3785

Source: IMF, UNCTAD

Table 3.5 Evolution of foreign investment flows (million USD) and the MSCI Socially Responsible Investment Index (SRI) in the post-adoption period of International Financial Reporting Standards

	Year									
	Brazil		Russia		India		China		South Africa	
Country	ISD	SRI	ISD	SRI	ISD	SRI	ISD	SRI	ISD	SRI
2007							156,249			
2008							171,535			
2009							131,057			
2010	77,687						243,703			
2011	97,422				36,497		280,072			
2012	82,060		30,188		23,995		241,214		4403	
2013	59,089		53,397		28,153		290,928		8296	
2014	14,884		11,288		9781		61,319		695	
2014	63,846		29,152		34,577		268,097		5772	
2015	49,961		11,858		44,009		242,489		1729	
2016	53,700		37,176		44,459		174,750		2235	
2017	66,585		25,954		39,966		166,084		2007	
2018	59,802	1.067	13,228	0.97	42,117	1.026	235,365	1.121	5447	1.036
2019	65,386	1.21	32,076	1.042	50,610	1.176	187,170	1.347	5125	1.167
2020	28,318	1.198	10,410	1.047	64,362	1.11	253,096	1.397	3062	1.095
2021	50,367	1.553	38,526	1.295	44,727	1.459	333,979	1.81	40,896	1.468
2022	73,352		−15,205		49,380		298,917		9231	
2023	65,897		8364		28,163		275,929		5233	

Source: UNCTAD (2024), MSCI INDEX

20% of the global share. During the period under review, China was the largest recipient of FDI within the group, followed by Russia, Brazil, India, and South Africa.

The adoption of International Financial Reporting Standards by companies in the BRICS countries has helped to maintain increased interest from Western investors, with the BRICS countries being a real competitor for other economies in attracting FDI. Basically, according to the data in Table 3.5, we can see that with the adoption of IFRS, FDI inflows to the BRICS countries have increased considerably. The convergence of national accounting standards to the international accounting benchmark has liberalised investors' access to BRICS markets. In terms of socially responsible investing, the adoption of IFRS has a positive impact on ESG disclosure in the BRICS economies. Brazil has seen a significant increase in socially responsible investment of 55.3% between 2017 and 2021, driven by the implementation of social and environmental policies, as well as progress in IFRS adoption. Within the group, Russia recorded the lowest growth in SRI, due to a lack of policies and regulations to conserve national resources. At the same time, Russia has also made the least progress on the path to harmonisation of the national accounting standards with the international benchmark, which may be a contributing factor to the stagnation of NIS. Overall, the adoption of IFRS can have positive implications for socially responsible investing, as it enhances the comparability and transparency of financial reporting and can facilitate the integration of ESG factors into investment decisions (Lee & Park, 2019). However, it is important to consider the potential limitations of financial reporting in reflecting all relevant ESG factors and to use a holistic approach to assess companies' sustainability performance.

Due to the fragility of the economy and slow growth in some economies, the level of foreign investment inflows fell substantially between 2016 and 2018. In 2018 compared to 2016, Brazil saw a −16.06% decrease in foreign investment inflows, Russia −64.13%, India −4.9%, China −3.98%, and South Africa −138%. These declines were mainly driven by a 22% reduction in cross-border acquisitions and the value of mergers, amplified by political uncertainty and weak investment in natural resources.

After a 4-year decline, foreign investment flows continued to fall, a decline amplified by the COVID-19 pandemic. During the pandemic period, when most of the world's economies were shut down to limit the spread of COVID-19 infection, foreign direct investment, according to UNCTAD (2021), fell by about 35% globally. The pandemic crisis had a much greater impact on foreign direct investments than the economic crisis in 2009, with the level of FDI inflows being 20% below the 2009 threshold.

Foreign investment inflows in the largest emerging economies (BRICS) fell in 2020 by about −13.7%, a rather small decrease compared to developed countries. This small fall was conditioned by several political and economic factors. China, the epicentre of the COVID-19 outbreak, was the largest recipient of foreign direct investment in 2020, with inflows of around $163 billion and GDP growth of 2.3%. However, in the first quarter of 2020, according to China's Ministry of Commerce, foreign investment inflows fell by about 10.8%. Even as the pandemic raged globally, China managed in a fairly short time to annihilate the spread of the virus, gradually eliminating the consequences of the pandemic on the economy. To improve the economic situation and to support foreign direct investments, the Chinese government has launched several fiscal, financial, and trade policies. For example, an important step in attracting foreign investments was to reduce the number of "blacklisted" sectors where foreign investment was either prohibited or restricted. Fang et al. (2021) believe that China will continue to remain an attractive destination of FDI, mainly due to its handling of the pandemic crisis and the advantages accumulated over time, such as a large-scale domestic market, medium to high GDP per capita, long and complex industries and supply chains.

India was the fifth largest recipient of foreign investment inflows in the world in 2020, receiving $64 billion in foreign investments. According to Reddy and Sudarshan (2021), the main factors that have made India an attractive country for FDI despite the COVID-19 pandemic are the reduction in corporate tax from 30% to 25%—a measure implemented from FY 2019 to 2020—simplification of labour laws by passing the three labour codes—Social Security Code, Industrial Relations Code, and SSM Code, and financial sector reforms, financial inclusion and digitisation of India and last but not the least, human capital. The Government of India's policies aim at creating a more favourable environment for investors, focusing in particular on creating appropriate mechanisms for economic development and improving socio-economic indicators. By the year 2024, the Indian government aimed to reach an economy of 5 trillion dollars. Another important factor supporting foreign investments in India during this period of instability is also the fact that India has risen 14 points in the World Bank's Ease of Doing Business 2020 survey, ranking 63rd out of 190 countries in terms of ease of starting a business.

The COVID-19 pandemic has had a devastating effect on Russia's foreign investment inflows, from $32 billion in 2019 to $10 billion in 2020, a drop of about 70%. The problematic business climate, corruption, ageing population, political conflicts, and embargoes make Russia an unattractive country for investors, with very high investment risk. The main attraction for foreign investment remains natural resources like oil, gas, and metals. Foreign investment flows are concentrated only in the big metropoles like Moscow and St. Petersburg. Although Russia declares itself to be a fairly independent country in terms of its economy, its economic development and prosperity are conditioned by foreign investment flows that come largely from the European Union, which is between 55% and 75% of the foreign investment sector (Domínguez-Jiménez & Poitiers, 2020). To support investors during the pandemic crisis, Russia has developed a government plan involving preferential credit programmes to maintain employment, reducing the tax burden during the period of restrictive measures, and finalising the "regulatory guillotine" programme—a programme that involves the elimination of unnecessary requirements for setting up a business. The government has also allocated significant funds for infrastructure projects. On September 23, 2020, the Russian government approved a nationwide action plan to launch a new investment cycle and improve the business climate. The plan entails the creation of a comprehensive mechanism to support large investment projects, private, public, and private-public, at the federal and regional levels, based on agreements on the protection and encouragement of capital investment. This plan also aims for a gradual improvement of the business climate, including improvement of the bankruptcy institution and company law, the creation of a programme mechanism for accelerating the socio-economic development of urban agglomerations and cities that are centres of economic growth, the implementation of the largest investment projects for infrastructure development with significant multiplier effects in related industries, which will become one of the factors of economic growth (Protocol N 36, Section VII, Government of Russia). According to Castiglione et al. (2012), foreign investors are looking for social and institutional stability and Russia appears as an "idiosyncratic country". As long as Russia has gas, oil, and metals, it will continue to benefit from a large flow of foreign direct investments. The global energy instability that made itself felt in the second half of 2021 with rising natural gas and electricity prices has tipped the balance of foreign direct investment in Russia's favour, as it is the largest exporter of gas and electricity at a global level.

Brazil, the largest recipient of foreign investment in Latin America, recorded a 62% drop in foreign investment inflows in 2020, the lowest level in 20 years, ranking 11th compared to 6th in 2019. The Brazilian government has implemented a strategy to promote foreign investment, giving foreign investors the same legal treatment as local investors. Priorities for the Brazilian government in terms of foreign investment are the automotive, oil, gas, renewable energy, and other industries. Foreign direct investments remain to be restricted by legislation in the areas of healthcare, telecommunications, media, maritime, and insurance. Brazil's high transportation costs due to poorly developed infrastructure, low domestic productivity, and political uncertainties hinder foreign direct investment.

Foreign direct investment fell in South Africa by 39% in 2020 to around $31 billion, a decline influenced by the COVID-19 pandemic, which caused a drop in cross-border mergers and acquisitions, and low energy commodity prices. As with other emerging economies, the determinants of foreign investment inflows to South Africa are natural resources, cheap human resources, government policies, infrastructure, inflation, etc. Foreign investment inflows to South Africa are mainly attracted by two uncontrollable factors: natural resources and market size, which denotes that resource-poor or small countries are limited in accessing foreign investment (Asiedu, 2006).

The global political, economic, and health instability harms business development and foreign direct investments. Russia, one of the largest recipients of foreign capital, following the invasion of Ukraine, has attracted a series of sanctions from major economic partners such as the European Union. EU economic sanctions on Russia have been in place since 2014, when Russia annexed Crimea, subsequently easing on the back of peace deals. In February 2022, when Russia attempted to annex other territories of Ukraine, several EU and non-EU member states condemned the invasion by imposing economic sanctions and even breaking political partnerships.

Economic sanctions harm the development of the business environment, affecting the performance of enterprises, considering the severing of economic ties, reduced exports, currency depreciation, and increased inflation. Political and economic instability has always been a determinant of sustainable economic, social, and environmental development. The literature has provided solid evidence of the negative impact of economic and political sanctions on the performance of firms in sanctioned countries. For example, Huynh et al. (2022) analysed the effects of economic sanctions over the past 20 years on firms in Russia. The research revealed that the performance of firms in the energy sector did not suffer from economic sanctions, while the performance of firms in other sectors was undermined. In particular, it was found that the negative impact of economic sanctions was strongly felt on capital expenditures, leading to an increase in the cost of capital and undermining

R&D. Economic sanctions generated other economic phenomena, which are determining factors in the sustainable development of business such as inflation, foreign investment flows, level of exports and imports, supply chains, etc. The evolution of the above-mentioned factors is in a close correlation with the level of performance of enterprises. Economic and political stability has an important role to play in creating an enabling environment for the sustainable development of multinationals. Economic sanctions, as other authors have said, are a "double-edged sword" affecting both sides. An eloquent example is the current EU and US sanctions against Russia, which have led to an unprecedented energy crisis, putting both domestic and non-domestic consumers in difficulty. Spiralling energy prices are driving up the cost of production, creating problems for businesses in various industries.

3.6 Summary Conclusions

The BRICS economies are a political and economic power and a real competitor for developed countries. The BRICS bloc has a crucial role to play in the global political and economic arena, especially in the current geopolitical context characterised by a fierce struggle for dominance. However, the BRICS economies are open to implementing mechanisms to facilitate foreign direct investment flows, both intra and extra-group. The convergence of national standards to international financial reporting practices and the introduction of concepts such as related parties, quality, financial reporting, etc., highlight an interest of the BRICS economies to respond to the needs of the business environment. Although the adoption of International Financial Reporting Standards is an arduous process for companies in BRICS countries involving quite high costs due to lack of infrastructure and especially specialised staff, they have realised their importance for international market access and have adopted IFRS to a lesser or greater extent.

Despite the crises, companies in the emerging BRICS economies remain a fairly strong magnet for foreign direct investments, and the most important factors that induce investors to invest in emerging economies even in times of crisis are natural resources, cheap labour, tax facilities, and market size. The role of economic and financial information in attracting investors can be considered important but insignificant compared to the other factors. By adopting IFRS, companies in the BRICS countries have improved the quality of financial reporting to some extent, but the level of adoption differs within the group. While Brazil has successfully adopted IFRS also for SMEs, Russia is in the process of adopting IFRS for listed companies and is the most reticent within the group on international accounting practices. The integration of BRICS companies into the international economy will strengthen supply chains and the flows of foreign direct and socially responsible investment. Another important step for the BRICS economies and for facilitating access to foreign direct investment is the adoption of accounting and tax policies on transfer pricing, which is currently a real problem for tax bodies and multinationals, which encounter obstacles in transferring capital between group subsidiaries, hampered by the lack or ambiguity of the relevant legislation. Strengthening accounting and financial reporting policies and practices within the group will contribute to the integration of the BRICS economies into the global economy.

References

Addison, T., & Heshmati, A. (2003). The new global determinants of ISD flows to developing countries: The importance of ICT and democratization. UNU-WIDER Research Paper DP2003/45. Retrieved from: https://www.wider.unu.edu/sites/default/files/dp2003-045.pdf

Agrawal, P. (2005). Foreign direct investment in South Asia: Impact on economic growth and local investment. In E. M. Graham (Ed.), *Multinationals and foreign investment in economic development* (International economic association series). Palgrave Macmillan. https://doi.org/10.1057/9780230522954_5

Asiedu, E. (2006). Foreign direct investment in Africa: The role of natural resources, market size, government policy, institutions and political instability. *The World Economy, 29*(1), 63–77. https://doi.org/10.1111/j.1467-9701.2006.00758.x

Bagaeva, A. (2010). The quality of published accounting information in Russia. In *Acta Universitatis Oulensis Oeconomica* (Vol. 4). University of Oulu.

Bao, D. H. (2009). Usefulness of financial information in evaluation of BRIC firms. *Advances in Accounting, 25*(2), 200–207. https://doi.org/10.1016/j.adiac.2009.08.006

Bhattarai, K., & Negi, V. (2020). ISD and economic performance of firms in India. *Studies in Microeconomics, 8*(1), 44–74. https://doi.org/10.1177/2321022220918684

Borker, D. R. (2012a). Accounting, culture, and emerging economies: IFRS in the BRIC countries. *Journal of Business & Economics Research, 10*(5), 313–324. https://doi.org/10.19030/jber.v10i5.6983

Borker, D. R. (2012b). Stepped-up progress on IFRS in Russia: History in the making. *International Business & Economics Research Journal, 11*(2), 255–268. https://doi.org/10.19030/iber.v11i2.6795

Callao, S., Jarne, J. I., & Laínez, J. A. (2007). Adoption of IFRS in Spain: Effect on the comparability and relevance of financial reporting. *Journal of International Accounting, Auditing and Taxation, 16*(2), 148–178. https://doi.org/10.1016/j.intaccaudtax.2007.06.002

Carneiro, J., Rodrigues, L. L., & Craig, R. (2017). Assessing international accounting harmonization in Latin America. *Accounting Forum, 41*(3), 172–184. https://doi.org/10.1016/j.accfor.2017.06.001

Castiglione, C., Gorbunova, Y., Infante, D., & Smirnova, J. (2012). ISD determinants in an idiosyncratic country. A reappraisal over the Russian regions during transition years. *Communist and Post-Communist Studies, 45*(1–2), 1–10.

Choi, F. D., & Meek, G. K. (2011). *International accounting*. Prentice-Hall.

Daske, H., Hail, L., Leuz, C., & Verdi, R. (2008). Mandatory IFRS reporting around the world: Early evidence on the economic consequences. *Journal of Accounting Research, 46*(5), 1085–1142. https://doi.org/10.1111/j.1475-679X.2008.00306.x

Doh, J., Rodrigues, S., Saka-Helmhout, A., & Makhija, M. (2017). International business responses to institutional voids. *Journal of International Business Studies, 48*(3), 293–307. https://doi.org/10.1057/s41267-017-0074-z

Domínguez-Jiménez, M., & Poitiers, N. (2020). FDI another day: Russian reliance on European investment. In *Policy contribution 03/2020, Bruegel.*

Evenett, S. J., & Fritz, J. (2021). *The 27th global trade alert global* (p. 33). Centre for Economic Policy Research. Retrieved from: https://cepr.org/voxeu/columns/fdi-big-trouble-insights-27th-global-trade-alert-report

Fang, J., Collins, A., & Yao, S. (2021). On the global COVID-19 pandemic and China's ISD. *Journal of Asian Economics, 74*, 101300. https://doi.org/10.1016/j.asieco.2021.101300

Ghio, A., & Verona, R. (2015). Accounting harmonization in the BRIC countries: A common path? *Accounting Forum, 39*(2), 121–139. https://doi.org/10.1016/j.accfor.2015.02.001

Gorodnichenko, Y., Svejnar, J., & Terrell, K. (2014). When does ISD have positive spillovers? Evidence from 17 transition market economies. *Journal of Comparative Economics, 42*(4), 954–969. https://doi.org/10.1016/j.jce.2014.08.003

Government of the Russian Federation. (1998). Program for Accounting Reform in Compliance with International Financial Reporting Standards approved by Resolution No. 283 of March 6, 1998. Retrieved from: https://www.consultant.ru/document/cons_doc_LAW_18125/

Gray, S. J. (1988). Towards a theory of cultural influence on the development of accounting systems internationally. *Abacus, 24*(1), 9–11. https://doi.org/10.1111/j.1467-6281.1988.tb00200.x

Grosu, V., Kholiavko, N., Safonov, Y., Zhavoronok, A., & Cosmulese, A. (2021). Quintuple helix model: Investment aspects of higher education impact on sustainability. *Management Theory and Studies for Rural Business and Infrastructure Development, 43*(1), 111–128. https://doi.org/10.15544/mts.2021.10

Guerreiro, M. S., Rodrigues, L. L., & Craig, R. (2012). Voluntary adoption of International Financial Reporting Standards by large unlisted companies in Portugal—Institutional logics and strategic responses. *Accounting, Organizations and Society, 37*(7), 482–499.

Gunby, P., Jin, Y., & Reed, W. R. (2017). Did ISD really cause Chinese economic growth? A meta-analysis. *World Development, 90*, 242–254. https://doi.org/10.1016/j.worlddev.2016.10.001

Hryckiewicz, A., & Kowalewski, O. (2010). Economic determinates, financial crisis and entry modes of foreign banks into emerging markets. *Emerging Markets Review, 11*(3), 205–228. https://doi.org/10.1016/j.ememar.2010.05.003

Huynh, T., Hoang, K., & Ongena, S. (2022). The impact of foreign sanctions on firm performance in Russia. CEPR Press Discussion Paper No. 17415. Retrieved from: https://cepr.org/publications/dp17415

International Accounting Standards Board (IASB). (n.d.). IAS 16 — Property, plant and equipment. Retrieved from: https://www.ifrs.org/issued-standards/list-of-standards/ias-16-property-plant-and-equipment/

Irvine, H. (2008). The global institutionalization of financial reporting: The case of The United Arab Emirates. *Accounting Forum, 32*(2), 125–142. https://doi.org/10.1016/j.accfor.2007.12.003

Kang, H., & Gray, S. J. (2014). Corporate financial reporting in the BRIC economies: A comparative international analysis of segment disclosure practices. In *Emerging market firms in the global economy* (Vol. 15, pp. 233–254). Emerald Group Publishing Limited. https://doi.org/10.1108/S1569-376720140000015010

Lee, K. S., & Park, S. (2019). IFRS adoption and socially responsible investment: Evidence from the Asia-Pacific region. *Journal of Business Research, 94*, 80–93.

Lehman, G. (1995). A legitimate concern for environmental accounting. *Critical Perspectives on Accounting, 6*(6), 393–412.

Li, H., Bhati, Z., Abbas, Q., Ahmad, I., Iqbal, N., & Aziz, B. (2020). Measuring low carbon energy. Economic and environmental sustainability performance of BRICS. *The Singapore Economic Review, 69*(1), 357–376.

Li, S., Ho Park, S., & Shuji Bao, R. (2014). How much can we trust the financial report? Earnings management in emerging economies. *International Journal of Emerging Markets, 9*(1), 33–53. https://doi.org/10.1108/IJoEM-09-2013-0144

Makin, A. J., & Arora, R. U. (2014). How solid are the BRICS? An economic overview. In V. Lo & M. Hiscock (Eds.), *The rise of the BRICS in the global political economy: Changing paradigms?* (pp. 11–26). Edward Elgar Publishing.

Ministry of Corporate Affairs (MCA). (2015). Press Release No. 11/10/2009 CL-V. Retrieved from: https://www.mca.gov.in/Ministry/pdf/PressRelease_06012015.pdf

Ministry of Finance of the Russian Federation. (2008). PBU Standard 1/2008. Enterprise Accounting Policies, paragraph 6. Retrieved from: https://www.consultant.ru/document/cons_doc_LAW_81164/2d52707f5a4d5314b9e470a9bf59cb826ec848dd/

Nair-Reichert, U., & Weinhold, D. (2001). Causality tests for cross-country panels: A new look at ISD and economic growth in developing countries. *Oxford Bulletin of Economics and Statistics, 63*(2), 153–171. https://doi.org/10.1111/1468-0084.00214

Naudé, W. A., & Krugell, W. F. (2007). Investigating geography and institutions as determinants of foreign direct investment in Africa using panel data. *Applied Economics, 39*(10), 1223–1233. https://doi.org/10.1080/00036840600567686

Nnadi, M., & Tanna, S. (2019). Accounting analyses of momentum and contrarian strategies in emerging markets. *Asia-Pacific Journal of Accounting & Economics, 26*(4), 457–477. https://doi.org/10.1080/16081625.2017.1284596

Peng, S., & van der Laan Smith, J. (2010). Chinese GAAP and IFRS: An analysis of the convergence process. *Journal of International Accounting, Auditing and Taxation, 19*(1), 16–34. https://doi.org/10.1016/j.intaccaudtax.2009.12.002

Pradhan, J. P. (2002). Foreign direct investment and economic growth in India: A production function analysis. *Indian Journal of Economics, 82*(327), 582–586.

Prather-Kinsey, J. (2006). Developing countries converging with developed-country accounting standards: Evidence from South Africa and Mexico. *The International Journal of Accounting, 41*(2), 141–116.

Puxty, G., Willmott, H. C., Cooper, D. J., & Lowe, T. (1987). Modes of regulation in advanced capitalism: Locating accountancy in four countries. *Accounting, Organizations and Society, 12*(3), 273–291. https://doi.org/10.1016/0361-3682(87)90041-9

Reddy, V., & Sudarshan, G. (2021). Foreign direct investment in India during COVID-19 pandemic vis-à-vis emerging economies. In *International scientific and practical online conferences: Investment attractiveness in providing economic stability of countries: Global problems and ways of their solution materials*. Tashkent.

Rodi, R. J. (2015). Implementing IFRS for SMEs-lessons from Brazil. Retrieved from: https://www.ifac.org/knowledge-gateway/supporting-international-standards/discussion/implementing-ifrs-smes-lessons-brazil

Rodrigues, L. L., & Craig, R. (2007). Assessing international accounting harmonization using Hegelian dialectic, isomorphism and Foucault. *Critical Perspectives on Accounting, 18*, 739–757.

Shatz, H. J., & Venables, A. J. (2000). The geography of international investment. The World Bank, Policy Research Working Paper No. 2338. Retrieved from: https://documents1.worldbank.org/curated/es/479241468764136437/pdf/multi-page.pdf

Sokolov, Y. V., Pyatov, M. L. (2009). Business optimism and methodology of accounting. *Finance and Business*, №4. Retrieved from https://finbiz.spb.ru/wp-content/uploads/2009/10/4_2009_sokol_pat.pdf

Spar, D., & Yoffie, D. (1999). Multinational enterprises and the prospect for justice. *Journal of International Affairs, 52*, 557–581.

Stephen, M. D. (2014). Rising powers, global capitalism and liberal global governance: A historical materialist account of the BRICs challenge. *European Journal of International Relations, 24*(1), 912. https://doi.org/10.1177/1354066114523655

Teodorescu, A. (2013). Impactul investițiilor străine directe asupra dezvoltării durabile. In *Conferința internațională Dezvoltarea durabilă în condiții de instabilitate economică, Satu Mare*.

UNCTAD. (2013). World Investment Report. Retrieved from: https://unctad.org/system/files/official-document/wir2013_en.pdf

UNCTAD. (2021). World Investment Report. Retrieved from: https://unctad.org/system/files/official-document/wir2021_en.pdf

UNCTAD. (2024). *World investment report 2024: Investment facilitation and digital government*. United Nations. Retrieved from: https://unctad.org/system/files/official-document/wir2024_en.pdf

Walton, P. J. (2004). IAS 39: Where different accounting models collide. *Accounting in Europe, 1*(1), 5–16. https://doi.org/10.1080/0963818042000262711

Zeghal, D., & Mhedhbi, K. (2006). An analysis of the factors affecting the adoption of international accounting standards by developing countries. *The International Journal of Accounting, 41*(4), 373–386. https://doi.org/10.1016/j.intacc.2006.09.009

Zhang, X., & Daly, X. (2011). The determinants of China's outward foreign direct investment. *Emerging Markets Review, 12*(4), 309–510. https://doi.org/10.1016/j.ememar.2011.06.001

Chapter 4
Accounting and Tax Policies Applied to Transfer Pricing in BRICS Economies

In the current global economic context, the business environment is showing a growing trend towards complex organisational forms, which are evident both in the structure of companies and in the geographical location of their activities, which are determined by the medium and long-term economic objectives of these companies. As a rule, they form multinational groups that operate in global markets and tend to expand into different jurisdictions. In these situations, various economic, legal, and tax issues start to arise, given the strong level of central decision-making that determines certain revenue management policies which, in turn, give rise to various particular legal situations. Although they are formally and legally independent, the expansion of these subsidiaries or branches entails several special legal relationships since they are part of a multinational group, and certain taxes and duties cannot be determined and calculated independently of the subject to which they are attributable. In recent years, the number of multinational entities has increased significantly and their role in world trade has doubled. This trend is also due to the phenomenon of globalisation, which is constantly expanding and has major implications for countries engaged in international trade.

In addition to the positive stimulating effect on the economy, this trend also entails challenges for both tax administrations and eco-entities, as tax systems differ from country to country. An important role here is played by the transfer prices at which multinational entities sell goods, intangibles, and services to associated enterprises.

Transfer pricing remains the most widely used and the simplest and most common method of minimising taxes. They represent the price set in commercial transactions between different subsidiaries of an enterprise or between members of a group or conglomerate of enterprises. In practical terms, transfer pricing and the artificial shifting of the tax base by redistributing the indicators that make up the tax base between the subsidiaries of the enterprise, allow the entity—without violating the regulatory provisions—to use a preferential tax regime. Thus, transfer pricing has become an important issue for tax authorities who want to ensure that income has been taxed where it has been realised.

A. Melega, *Geopolitical Risks in Financial Reporting and Transfer Pricing*,
Contributions to Finance and Accounting,
https://doi.org/10.1007/978-3-031-76600-8_4

4.1 Bibliometric Analysis of the Term "Transfer Pricing"

In recent years, researchers' interest in the topic of transfer pricing in economics has increased at a rapid pace due to the phenomenon of globalisation and hence the emergence of multinational entities (Rogers & Oats, 2022). This sub-chapter aims to review the literature on transfer pricing with a focus on emerging themes and their tangential topics. To achieve the proposed objective, a bibliometric analysis of scholarly papers in the ISI Web of Science and Scopus databases—both of which are internationally recognised as ensuring high-quality works—(Mongeon & Paul-Hus, 2016) was used as the research method. The research was conducted and structured following a protocol suggested by other researchers (Massimo & Corrado, 2017) in 2 stages:

(a) Data collection
(b) Data analysis and visualisation

Data Collection
The search term "transfer prices" was used to collect the papers. The criteria for filtering the results were the areas relevant to the paper, as highlighted in Table 4.1.

Data Analysis and Visualisation
According to Small (1999), bibliometric analysis is a technique by which we can spatially represent the various relationships between keywords, disciplines, fields, documents, or authors and is used to reveal elements that at first glance might not be relevant, such as hidden topics or themes of research areas (Huang & Chang, 2014).

Selected papers from the Web of Science were processed in the VOSviewer and Bibliometrix software to identify the main research clusters formed by the keywords of the selected papers, the links between them, and to represent them as thematic clusters using a two-dimensional diagram (Callon et al., 1991).

Regarding the articles on ISI Web of Science, in the data collection phase, 4166 articles with the topic *transfer prices* were identified and selected, while on Scopus we identified 3463, only the first 2000 being included in the analysis, based on the number of citations. The evolution of the number of identified publications from 2000 to 2024 can be observed in Fig. 4.1.

According to the figure above, we observe that authors' interest in transfer pricing has been increasing, peaking in 2021, when 249 articles with the selected topic were registered on the ISI Web of Science. The situation is similar for the selected articles on Scopus, reaching the peak during the analysed period, 229 in 2022. Although there is a higher number of publications referring to transfer pricing on the Scopus database, the number of them in the focus areas of our analysis is lower compared to that on Web of Science. These results suggest an increasing role of transfer pricing, highlighting the importance of our research. Also, the linear regression performed on the evolution of the number of publications on both databases indicates that the number of those on Web of Science will increase at almost double the rate of those on Scopus (the β-coefficient on WOS being 69.65 and that on Scopus 48.65). At the same time,

Table 4.1 Data collection methodology

Database: ISI Web of Science		*Database:* Scopus	
Topic: "transfer prices"		*Topic:* "transfer prices"	
Inclusion criteria: – Research areas: Business finance, business, economics, economics, management, operations research and management science.		*Inclusion criteria:* Research areas: Economics, econometrics, finance, business, management, accounting.	
Exclusion criteria: – All other research areas – For the topic transfer prices on the Scopus platform, we have selected the top 2000 documents in order of number of citations, as the platform limits the maximum download to 2000			
WOS results		*Scopus results*	
No exclusion criteria	10.775	No exclusion criteria	11.396
With exclusion criteria	4.166	With exclusion criteria	3.463
Date of access	20.06.2024	Date of access	20.06.2022
Selected articles	*3.324*	*Selected articles*	*2.000*
WOS search link: https://www.webofscience.com/wos/woscc/summary/734d8212-de2f-4f7d-be8a-5acdb1055bb9-fb843acb/relevance/1			
SCOPUS search link:: https://www-scopus-com.am.e-nformation.ro/results/results.uri?sort=plf-f&src=s&st1=transfer+pricing&sid=0bbe00db479f9314a105733d827d05c5&sot=b&sdt=b&sl=31&s=TITL			

Source: Developed by the author

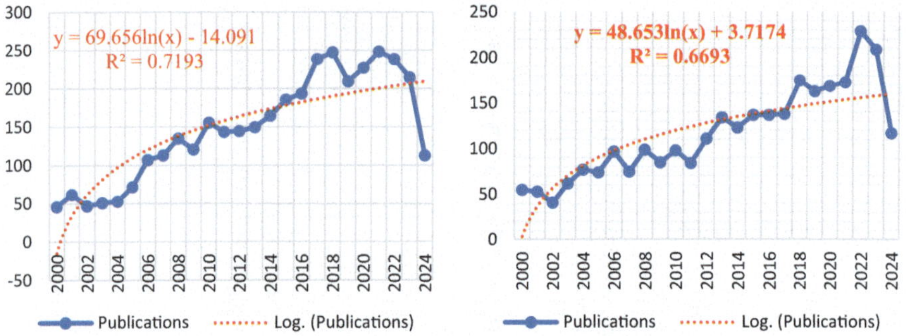

Fig. 4.1 Evolution of the number of publications with the topic transfer prices on Web of Science and Scopus. *Source*: Own processing based on WOS and Scopus data

we observe a decrease in the number of publications in 2023, this is caused by the beginning of the pandemic, researchers refocusing on analysing its impact, and the interest in transfer pricing being diminished in that year.

We have also identified the areas of the publications and to get an overview, Fig. 4.2 can be analysed.

In Fig. 4.2, we can visualise the incidence hierarchisation of the topic *transfer prices* according to research fields. As we can observe, the *economics* domain is the first at the top, with a number of 2030 publications in the Web of Science database and 1997 in Scopus, which denotes the importance and impact of transfer prices in the field of globalised economics. We can observe that most of the articles in the database dealing with transfer pricing are in correspondence with the fields of *economics, business finance, management, accounting,* and other adjacent fields, both on Web of Science and Scopus. Given that efficient transfer pricing management allows global companies to avoid paying unnecessary taxes or even reduce the tax burden to achieve the best possible financial outcome, we find this increased interest from economics as a natural one.

To capture the countries that have a high interest in the topic of transfer pricing, we have mapped the number of publications, according to the countries of origin of the authors, as can be seen in Fig. 4.3.

The US ranks first on both platforms with 2623 publications on WoS and 944 on Scopus. The following countries with a significant number of publications are China, UK, Germany, Canada, and France. Thus, there is a growing interest from developed countries in transfer pricing, especially in the Americas and the European Union, which are the areas with the largest number of multinationals. The fewest papers are found in Africa, a normal result given that most of these countries are developing.

Table 4.2 presents the authors with the most citations in the selected papers.

Reichelstein is the author with the most citations in our WoS selection. He analysed the influence of transfer pricing on investments and showed that transfer pricing negotiation leads to increased entity efficiency and performance compared to standard setting (Edlin & Reichelstein, 1995). The author also provides solutions to double taxation issues and some methods of reducing the tax burden of entities

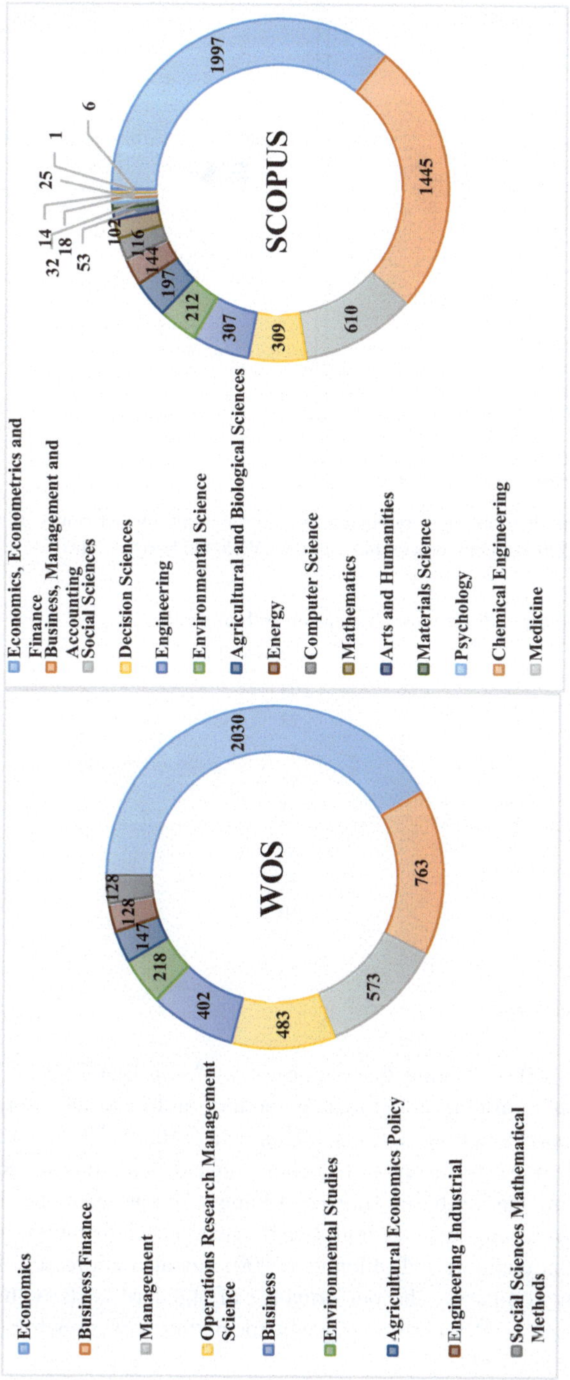

Fig. 4.2 Top 10 research fields with the topic transfer prices on the Web of Science and Scopus platforms. *Source:* Own processing based on WoS and Scopus data

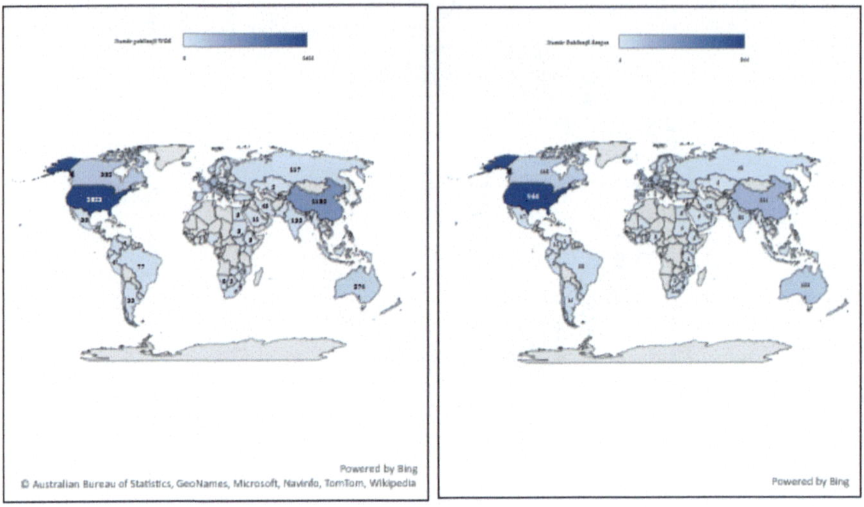

Fig. 4.3 Geographical distribution of publications with the topic transfer prices on the WoS and SCOPUS platforms. *Source:* Own processing based on WoS and Scopus data

Table 4.2 Top 10 authors with the most citations on Web of Science

Author	Number of citations
Reichelstein	108
Baldenius, T.	78
Srinidhi, B.	57
Clausing, K.A.	54
Melumad, N.D.	52
Grubert, H.	49
Goetschalckx, M.	46
Mutti, J.	46
Vidal, C.J.	46
Bartelsman, E.J.	42

Source: Author's processing

(Baldenius et al., 2003). Among his important works, a literature review on the importance of transfer pricing in the management of multinational companies with a focus on the tax burden of multinationals (Hiemann & Reichelstein, 2012) is listed.

Another notable paper is the one of Reilchelstein and Baldenius and Reichelstein (2006) who examine market-based transfer pricing when an upstream division has monopoly power in selling an asset both to a downstream division within the same firm and to external customers. Baldenius (2000) has also addressed the issue of transfer pricing by comparing the performance of standard costs with negotiated transfer prices when the information known by the parties is asymmetric (Baldenius, 2009; Baldenius et al., 1999).

The author Srinidhi B. examines how differential taxation affects both resource allocation and profitability of a decentralised multinational enterprise that uses the same transfer pricing for tax and performance measurement purposes (Halperin & Srinidhi, 1991). He also analysed the impact of differential tax rates and transfer pricing regulations on production and pricing decisions (Halperin & Srinidhi, 1987).

Regarding Goetschalckx et al. (2012), the authors describe the primary model and heuristics for the strategic configuration problem of supply chain design, which determines the optimal location of new production or capacity expansion facilities at a given transfer pricing rate by maximising net after-tax income.

4.1.1 Bibliometric Analysis of the Transfer Pricing Literature

To explore the main research themes in the analysed theme, a bibliometric analysis of the selected papers was performed using the VOSviewer software. The total number of keywords subjected to bibliometric analysis is 10,512 from the Web of Science selection, a number far too large to be represented in a table. Therefore, we have chosen a minimum threshold of 5 occurrences as a criterion, met by 725 keywords out of the 10,512. The network of keywords by cluster and by frequency of occurrence can be seen in Fig. 4.4.

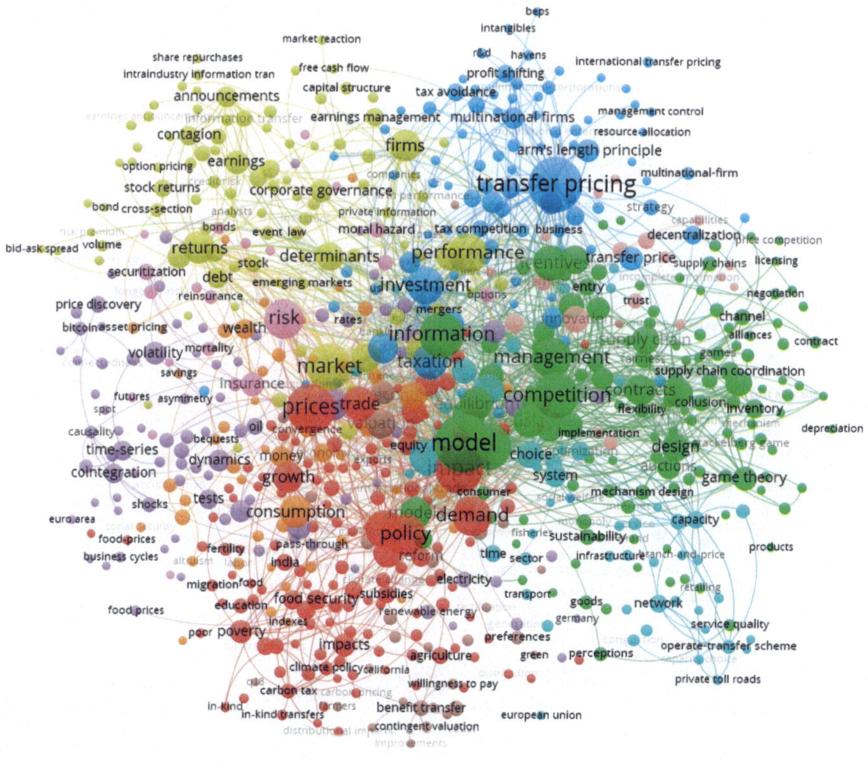

Fig. 4.4 Keyword network of the main WoS clusters. *Source:* Author's processing in VOSviewer

Processing the selected publications resulted in 10 clusters as shown in the image above. The main cluster formed is coloured red and has as central themes concepts like impact, prices, policies, demand, and supply. This cluster is relevant as it forms links with the transfer pricing cluster, especially on topics such as price and policy. We believe that this cluster discusses issues related to transfer pricing tax policies and all sorts of other factors that may have an impact on transfer prices.

The next largest cluster is represented in green and includes topics such as information, competition, and management, topics that relate to an entity's stakeholders and are important because knowledge of these transfer prices and the decisions made based on them by management are of great importance.

The third most important cluster is transfer pricing and we can observe the strong links formed between this main keyword and the other keywords in the other clusters: market, firms, competition, performance, information, demand, etc. All these words refer to transfer pricing and other traditional topics, but we observe a greater interest among researchers in information, policies, and models and less in performance. This denotes the researchers' main interest, which is primarily to improve the way and the policies for realising transfer prices and to smooth this process, followed by the performance and profit of the entities. The other clusters are significantly smaller, so we cannot comment on them.

Next, we analyse the keyword network by cluster and by frequency formed from the analysis of Scopus publications. The word network map obtained from the processing can be seen in Fig. 4.5.

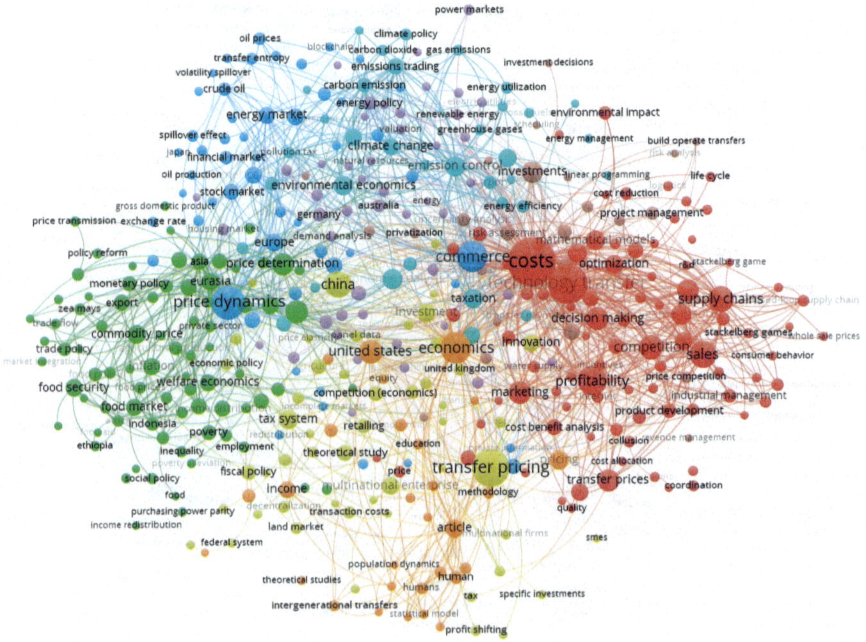

Fig. 4.5 Keyword network of the main clusters in Scopus. *Source:* Author's processing in VOSviewer

The total number of keywords subject to bibliometric analysis is 7436 from the Scopus selection, out of which 410 met the minimum occurrence threshold of 5. The processing resulted in 8 clusters as shown in the image above.

The first cluster—which is also the most numerous in terms of keywords—is coloured red and contains words such as cost, technology transformation, supply chain, and profitability. As a main theme, this cluster deals with the impact of technology development on costs, an impact that will also be felt in the area of transfer pricing, as it has multiple links with the cluster dealing with this theme. The next cluster, the one in blue, deals with trade and price dynamics, focusing more on cost drivers, i.e. the economic domain. We observe that this cluster also has multiple connections with the yellow cluster, which deals with transfer pricing. Therefore, we can see a difference between Web of Science publications and Scopus publications: the former is more focused on management, decisions, and policies, while the latter is focused on technology, innovation and how this influences the economic domain, including transfer pricing.

To visualise more easily, as well as to form an overview of the themes present in the field of transfer pricing research, we have processed the previously selected data in Bibliometrix software, mapping these themes in the form of a two-dimensional diagram. This type of representation allows us to visualise four typologies of themes: niche, emerging or declining, general, and *motor themes*. The results of the data processing can be seen in Fig. 4.6.

The top-right quadrant of Fig. 4.6 represents current and particularly relevant

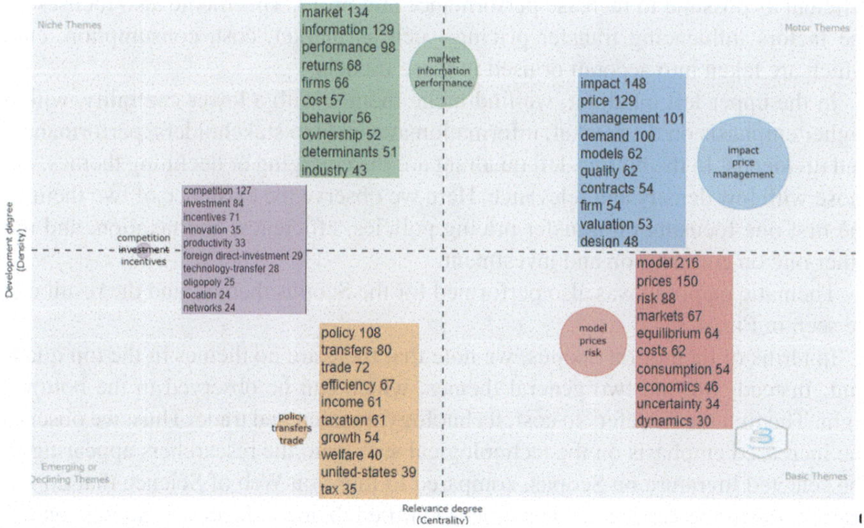

Fig. 4.6 Thematic mapping of keywords in the selected WoS literature. *Source:* Author's processing in VOSviewer

research topics, i.e. those topics whose keywords have a high density and centrality. The central theme of this quadrant indicates an increased interest of researchers in

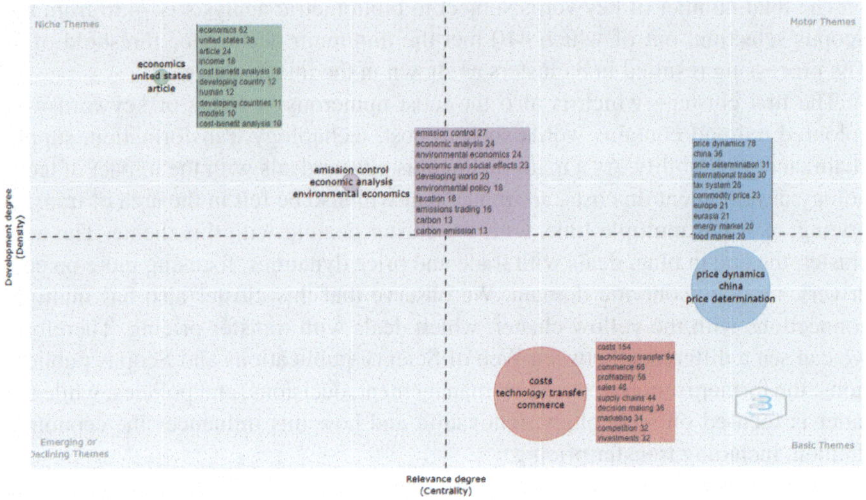

Fig. 4.7 Thematic mapping of keywords in the selected Scopus literature. *Source:* Author's processing in VOSviewer

the impact that transfer pricing has on the entity, as well as on management's transfer pricing decisions. In the bottom-right quadrant, we find general themes, i.e. those with high centrality and medium or low density, among which we mention the *model* theme, which aims at analysing transfer pricing by making their models as efficient as possible to increase performance and profit. This theme also focuses on the factors influencing transfer pricing, such as market, cost, consumption, etc., which are taken into account or used in these models.

In the upper-left quadrant, we find niche themes with a lower centrality, with a higher emphasis on the market, information available to stakeholders, performance, and dividends. In the bottom-left quadrant are the emerging or declining themes, i.e. those with low density and relevance. Here we observe the existence of two themes, the first one focusing on transfer pricing policies, efficiency, and taxation, and the other one on competition and investment.

Thematic mapping was also performed for the Scopus themes, and the result can be seen in Fig. 4.7.

In terms of themes on Scopus, we note that there are no themes in the top quadrant. Instead, we find two general themes, which can be observed in the bottom-right. The first theme refers to cost, technology transfer, and trade. Thus, we observe the increased emphasis on the technological side from the researchers appearing in the selected literature on Scopus, compared to those on Web of Science that do not address this topic very often. The other identified theme indicates an interest on the part of researchers in how transfer pricing is calculated. In the top-left, we find the niche themes, with low centrality but high density where we observe concepts related to carbon emission, environmental impact, sustainability, etc.

Thus, following the analysis of the two databases, we find that there are more topics of interest in Web of Science articles compared to Scopus articles, the former being more specific and much more centralised in terms of word linkage, indicating that there is a general direction of interest for most researchers in the transfer pricing approach. In contrast, the publications on Scopus are more focused on the impact of the technology and its development and do not have a topical focus that captures the interest of most researchers.

4.1.2 Modelling the Behaviour of Research Clusters

Keyword analysis is an effective tool in qualitative research that provides a clear picture of the scientific output, i.e. research trend. To identify the latent dimensions of research niches, keyword mining is one of the most effective methods (Kaur & Gupta, 2010). The distance between words or link between words is a very important variable in co-occurrence analysis. Statistical information on the relationships between key terms improves TL (total links) frequency results, helping to identify and capitalise on emerging research themes. According to Miyosawa et al. (2016), the combination of co-occurrence and frequency information provides clearer information in terms of scientific output and research areas. In this vein, to analyse the co-occurrence and frequency links, we applied the econometric model to the data collected and provided by the VOSviewer software on keywords extracted from scientific publications having the topic "transfer pricing".

Considering that scientific output is influenced by the correlations between key terms, the frequency of their occurrence, and the number of citations of scientific publications—based on the data provided by the VOSviewer software—we developed an econometric model that allows us to identify the correlations between existing research directions and to highlight the research directions that have not been addressed.

$$TL = \alpha + \beta_1 \text{cluster} + \beta_2 L + \beta_3 O + \beta_4 NC$$

where:

TL—Total links
L—Links
O—Occurrences
NC—Normalised number of citations

Total links or total link strength indicates the number of publications in which two keywords appear together. The links variable shows the co-occurrence connection between two keywords. According to the VOSviewer manual, each link has a strength represented by a positive numerical value. The higher this value, the stronger the link. The variable occurrence indicates the number of articles in which the

Table 4.3 Correlations on Total links and links, cluster, occurrence, and number of citations

		TL	CL	L	O	NC
Pearson correlation	TL	1.000	−0.097	0.981	0.984	0.065
	CL	−0.097	1.000	−0.088	−0.089	−0.073
	L	0.981	−0.088	1.000	0.956	0.073
	O	0.984	−0.089	0.956	1.000	0.033
	NC	0.065	−0.073	0.073	0.033	1.000
Sig. (1-tailed)	TL	.	0.005	0.000	0.000	0.040
	CL	0.005	.	0.009	0.009	0.024
	L	0.000	0.009	.	0.000	0.025
	O	0.000	0.009	0.000	.	0.188
	NC	0.040	0.024	0.025	0.188	.
N	TL	725	725	725	725	725
	CL	725	725	725	725	725
	L	725	725	725	725	725
	O	725	725	725	725	725
	NC	725	725	725	725	725

Source: Developed by the author with SPSS

Table 4.4 Model summary

Model	R	R square	Adjusted R square	Std. error of the estimate	Durbin–Watson
1	.994[a]	0.987	0.987	11.412	1.960

Source: Developed by the author with SPSS
[a]Predictors: (Constant), NC, O, CL, L
[b]Dependent variable: TL

keyword appears or its frequency. The normalised citation number indicates the number of citations of the document divided by the average number of citations of all documents published in the same year and included in the data that are provided by VOSviewer. Normalisation corrects for the fact that older papers have had more time to receive citations than more recent papers (Van Eck & Waltman, 2018).

According to the data in Table 4.3, regarding the correlations between the analysed key terms from the two databases (Web of Science and Scopus), it can be observed that between the variable TL (total links) and the variables L (links) and O (occurrence), there is a very strong correlation in the value of 0.984 and 0.981, respectively. In other words, the total number of links between keywords is influenced by the frequency of their occurrences within publications and the links they generate within and outside the cluster.

Keyword frequency and co-occurrence are important indicators that contribute to the growth of scientific output in certain fields. In antithesis to the above, the data in Table 4.3 show a weak correlation between Total Links and both the number of citations (0.065) and cluster variables (–0.097). This suggests that many publications around on the same key terms without generating other variables, additional clusters, or distinct research niches.

According to the data in Table 4.4, the R-squared indicator has a value of 0.987, which explains the strength of the relationship between the dependent variable Total

Table 4.5 ANOVA

Model		Sum of Squares	Df	Mean Square	F	Sig.
1	Regression	7296138.152	4	1824034.538	14006.558	.000[b]
	Residual	93763.567	720	130.227		
	Total	7389901.719	724			

Source: Developed by the author with SPSS
[a]Dependent variable: TL
[b]Predictors: (Constant), NC, O, CL, L

Table 4.6 Regression coefficients

Model		Unstandardised coefficients		Standardised coefficients			95.0% confidence interval for B	
		B	Std. Error	Beta	t	Sig.	Lower bound	Upper bound
1	(Constant)	−14.119	1.182		−11.948	0.000	−16.439	−11.799
	CL	−0.310	0.176	−0.007	−1.762	0.079	−0.655	0.035
	L	0.913	0.029	0.451	31.094	0.000	0.856	0.971
	O	2.644	0.069	0.552	38.135	0.000	2.508	2.780
	NC	1.711	0.529	0.014	3.232	0.001	0.671	2.750

Source: Developed by the author with SPSS
[a]Dependent variable: TL

links and the independent variables NC, O, cluster, and Links. The variation of these independent variables, i.e. their increase or decrease, implicitly leads to the variation of the dependent variable Total Links. The strong relationship between the variables can be explained by the fact that the total number of links between the keywords is generated by the frequency of their occurrence as well as by the number of clusters that generate new links, i.e. new research niches that have not been highlighted or have been explored less.

By applying the ANOVA test, we were able to statistically validate the multiple linear model (Anghelache et al., 2020), as shown in Table 4.5.

According to Table 4.5, the Fisher coefficient value is $F = 14006.558$. It can be observed that the Sig. value for the *F-test* is less than 0.05, i.e. the constructed model explains the significant dependence between the analysed variables by a multiple linear relationship (Table 4.5).

The estimated equation of the multiple linear regression model, according to the model coefficients presented in the Table above, is presented as:

$$TL = -14.119 - 0.310CL + 0.913L + 2.644O + 1.711NC$$

According to the data in Table 4.6, the total number of links (total links) is influenced to a very large extent by occurrence, followed by links, the normalised number of citations and clusters. If we take it logically, the number of occurrences of keywords in other articles generates new links which implicitly leads to an increase in the number of publications in which two keywords appear together (total links). An increase in the

Table 4.7 Residual statistics

	Minimum	Maximum	Mean	Std. Deviation	N
Predicted value	2.07	919.80	72.28	100.387	725
Residual	−63.474	85.176	0.000	11.380	725
Std. predicted value	−0.699	8.443	0.000	1.000	725
Std. residual	−5.562	7.464	0.000	0.997	725

Source: Developed by the author with SPSS
[a]Dependent variable: TL

normalised number of citations leads to an increase in the number of clusters which may represent new research niches (emerging themes) that detach from the old network, creating a new, often independent, or in very rare cases with small links to nearby clusters. This leads to a decrease in the total number of links, as the creation of a new cluster deliberately causes the network to break up by creating another one that is of more interest and topical, representing an emerging theme. Analysing the regression coefficients, we conclude that the co-occurrence (links) of words within these topics of analysis indicates the importance of certain topics within a discipline, while also influencing the number of publications in which two keywords appear together (TL). The analysis of the overlapping word clouds in different scientific publications as well as the relationships between Total Links, Links, and Occurrence highlights broader research topics, contributing to the increase of scientific output (Melega et al., 2022). The relationship between TL, Cluster, and NC variables gives an impression of related topics in a continuous two-dimensional space but misses a clear discrimination between different higher-order topics in a categorical space.

Often occurrences or frequency are not variables that can provide clear information, as stand-alone keywords that occur infrequently do not reveal latent flows, although separating frequently co-occurring longitudinal from temporary terms will do this. Applying residual statistics (Table 4.7), we identify topics or themes that do not fit the model, i.e. have been analysed and exploited extensively in the literature: competition, transfer pricing, efficiency, valuation, and returns. In other words, much of the scientific output revolves around these key terms, which are no longer topical. The following have been identified as research topics that fit the model: political economy, rents, transportation, house prices, and price discrimination. In practice, future research on enterprise performance should orbit around the topics listed above, which have been less explored, either because they are not topical or because they have simply been neglected by researchers.

The histogram represented in Fig. 4.8 shows an asymmetric distribution towards the right side (on the decreasing slope of the Gaussian curve), which means that the scientific output on transfer pricing has—according to the obtained model—a predominantly favourable evolution, developing new research niches, which means high exposure to exogenous and endogenous factors that may influence this perception.

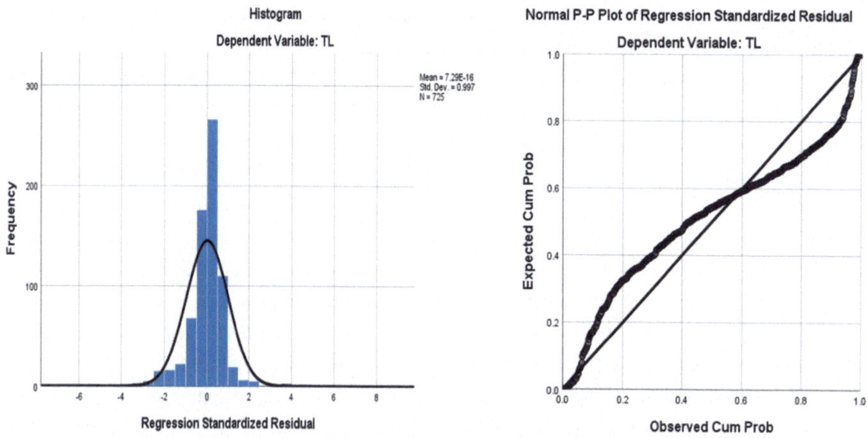

Fig. 4.8 Error histogram. *Source:* Developed by the author with SPSS

4.2 Accounting, Legal, and Fiscal Approaches to Transfer Pricing

The concept of transfer pricing dates back to the late 1880s when it referred to managerial accounting issues, and as companies increasingly organised themselves around divisions and segments, their management devised a methodology for internal profit allocation among them using this transfer pricing mechanism (Bradley, 2015). Petruzzi and Tavares (2019) identified several significant stages in their evolution as follows:

1. *Late nineteenth century–1930.* The first mention of transfer pricing in certain industries takes us to the late nineteenth century in England, which was also the period when multinational companies emerged due to the internationalisation of production and capital; in 1915, the arm's length principle was first mentioned in the UK in a law allowing non-residents to be taxed if profits were generated in the course of their business activities with a resident with whom they were deemed to be connected by close links and substantial control.
2. *Period 1930–1960.* This period is characterised by massive sales, the operational diversification of industrial enterprises in the USA, Japan, and Germany, the formation of financial and industrial groups, and an increasing level of organisational complexity of enterprises, which gave impetus to the transfer pricing theory. Also in 1935, the Draft Convention on the Allocation of Profits from Commercial Profits was drawn up, containing articles which served as the basis for Articles 7 and 9 of the current OECD Model Convention. It was the first time the issue of transfer pricing was formalised in economics by Hirshleifer (1956) who stated that the transfer price is the "correct" price only when the transaction is carried out in a perfectly competitive market, and if this does not exist, then

the "correct" price is the applicable marginal cost, taking into account some specific requirements (Chitic & Birman, 2012).

3. The *period 1960–1990* when in England, the USA, and Japan large holding companies were formed, and transfer pricing became an instrument of the corporate production management mechanism. From the 1960s and 1970s, legal regulations in this area developed in parallel in the USA and Europe, with the OECD Model Convention on the avoidance of double taxation of income and capital being adopted in 1963.
4. *1990–present.* In 1992, the Model Tax Convention on Income and Capital was adopted and has been revised 10 times, most recently in 2017 (OECD, 2017a, 2017b, 2017c). In 1995, the Transfer Pricing Guidelines for Multinational Enterprises and Tax Administrations were adopted, a document that represented a consensus among OECD member states, which have widely adopted and implemented these regulations and recommendations (TPG, 2017). In 2015, the BEPS (Base Erosion and Profit Shifting) Action Plan was adopted by the G20/OECD whose objective was to achieve coherence, substance, and transparency in global tax strategies and policies, with three actions dedicated to transfer pricing, addressing issues related to intangible assets, risk and capital, and other high-risk transactions (Chirag Sheth, 2018).

Therefore, it can be noted that the rules and the international framework on transfer pricing guidelines have been constantly changing and adapting to the requirements and challenges of the economic environment, and these changes have been increasingly accentuated in recent times. The race for new international transfer pricing obligations could be seen as an opportunity for professionals in the field to improve their skills, opening up new horizons and prospects for their development and the expansion of their expertise in new areas of practice. This trend towards digitisation of the economy and the increased need to adapt the international tax regulatory framework has not gone unnoticed by the OECD, which is also the main international body dealing with such global problems, issuing recommendations and guidelines that are not legally binding but are widely appreciated and adopted by the governments of many countries, which reinforces its role and international importance in shaping international tax rules. Therefore, having an interest in addressing the challenges brought by the massive digitisation of the economy whose characteristics further accentuate the risks of erosion of the tax base and profit shifting, the OECD has identified those with significant impact on international taxation and the business environment (Petruzzi & Buriak, 2018). These characteristics relate to issues such as the mobility of intangibles, users and business functions, information trust, network effects in terms of user participation and integration, the use of multilateral business models, the tendency towards monopoly or oligopoly, volatility generated by low entry stringency, and rapid technological change (OECD, 2015a, 2015b). All these aspects may more or less influence the procedure for analysing the transfer pricing practised by multinational enterprises (MNEs), as well as the way they allocate their tax bases between the different countries in which they operate, while also highlighting areas of interest for future improvements.

Given the evolution and the direction of development of the international business context, which is increasingly subject to globalisation and digitisation, there are generated or highlighted certain issues and challenges specific to this context that derive from the very complexity and breadth of the existing system, given the multitude of actors involved and their different interests, the need for communication between them, the level of territorial extension, the legislative systems that make it up, and so on. Some of the biggest problems, however—specific to the current period—are represented by the phenomena of organised economic crime, such as tax evasion, money laundering, smuggling, underground economy, shell companies, and other forms of these (Albanese, 2021; Popko & Popko, 2021) which still occur in the current international context, despite the existence of various legislative and administrative measures aimed at reducing their frequency and intensity, as well as various scientific studies aimed at identifying appropriate methods and techniques to prevent, combat, and manage these phenomena (Oliinyk et al., 2021; Akinbowale et al., 2020; Markina et al., 2021). Although all economic crime phenomena have in common aspects such as the misuse of anonymous corporate vehicles, professional facilitators (accountants, lawyers, etc.), and the co-opting of public officials (Duri, 2021), they have certain specific characteristics that differentiate them. Their frequency and intensity differ from country to country (Achim et al., 2021) depending on the level of economic development, the level of digitisation, the rigour of the applicable legal system, and other aspects.

These phenomena are also manifested in the practices of multinational companies, which are very often accused of tax evasion and of avoiding and minimising taxes and duties by using various mechanisms and techniques at their disposal, including transfer pricing (a concept that is increasingly being used in correspondence with various illicit behaviours of large corporations that generate financial and social harm to the entire global community (Faccio & Ghosh, 2021)), in a context where they dominate the economic, political, and social scene of most nations (Sikka & Willmott, 2010) by expanding their activities in different tax jurisdictions. According to Brugger and Engebretsen (2022), more than one-third of international trade takes place within corporations rather than between corporations; therefore, in this international business context, the role and importance of transfer pricing is increasing. This mechanism is also used by large corporations to increase shareholders' value through tax minimisation and avoidance strategies (Arafat & Haga, 2020). Transfer pricing is not per se an illicit practice, but it acquires this character when it becomes manipulative, aggressive, and abusive in the context of non-compliance with the principles underlying the legal basis of this mechanism (Ciubotariu & Petrescu, 2021), thus leading to the erosion of the tax base and the illicit transfer of multinationals' profits from jurisdictions with a rigid tax system and high level of taxation to jurisdictions with a flexible tax system and low level of taxation (Tørsløv et al., 2018), also called tax havens. These are defined by the Tax Justice Network (2022) as countries or jurisdictions that allow multinational corporations and individuals to evade the obligations of the rule of law in the countries where they operate and reside by paying less tax than they would be required to pay by law in those countries.

As for the principles that should govern the transfer pricing mechanism, they refer to the arm's length or market value principle whose basis can be found in Article 9 of the OECD Model Tax Convention (2017b), which outlines the premises of the bilateral tax treaties of the OECD member states, stipulating that when between two associated enterprises certain conditions are laid down or imposed in their commercial or financial relations which differ from those which would have been laid down between independent enterprises, then any profits which, but for those conditions, would have accrued to one of the enterprises, but which, because of those conditions, have not so accrued, may be included in the profits of that enterprise and taxed accordingly. Thus, by attempting to adjust profit for the conditions that would have existed between independent enterprises in comparable circumstances and transactions, the arm's length principle involves treating the members of a multinational group as operating as separate entities and not as inseparable parts of a single unified enterprise, as stipulated in the OECD Transfer Pricing Guidelines for Multinational Enterprises and Tax Administrations (2022a). Therefore, transactions within multinationals should be conducted at a price that reflects compliance with the arm's length principle, which involves comparing the price charged for goods or services transferred in a controlled transaction with the price charged for goods or services transferred in a comparable uncontrolled transaction under similar circumstances, and if a difference is found between them, it can be concluded that the commercial and financial relations of associated enterprises are not conducted at arm's length (Choi et al., 2018). The purpose of this principle is to ensure that profits are taxed where the business activity takes place, i.e. where its resources are located and directed and economic value is created (Greil, 2021). However, aggressive tax avoidance strategies practised by multinationals in diverse economic sectors cost governments an estimated €36 billion per year in the European Union, €24 billion in Japan, and €100.8 billion in the United States (Álvarez-Martínez et al., 2021).

Therefore, despite all the regulations related to this principle underlying international tax systems, since the beginning of the twentieth century, there have been several researchers questioning its effectiveness (Cobham & Janský, 2018; Ylönen & Teivainen, 2018), considering it as one of the main facilitators of profit shifting, especially in transactions that are difficult to quantify in terms of market value, such as those whose subject matter is intangible assets or intellectual property rights (Lips, 2019). According to Pleune et al. (2017), this principle that has prevailed in international tax systems for decades has lost its topicality as a result of the accentuation of globalisation and European integration phenomena, the increase in the number of multinational enterprises and the value of their intangible assets, the world of a century ago has changed considerably, especially if we look from the perspective of the digitisation process that increasingly monopolises international relations and transactions. Due to these issues, some subjective interpretations may be generated, which also leads to difficulties in the enforceability of existing regulations, as in some contexts, there might not be a "fair" market price because there are no comparable transactions with third parties (Beer et al., 2018) for various reasons such as monopoly situations (Choi, Furusawa, & Ishikawa, 2020a), the arm's length principle aiming to help combine the planned price anomaly with an analytical framework of "free" markets (Ylönen & Teivainen, 2018).

Thus, when talking about multinational enterprises engaging in cross-border transactions with related units of the group (subsidiaries, affiliated entities)—through which final and intermediate products, capital goods, licenses, fees for technical and management services, intra-firm loans or credits, and services are transferred (Lecraw, 2017)—it is also impossible not to enter into the concept of transfer pricing, as it is defined as referring to the prices set by a multinational enterprise on its intra-group transactions to allocate revenues and costs between divisions, subsidiaries, and joint ventures within a group (Rogers & Oats, 2022). According to Chitic and Birman (2012), the price of a good or resource is an indicator of what has to be given up to obtain that good or resource and is expressed in monetary terms, although the payment does not necessarily have to be in monetary form. Kumar et al. (2021) have also referred to transfer pricing as the practice of pricing transactions between and within enterprises under common ownership and control, which is similar to Asongu et al. (2019) who what emphasised that transfer pricing is a process by which goods are traded between legal entities or subsidiaries within a corporation. Despite the high level of transfer pricing regulation and the existing frameworks and implementation guidelines—which generally relate to the permitted methods for determining arm's length prices, documentation requirements, setting penalties for non-compliance, and determining the likelihood of a transfer price adjustment (de Mooij & Liu, 2018)—these continue to be the subject of an ongoing controversy between multinationals and the governments of the states in which they operate because we can see a conflict of interest between these two parties, as governments want the highest possible tax and duty receipts, and multinationals want the highest possible minimisation of tax expenditures, which is one of the main revenue management policies (Amidu et al., 2019). Lecraw (2017) identified three main reasons why these controversies exist:

- The impact on host and home economies of the prices charged by MNEs for intra-firm exports and imports, which also affect their profitability and their ability to allocate resources within the group
- The existence in many cases of a considerable degree of room for manoeuvre between the transfer price that is optimal for the multinational enterprise and the price that is optimal for the government and the market price
- The non-existence in some situations of a competitive market price for a given product or service and therefore there is no benchmark against which transfer prices can be assessed.

This explanatory memorandum emphasises the discrepancy between the idealistic nature of the legal regulations and the practical situations in which multinational companies may find themselves and in which it is quite difficult to make decisions that reflect the principles underlying the transfer pricing mechanism. As already mentioned, this context offers a high degree of interpretability and is nothing more than an opportunity for multinationals to strengthen their strategies for minimising and avoiding tax liabilities. Despite highlighting the loopholes in the transfer pricing legislative framework, it can still increase the tax burden on multinationals, thereby protecting domestic revenues and levelling the playing field against domestic companies (de Mooij & Liu, 2018). Some research has identified that profit-shifting activities of multinationals are significantly discouraged and reduced when countries introduce or tighten transfer pricing documentation requirements, which reinforces the role and importance of regulations in combating tax base erosion and profit shifting.

It can be seen that in the context of transfer pricing, there is an emphasis on concepts such as group, subsidiary, affiliated party and divisions, which emphasises the requirement that there must be some level of "relatedness" between the entities involved in the transaction to be able to talk about transfer pricing. Thus, we can appreciate that a group consists of several companies that are related through ownership and/or other mechanisms to exercise control (Sørensen, 2021), and, according to the OECD Glossary (1993), a subsidiary is defined as a company controlled by another company that owns more than 50% of its ordinary shares.

Therefore, it can be seen that for a company to be considered a subsidiary, it needs to be at least 50% controlled by the parent entity and to be considered an affiliated entity it needs to be at least 25% controlled by another company. According to Accounting Rule 15 of the European Commission, affiliated relationships may be reflected in situations where one party can control the other party if one party exercises significant influence over the other party in making financial and operating decisions, and if the related party entity and another entity are subject to common control (European Commission, 2009). According to the same source (European Commission, 2009), related party relationships may arise where an individual is either a member of the management body or is involved in the financial and operating decisions of the reporting entity or in the context of external operational relationships between the reporting entity and the related party, often involving some level of economic dependence. We can therefore appreciate that relationships between companies within the same group are complex, which creates the need for tailored regulations that address each side of these types of relationships in as much detail and realistically as possible so that the risks associated with them are minimised.

4.3 Determinants in Building the Transfer Pricing Case and Attracting Foreign Direct Investment

The issue of tax evasion or tax avoidance through the transfer pricing mechanism is a topic of major interest in today's globalised economy, with national and international legislative authorities paying more and more attention and concern to this topic (Barrera & Bustamante, 2018) in an attempt to optimise the legal system and practices in this area, since with the increase in transactions and capital turnover at the international level, the risks and likelihood of economic crime phenomena increase, especially in multinational companies. The author has identified three main reasons for practising transfer pricing that a multinational company may consider and they refer to the fact that this mechanism can increase the efficiency of the management system, it can help tax planning and thus avoid paying various taxes and duties, and the fact that they are imposed by government authorities. Therefore, multinational companies are certainly aware of the administrative and financial benefits of implementing a transfer pricing system, even if it is imposed by the authorities or even if it requires significant additional costs, which in any case are covered by the benefits generated by its efficient management.

According to Cooper and Nguyen (2020), tax planning refers to the ability of national companies to structure and organise their tax affairs through various mechanisms to reduce taxes and duties legally—in the context of multinational companies, we can speak predominantly of transfer pricing mechanisms, these measures "focusing on the annual corporate income tax due or other tax implications of the activities carried out or the structure of the firm, including after merging and acquisition procedures". Other existing research shows that the main tax planning techniques or strategies used by multinational companies to mitigate, avoid, and evade tax liabilities relate to the use of transfer pricing to move income to countries with low tax rates from those with high ones (Padhi, 2019). The use of thin capitalisation, deduction of intra-group interest payments, use of tax havens and tax incentives (Bradley, 2015), trading at over- or underpricing (Sebele-Mpofu et al., 2021), allocating valuable intangible assets to low-tax jurisdictions, and hoarding cash in foreign subsidiaries are other methods used by multinationals to reduce or avoid taxation. All of these point government authorities in the optimisation directions on which they should focus their attention and efforts to minimise their impact on savings. At the same time, we can mention that under the management of an aggressive and manipulative transfer pricing strategy or policy, a significant impact is exerted on the locally declared tax base—in the sense of decreasing it—which economically and socially affects the communities where the subsidiaries carry out their economic activity.

Thus, in the vast majority of cases, transfer pricing policies and strategies are implemented as an exploitation or an extension of cost management or tax planning by multinational companies. Mashiri et al. (2021) provide an interesting insight into the avoidance behaviour of multinational companies through transfer pricing policies and strategies, arguing that it is also largely encouraged by tax consultants who have a rich and detailed knowledge of complex tax issues, offering their expertise to support non-transparent and illicit practices that generate a high level of social and economic inequity. Of course, we cannot generalise this statement for all professionals who are tax consultants, but we can appreciate that they are in a rather uncomfortable position, since on the one hand they have to demonstrate loyalty to the companies that have requested their services and contribute to optimising their tax costs, and on the other hand, they have to ensure compliance with the rules and legislative (Fogarty & Jones, 2014), which requires a high level of objectivity and verticality that is quite difficult to achieve, given that in most situations there is a tendency to be more biased towards one side or the other. Therefore, governments need to have well-trained human resources with expertise in the field of taxation, who are particularly knowledgeable and understand abusive transfer pricing strategies and policies, including how they manifest themselves to be able to identify them efficiently and timely (Cooper et al., 2016), so that there is a high counter-attacking capacity of governments against these phenomena, precisely to protect the economy by reducing the frequency or intensity of their impact.

With the increasing digitisation of the international trading system and with the more and more intensive introduction of artificial intelligence in international economic relations, the economic and fiscal environment will face new and demanding challenges which, once overcome, will add value and efficiency to the knowledge, procedures, and regulations related to this field, allowing the creation of a more transparent and secure international economic system, closer to the real needs and requirements of the business environment.

4.4 Transfer Pricing Documentation

Transfer pricing documentation is one of the main tools that can be used to assess the legality and compliance of intra-group transactions with existing national and international principles, guidelines, and regulations. The documentation is useful for several categories of stakeholders, but especially for auditors and government authorities as they have a high interest in the reality, fairness, and legality of the transfer policies practised by the entities, as they can significantly influence various reported performance indicators and the amount of corporate income tax paid. Therefore, in order not to be subject to adjustments that would entail additional costs, companies should consider building a detailed and complete transfer pricing file that demonstrates good faith compliance with legal principles and regulations regarding the terms of transaction prices with other companies in the same group and should also contain detailed information on the practised transfer pricing method and the rationale for its choice (Fun & Raiahu, 2018), thus facilitating the conduct of tax audits.

According to the OECD Transfer Pricing Guidelines for Multinational Enterprises and Tax Administrations (2022b), the objectives of transfer pricing documentation requirements are to:

- Ensure that the specific requirements are properly taken into account by taxpayers when setting the prices and other terms of their transactions with other associated enterprises and when reporting the income from such transactions in their tax returns
- Provide tax administrations with the necessary information to make an informed assessment of transfer pricing risks
- To provide tax administrations with useful information that they can use to conduct a thorough and proper audit of the transfer pricing practices of entities subject to taxation in their jurisdiction

It can thus be seen that among the main objectives of transfer pricing documentation is to provide detailed information to subjects interested in these policies. Lohse and Riedel (2013), Marques and Pinho (2016) identified that transfer pricing documentation provisions have some effectiveness in limiting mispricing and illicit pricing behaviour. The application of the arm's length principle requires transfer pricing to be calculated before the benchmark transactions take place, which means that the transfer pricing documentation or file needs to be constructed during the business and not at the end of the tax period or when required by the authorities (Transfer Pricing Asia, 2018). This implies a permanent and constant involvement of companies in this area, a concern that materialises either by outsourcing this activity or by including an internal department in the organisational structure to deal with it.

According to the OECD, there are three levels of a standardised approach to these transfer pricing documentation requirements, the objective of which is to determine the actual profit of multinational companies that has been generated in each national tax jurisdiction, which may indicate that there is an intention of states to control these companies to some extent, which is also because, at the international level, there are hardly any general regulations for this category of companies (Velikorossov et al., 2019). As stipulated in the OECD Transfer Pricing Guidelines, this three-tiered approach refers to:

- A Master File containing standardised information relevant to all MNE group members
- A Local File which relates specifically to the material transactions of the local taxpayer
- A Country-by-Country (CbC) Report which contains certain information on the overall allocation of the enterprise group's income and taxes paid, as well as some indicators on the location of economic activity within the group.

Action No. 13—*Transfer Pricing Documentation and Country-by-Country Reporting* of the BEPS Action Plan addresses this topic of the documentation required for optimal transfer pricing records, providing insights on how to approach this topic as well as details on what information should be included in these categories of reports (OECD, 2015a, 2015b). The master file provides tax administrations with an overview of the economic, legal, financial, and tax arrangements within an MNE and a structure of its operations (Transfer Pricing Asia, 2018), which helps to assess the company's position on transfer pricing and the related risks from a general perspective (Güvemli et al., 2017). This report should include information on the organisational structure, description of various activities, intangible assets used in the activities, financial transactions between companies, and financial and tax positions (KPMG, 2016). While the OECD guidelines outline this information requirement, there is still some flexibility in how structured the information should be presented, with centralised functions and transactions having to be documented in detail (Valentiam Group, 2021). For the preparation of this file, there is no need for MNEs to reach a certain threshold of any economic-financial indicator, rather these issues are addressed in the national regulations of the countries that apply the OECD provisions related to this topic (Transfer Pricing Asia, 2018). Although this file should also be made available to local tax authorities, the burden of its preparation does not fall on all group entities, but only on the parent entity (Valentiam Group, 2021).

As for the local transfer pricing file, it complements the main file and relates to a specific taxpayer in a specific country, providing a detailed picture of the financial information and related party transactions entered into by that taxpayer, which supports the work of local tax authorities in identifying the legality and arm's length compliance of these categories of transactions (Transfer Pricing Asia, 2017). According to the OECD Transfer Pricing Guidelines, the local file must contain information on the management structure of the local entity, a local organisational chart, a description of the persons to whom the entity reports, a description of the business activity and strategy pursued by the entity, and information on the main competitors. As with the main file, the requirements related to the obligation to prepare the local transfer pricing file differ from country to country, with some countries requiring almost all transactions to be documented, while others show interest only in major transactions with a significant impact on the local entity's tax liabilities (Nehoray et al., 2015).

The third level of transfer pricing documentation approach promoted by the OECD is the CbC report, as mentioned above. It is part of a series of international measures to combat tax avoidance, with the ability to identify multinational corporations that shift their profits to tax havens to pay less tax than they should (Tax Justice Network, 2020), which is made possible by full information exchange between participating jurisdictions (Australian Taxation Office, 2022). Action 13 of the BEPS Action Plan provides MNEs with an annual reporting template for each tax jurisdiction in which they operate (OECD) and the information that it must provide and refer to (Nehoray et al., 2015):

- "income on related and unrelated parties and the amount, including royalties, service charges, service fees, interest income premiums and any other amounts derived from transactions with related and unrelated parties, but excluding dividends;
- pre-tax profits;
- income tax paid, including withholding tax;
- accumulated corporate income tax, i.e. the sum of current accrued tax expense recognised on the taxable profit for the reporting year, excluding reversals or deferred taxes and provisions for uncertain tax liabilities;
- number of full-time employees;
- stated capital;
- retained earnings;
- tangible assets, other than cash and cash equivalents".

It can be noted that the information contained in the CbC report is more complex than that in the other two reports presented above, and its preparation applies to multinational companies with a consolidated revenue of €750 million or more (Deloitte, 2016). By its nature, the CbC report involves the transfer and exchange of financial and tax information from one jurisdiction to another, which encourages increased transparency and accountability of multinational companies in their dealings with other stakeholders. According to OECD (2022a), as of March 2022, there were more than 3000 activated bilateral exchange relationships for the exchange of CbC reports, with the first automated exchanges of CbC reports taking place in June 2018. These include exchange relationships between the 92 jurisdictions that are signatories to the Multilateral Competent Authority Agreement on The Exchange of Country-By-Country Reports (CbC MCAA), under which each competent authority will automatically exchange the CbC report received from each reporting entity that is tax resident in its jurisdiction with all other competent authorities in its signatory jurisdictions on an annual basis.

As mentioned above, among the most significant guidelines related to transfer pricing documentation are the *OECD Transfer Pricing Guidelines for Multinational Enterprises and Tax Administrations* and Action No. 13—*Country-by-Country Reporting* which is part of the BEPS Action Plan. Its implementation is being closely monitored by the OECD which in 2021 issued its fourth peer review report to 132 jurisdictions across the globe, the purpose of which is to ensure effective and consistent implementation of the standard assessed and to recognise the progress made by jurisdictions in this regard (OECD, 2021c). The main results of this peer review are as follows:

- *Related to the national legal and administrative framework:* More than 100 tax jurisdictions have a national legal framework for CbC reporting, and several jurisdictions have final approved legislation awaiting formal publication.
- *Related to the information exchange framework:* 83 jurisdictions have multilateral or bilateral competent authority agreements in place; as of October 2021, more than 4500 activated bilateral exchange relationships have been registered with more than 110 jurisdictions engaged in the Common Reporting Standard (CRS) (activated relationships for the exchange of CRS information), which are covered by the Multilateral Convention (MLI),[1] The CRS Multilateral Competent Authority Agreement (CRS MCAA), the European Union (EU) framework, and bilateral agreements (OECD, 2021a, 2021b).
- *Privacy-related:* 89 of the jurisdictions surveyed have undergone an assessment by the Global Forum on Transparency and Exchange of Information for Tax Purposes on privacy and data protection in the context of the implementation of the Automatic Exchange of Information (AEOI) standard and have not received any action plans, while 10 of them have been issued with such action plans providing recommendations for improvement.

Based on the same categories of reports previously issued by the OECD, Table 4.8 shows the following evolution of the main results of the peer review of jurisdictions' progress in implementing Action 13 of the BEPS Action Plan:

[1] The Multilateral Convention to Implement Tax Treaty Related Measures to Prevent Base Base Erosion and Profit Shifting entered into force on July 1, 2018 and already covers 99 jurisdictions, its role is to provide concrete solutions to close loopholes in existing international tax rules by translating the results of the OECD/G20 BEPS project into bilateral tax treaties around the world, according to https://www.oecd.org/tax/treaties/multilateral-convention-to-implement-tax-treaty-related-measures-to-prevent-beps.htm

Table 4.8 Implementation of Action No. 13 of the BEPS Action Plan at the jurisdiction level

Reference year	Year of report publication	National legal and administrative framework	On the information exchange framework	On privacy
2017	2018	60 jurisdictions	58 jurisdictions	–
2018	2019	>80 jurisdictions	67 jurisdictions	73 jurisdictions
2019	2020	>90 jurisdictions	73 jurisdictions	78 jurisdictions
2020	2021	>100 jurisdictions	83 jurisdictions	89 jurisdictions

Source: Information from Country-by-Country Reporting—Peer Review Reports (2018, 2019, 2020, 2021a)

From the above table, it can be seen that over the years under review, there has been significant progress in the number of jurisdictions involved in the global initiative to increase corporate information transparency and the number of bilateral or multilateral information exchanges by designing, developing, and supporting a legal framework that creates an optimal environment for their development and discourages the secrecy of corporate economic, financial, and tax information, which is often the premise for the manifestation of economic crime. We can therefore appreciate that more and more governments are becoming aware of the importance and role of legislative regulation in strengthening the most transparent possible relationship between multinational companies and their stakeholders, which will reduce the opportunities or circumstances for economic crime. These transparent and optimal relations between multinational companies and their stakeholders—in particular government authorities and investors—concerning economic, financial, and tax information suppose nothing other than correct, complete, and timely communication between them, which can be achieved by preparing transfer pricing documentation, i.e. the related reports that have been analysed above. Therefore, we consider the role of transfer pricing documentation to be a rather significant one in managing the need for transparent information of the stakeholders, as it provides an overview of the economic relations, financial and tax status, and structure of the company that is subject to analysis.

4.5 Transfer Pricing Assessment Policies and Methods According to OECD Guidelines

To be able to understand how transfer pricing is valued, it is very important to first understand what transfer pricing is and when it is practised. According to the OECD guide definition, "transfer prices are the prices at which transactions between companies that are parts of the same group, called related parties, are carried out, transactions that must be concluded at a market price as if they had been concluded between independent parties under comparable economic conditions" (Rus, 2020). The transfer pricing problem is usually described as a problem of finding the price or pricing schedule that comes closest to inducing an efficient level of trade between two divisions of a firm (Clausing, 2003; Cristea & Nguyen, 2016; Grubert & Mutti, 1991; Holmstrom & Tirole, 1991; Riedel et al., 2015).

The overlapping crises of recent times have led to a downturn in economic activity and a fall in corporate profits, which has increased pressure on multinationals to find ways to reduce their tax liabilities, leading them to possibly resort to transfer pricing strategies aimed at shifting profits to low-tax jurisdictions. To meet these challenges, governments around the world have implemented new transfer pricing regulations, strengthened existing regulations, and stepped up tax controls and enforcement. They are also continuing to monitor the impact of the crisis on transfer pricing policies and practices to ensure that multinational companies meet their tax obligations. The current crisis has underlined the importance of transfer pricing and the need for governments to ensure that multinational companies pay their fair share of taxes in each country where they operate.

Therefore, tax planning is one of the main sources of profits for modern enterprises, especially for those companies operating in countries with different tax regimes whose aim is to realise profits through localisation options of affiliated companies, such as tax reduction (Eden, 2009; Graham et al., 2017; Lo et al., 2010). A transfer price refers to the cost at which a product, asset, or service is provided by one subsidiary of a company to another subsidiary within the same corporation. These prices are used to calculate the revenues of both parties involved in cross-border transactions. They also have an impact on the taxable income of the countries involved in the transaction. In any cross-border tax situation, the parties involved are the group entities and the tax authorities of the respective countries (Dallyn, 2017; Devereux & Vella, 2018; Jost et al., 2014). When the profits of a group member in one country change, this can have an impact on the taxable income of another country.

Most commonly, multinational companies use transfer pricing to artificially shift profits to jurisdictions with flexible tax systems, charging high prices for goods and services sold to subsidiaries in high-tax jurisdictions and low prices for those sold to subsidiaries in low-tax jurisdictions. This transfer pricing manipulation can significantly reduce the amount of taxes a company pays in high-tax jurisdictions (De Wulf, 2015; Durst, 2010). Multinational corporations take advantage of the different tax rates imposed in different jurisdictions to reduce the overall tax liability for the group as a whole (Awodiran, 2014; Zetter et al., 2009). Consequently, the transfer pricing process and the selection of the transfer pricing method are of significant importance to both multinational corporations and the nations in which they are located (Cools et al., 2008; Smolarski et al., 2019).

Today, profitable businesses are turning their interests to organisational structures called global value chains (Antràs, 2020; Lee & Yi, 2018). Thus, to minimise operating costs, entities recognise a new variable to avoid legal barriers by dividing global processes through vertical corporate structures. Based on the aforementioned, the topic is of particular interest in the spectrum of countries tending towards liberalisation of economies, as such business strategies are likely to produce conflicts with their economic policies and interests. A concrete example of such a problem arises when multinational companies conduct intra-group operations and distort market price dynamics to minimise their overall tax rate. Essentially, this phenomenon refers to the manipulation of the "transfer pricing" of a transaction and takes on particular importance when the economic linkage situation is instrumented to set prices that allow the allocation of revenues across business units of the same group (Duong, 2018; Nguyena et al., 2019).

The above-mentioned gap reiterates that the transfer pricing issue is topical, but does not captivate contemporary economic theory intensively. To exemplify the situation addressed, at the moment, the persistent approach to transfer pricing issues is tax law, the maximum exponent of which is concentrated in the Transfer Pricing Guidelines for Multinational Enterprises and Tax Administrations of the Organisation for Economic Cooperation and Development (OECD, 1995, 2010, 2015a, 2015b, 2017a, 2017b, 2017c).

Establishing and identifying an optimal method of transfer pricing is the main concern for multinationals and regulators. In selecting an optimal transfer pricing method, multinationals need to consider the advantages and disadvantages of the methods recognised by the Organisation for Economic Cooperation and Development, as well as other methods applied at the national level. The suitability of a method is primarily determined by a functional analysis and the availability of reliable data needed to implement the chosen method or alternative methods. Another important factor is the level of comparability between controlled and uncontrolled transactions, including the reliability of any comparability adjustments that may be needed to eliminate significant disparities between them (Ainsworth & Shact, 2012).

Transfer pricing methods refer to the way of calculating the prices at which transactions between two or more affiliated companies are carried out, and the choice of the most optimal method among those available may be determined by various internal or external factors, such as the overall profit of the company, the interest of the host country subsidiary and its requirement to maintain adequate cash flows, demographic and behavioural characteristics, and differences found in the tax regulations in general and transfer pricing regulations in the respective countries (Amidu et al., 2019). The transfer pricing methods proposed by the OECD Transfer Pricing Guidelines can be visualised in Fig. 4.9:

There are, therefore, five established methods for calculating transfer pricing, the applicability, relevance, and efficiency of each one being determined by the nature and subject matter of the transactions for which the calculation is intended, as well as market conditions related to competition and the availability of information. None of these methods can be considered appropriate in every context, as it is up to the taxpayer to select the one that provides the best estimate of a normal competitive price for a given transaction (Challoumis, 2019; Vissio & Samperna, 2022), identifying this process as a core criterion of transfer pricing (in addition to comparability analysis and the arm's length principle), naming it as the best method rule.

Traditional commercial methods for transfer pricing are considered to be the simplest methods for determining the value of transactions between related parties

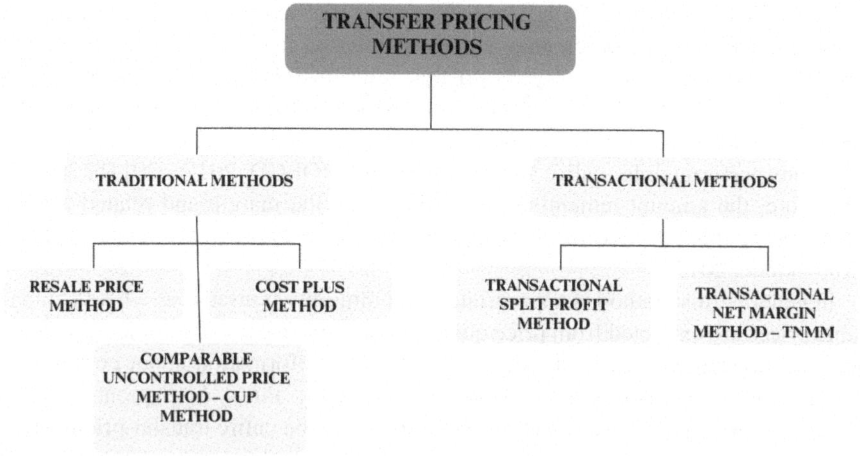

Fig. 4.9 Transfer pricing methods. *Source*: Adapted from OECD

(Boro, 2013; Grondona, 2017; OECD, 2017a, 2017b, 2017c). For example, when determining the price of an uncontrolled comparable transaction, any price variation can be directly attributed to the commercial and financial links established or imposed between the entities. The competitive market conditions can then be aassessed by substituting the uncontrolled transaction price for the controlled transaction price (Chong et al., 2018; Cools & Slagmulder, 2009; OECD, 2017a, 2017b, 2017c).

As for the Comparable Uncontrolled Price (CUP) method, it is considered the closest to the concept of the arm's length principle and is recommended by the OECD guidelines when its application is feasible, as it requires the existence of a fair price of a similar and comparable transaction. This approach relies on direct price comparisons and can only be accepted if the goods are available in the open market (Septiani et al., 2021). According to Heckemeyer et al. (2017), the CUP method is commonly used in the financial services sector, which indicates a high level of information availability related to the prices of similar and comparable independent transactions within this sector.

This method involves a comparison of the price charged or paid for the goods or services provided in a transaction or a series of similar, uncontrolled transactions, adjusting for any differences between the transaction and the comparable uncontrolled transaction or between the firms involved in the transactions that may affect prices. The adjusted price is considered to be the arm's length price for the goods or services provided in the transaction (Abidoye & Chan, 2018). The criteria for comparability between an uncontrolled transaction and a controlled transaction require that two essential requirements are met: first, there must be no variations that could have a significant impact on the market price and second, reasonable adjustments to the price can be made to achieve a higher degree of comparability (United Nations, 2021). Meeting the two criteria contributes to setting a fair price under competitive market conditions.

The OECD Transfer Pricing Guidelines state that the basis of the resale price method is the price at which an asset was purchased from an affiliated party and resold to an independent party. From this price is subsequently subtracted "an appropriate gross margin appropriate to it, which is the amount from which the reseller would seek to cover its selling and other operating expenses and given the functions performed, to realise an adequate profit" (OECD, 2017a, 2017b, 2017c). Therefore, the amount remaining after subtracting the margin and related adjustments is the market price for the original transaction between the related entities (Rudzikiene, 2017).

In general, this method is appropriate for commodity transactions where comparable prices are extracted from price quotations obtained from government agencies that are transparent statistical entities that disclose information about commodity indices to the general public (Lang et al., 2018; Putra & Saptono, 2021). Comparability analysis is, in fact, the centrepiece of the entire transfer pricing process, as it is an action that juxtaposes a controlled transaction between two affiliated entities with independent or uncontrolled transactions to determine the level of comparability between controlled and uncontrolled transactions (Agana et al., 2018; Barsch et al., 2019; Lips, 2019). In other words, a higher degree of understanding and comparability analysis inherently encompasses two distinct but interrelated analytical processes. The initial process aims to understand the transaction under consideration and simultaneously identify the economic characteristics that have a significant impact, including the roles and responsibilities held by each participant to establish a functional profile that is vital in the selection of the transfer pricing method and associated indicators (Cobham & Janský, 2018; Ohnuma & Sakurada, 2017; Omodero & Ogbonnaya, 2018). The second stage of the comparability analysis focuses on examining and comparing the prices, margins, or other terms of the transaction under analysis with those of independent companies in circumstances considered comparable (Overesch, 2006; Sikka & Willmott, 2010; United Nations, 2021).

As for profit-based transaction methods, they are relatively unrepresentative in the IT and telecommunications sectors, whereas in the wholesale, retail, logistics, biochemical, or pharmaceutical sectors they have a high level of representativeness (Heckemeyer et al., 2017).

The cost-plus method, also known as CPM, is another commonly applied method in transfer pricing. It involves determining the arm's length price by adding a markup to the actual costs incurred by the supplier in providing goods or services to the associated undertaking. This markup is intended to reflect the value of any additional elements, such as profits, that would have been present if the transaction had been between independent parties. This method is typically used for transactions that involve the provision of unique goods or services or have high value-added elements (Gox & Schiller, 2006; Marcuta et al., 2021; Matei & Pirvu, 2011). This price, which is formed by adding a markup to the actual costs, is adjusted for any functional or other differences between the controlled transaction and comparable uncontrolled transactions or between the entities involved to determine the arm's length principle application (Falcão, 2021; Huh & Soo, 2013).

Transactional Net Margin Method supposes that the net profit resulting from a transaction between unrelated companies is determined in relation to a given parameter (costs, revenues, fixed assets). For example, they identify that the cost-plus method is prevalent even in the context of intra-group transactions involving intellectual property assets, although this is contrary to generally accepted international tax recommendations that suggest the use of transactional profit-based methods in such circumstances. Also, Güvemli et al. (2017) identified that this method is also typically chosen by manufacturing companies in the context of reselling goods to affiliated distributors, as "this is more of a gross profit rather than a net profit method, as the markup is applied to direct and indirect production costs to adjust the price to market value". This is in line with the OECD Transfer Pricing Guidelines (2022b) where the cost-plus method is considered to be the most useful method for transactions in semi-finished products between related parties, where they have entered into various joint facility or long-term purchase-supply agreements. The positive aspects of this method are that only one party's financial data are examined, net margins are less influenced by functional product differences and allow for high data availability. There are also some disadvantages since it is used by only one party and inconveniences may arise especially when there are unique intangible assets (Choi, Ishikawa, & Okoshi, 2020b; Sari et al., 2020; Susanti, 2018).

Whichever methods are chosen to determine transfer prices, there is an OECD reference practice, namely *BEPS Action 13* (*Transfer Pricing Documentation and Country-by-Country Reporting*). Base erosion and profit shifting (BEPS) refers to the tax avoidance strategies used by multinational corporations to reduce their overall tax burden by eroding the tax base in the countries in which they operate (Abu et al., 2020; Adu, 2016; Burnett, 2019). This can be accomplished by shifting profits to subsidiaries in low-tax jurisdictions, through the use of transfer pricing techniques, or other means, such as the use of tax havens or aggressive tax planning. The BEPS project, launched by the Organisation for Economic Co-operation and Development in 2013, aims to address these problems by developing a coordinated international response to tackle these tax avoidance strategies. The project includes 15 action points, including a focus on transfer pricing and the development of a global standard for the exchange of tax-relevant information between countries. BEPS is a term that refers to the use of tax planning strategies that exploit loopholes and inconsistencies in tax rules to artificially shift profits to entities or jurisdictions with lower tax rates (Burgers & Mosquera, 2017; Irma, 2015). This leads to a reduction in overall tax liabilities, while the underlying economic activity and corresponding profits remain in higher-tax jurisdictions. This practice is considered problematic because it undermines the fairness and integrity of the international tax system and is not limited to the actions of individuals or non-compliance with national tax rules by companies, but goes further by creating an artificial separation between income and the activities that generate it. A distinction should be made between tax evasion by individuals and non-compliance by businesses towards national tax rules (OECD, 2015a, 2015b).

The BEPS package comprises 15 measures that provide governments with the domestic and international tools needed to combat tax evasion (OECD, 2017a,

2017b, 2017c). These measures enable countries to ensure that profits are taxed in jurisdictions where profit-generating and value-creating economic activities take place. In addition, they provide greater certainty for businesses by reducing disputes over the application of international tax rules and standardising compliance requirements (OECD, 2017a, 2017b, 2017c).

Thus, the main objective of the Base Erosion and Profit Shifting (BEPS) plan is to combat tax avoidance by multinational companies by creating a more coordinated and efficient approach to international tax rules (Lips, 2019; Stuart, 2009; Shukla et al. 2020). At the same time, the plan is designed to ensure that profits are taxed where the economic activity and value creation that generate those profits take place, rather than allowing companies to shift profits to lower-tax jurisdictions through the use of artificial structures and transfer pricing techniques.

As part of its ongoing initiative to combat tax evasion by multinational companies, the Organisation for Economic Co-operation and Development has published a series of papers on Base Erosion and Profit Shifting (BEPS). These papers cover a range of BEPS-related topics, including transfer pricing, digital economy, treaty abuse, and country-by-country reporting. The documents provide detailed explanations of the issues addressed under the BEPS initiative and the specific actions taken to address them.

Based on the OECD hypothesis that "multinational enterprises use tax-based transfer pricing strategies within the corporate group to shift profits to low-tax or no-tax jurisdictions", Schoen (2015) argues that "the factual context lies to a large extent in the growing importance of intangible assets, as these assets combine three critical characteristics: they are highly mobile, i.e., they are easily transferable to subsidiaries in low-tax jurisdictions, and they are difficult to value, i.e., multinational enterprises enjoy a high degree of discretion both in the pricing of intangible assets when they are transferred to a low-tax jurisdiction and when they are licensed to other subsidiaries in high-tax jurisdictions". In other words, most often used in related party transactions are transactions involving intangible assets that are difficult to value and the determination of the transfer price can be manipulated.

The Organisation for Economic Co-operation and Development and G20 countries are working together to tackle Base Erosion and Profit Shifting by multinational companies. Over 135 countries are participating in this effort to eliminate tax strategies that artificially shift profits to tax haven jurisdictions.

To determine appropriate BEPS countermeasures and to assess the effectiveness of tax policy changes, it is essential to have accurate information on the distribution of corporate income across countries. To this end, efforts have been made to develop methods to measure BEPS, but relatively little attention has been paid to assessing how different data sources capture the appropriate distribution of income. This is an important issue because the way accounting methods are used can significantly affect the empirical distribution of group profits. Therefore, a better understanding of how accounting methods influence BEPS measurement is needed to improve the effectiveness of BEPS countermeasures (Blouin & Robinson, 2020).

4.6 Tax Policies Applied to Transfer Pricing in BRICS Economies

Currently, in the emerging BRICS economies, there are no clear transfer pricing regulations, and in particular concerning the taxation of multinationals and their subsidiaries. The lack of a mechanism to regulate the use of transfer pricing harms the implementation and enforcement of tax policies, reducing the ability of the state to collect budget revenues while providing a free avenue for tax avoidance practices. The importance of studying transfer pricing regulation in the emerging BRICS economies is justified by the fact that they are the main recipient of FDI inflows at the global level, with a substantially large number of holding companies with subsidiaries in different economic environments applying this preferential taxation mechanism. Thus, in this sub-section, we aim to analyse the transfer pricing regulations, in particular tax legislation in the BRICS economies.

The first regulation covering transfer pricing in Brazil is Law No. 9430 of 1996, which was enacted to combat tax evasion and restrict the improper transfer of taxable income from Brazil to a foreign country by corporate income tax and social contribution on net profit, as a result of more favourable terms negotiated between related parties. According to Article 23 of Law 9430/1996, the following are considered affiliated persons:

1. "parent company when located abroad;
2. its main subsidiary located abroad;
3. natural or legal person, resident or located abroad, whose participation in the equity capital characterises it as a controlling person or associate;
4. a legal entity located abroad characterised as its controlled entity or associate;
5. a legal entity located abroad, when this legal entity and the company located in Brazil are under common corporate or administrative control or when at least 10% of the share capital of each is held by the same individual or legal entity;
6. an individual or legal entity, resident or located abroad, which, together with the legal entity located in Brazil, holds a participation in the share capital of a third entity; the total amount of which it holds gives them the ability to be considered controlling persons or associates;
7. the natural or legal person, resident or located abroad who is its associate, in the form of a consortium or condominium, as defined in Brazilian law, in any enterprise;
8. an individual resident abroad who is a relative or a relative by affinity up to the third degree, the spouse or life partner of any of its officials or its controlling partner or shareholder in a direct or indirect holding;
9. natural person or legal entity, resident or located abroad, who holds an exclusive right as its agent, distributor or licensee to buy and sell goods, services or rights; and
10. the natural or legal person, resident or located abroad, in relation to which the legal person located in Brazil holds an exclusive right, as agent, distributor or concessionaire, to purchase and sell goods, services or rights" (Article 23 of Law 9.430, 1996).

Although Brazil has adopted regulations on transfer pricing, the term itself is not expressly defined and therefore it is not stipulated that the best method approach should be used for transfer pricing. In practice, an objective application of the methods laid down in the legal text prevails, applying the most advantageous method for taxpayers, regardless of whether or not it is in line with real market conditions. Although the idea of standardisation of market conditions is the key feature of the principle of competition, in Brazilian tax law this principle can only be adopted through an integrated application of the principles effectively provided for in the Brazilian Constitution. This requirement derives not only from the fact that Brazil is not yet a member country of the OECD, but also from the lack of an express provision dealing with the principle of freedom in the constitutional text and federal laws.

Brazil has taken important steps to align national transfer pricing regulations with international OECD regulations and practices. As of 2018, the Brazilian Tax Authority (RFB) and the OECD are working together to align national transfer pricing regulations with the OECD Guidelines as part of Brazil's entry into the OECD. Reasons for aligning Brazil's transfer pricing system with OECD rules include the following:

1. Brazil's integration into the global value chain of MNEs
2. Avoiding double taxation and double non-taxation scenarios
3. Fulfil Brazil's development objectives (preventing revenue loss due to current Base Erosion and Profit Shifting practices)
4. Facilitating Brazil's entry into the OECD

In this regard, on April 12, 2022, the Brazilian Tax Authority and the Organisation for Economic Cooperation and Development met to discuss Brazil's proposal for a new transfer pricing (TP) system implementing the arm's length principle. Full implementation of this principle would be an important step for Brazil as it would align its TP system with the OECD Guidelines on Transfer Pricing Guidelines for Multinational Enterprises and Tax Administrations (OECD Guidelines).

The tax legislation of Russia does not contain concepts such as "transfer pricing", however, this term is widely used in practice. According to the Federal Tax Service of Russia, transfer pricing is the simplest and most common scheme of minimising taxes paid by redistributing a group of persons' total profit to persons in lower-tax countries. The regulation and control of transfer pricing transactions in Russia fall under the competence of the Federal Tax Service. The first mention of the concept of "related parties" in Russia's regulations is made in the Tax Code of 1998, Article 20, which sets out the definition of related parties in detail. A set of principles for the pricing of goods and services for tax purposes was introduced in practice by the Tax Code of 1998, Article 40 to stop tax evasion through transfer pricing. However, applying these principles has not contributed significantly to reducing tax evasion, which remains high.

In 2011, Articles 20 and 40 of the 1998 Tax Code were replaced by Chap. V.I. "*Related parties. General provisions on pricing and taxation. Tax control in connection with transactions between related parties. Pricing agreement*" (Federal Law No. 227-FZ of July 18, 2011). This section of the Tax Code essentially transposed the basic principles and rules on transfer pricing from the OECD Guidelines on *"Transfer Pricing for Transnational Corporations and Tax Authorities"*, based on the "arm's length principle".

With the new amendments to the Tax Code, a declaration for intra-group transactions has also been introduced, in which the taxpayer justifies the transfer pricing applied in transactions with related parties. Considering the introduction of the definition of controlled transactions in the legislation and the establishment of a closed list of controlled transactions, the Code obliges organisations carrying out such transactions to notify the tax authorities about these and give details on the principles applied in transfer pricing. As a general rule, transfer pricing is not a method of avoiding tax liability, but rather the pricing of transaction between related parties. Taxpayers have the right to justify the prices used in controlled transactions by applying generally accepted methods, provided supply tax authorities with reliable information on the transaction at the time of its completion.

Tax control of transfer pricing by the Federal Tax Service is performed only in connection with the controlled transactions and transactions equivalent to them. According to Article 105.17 of the Tax Code of Russia, "transfer pricing control for compliance with market prices is an independent type of tax control and cannot be subject to on-the-spot and office controls" (Tax Code of Russian Federation, n.d.). These regulations oblige companies operating in this country to prepare and maintain transfer pricing documentation and to submit it to the tax authorities upon request. This documentation must include details of the company's organisational structure, a description of the transactions subject to transfer pricing, and a thorough examination of the prices charged for these transactions.

Russia has adopted the arm's length principle, which requires companies to charge prices for transactions between related parties that are comparable to those charged for similar transactions between unrelated parties. The Russian transfer pricing regulations also guide the determination of the arm's length price, including the use of the uncontrolled comparable pricing method, the resale price method, and the cost-plus method.

In addition, Russia has implemented transfer pricing regulations to discourage tax avoidance through the use of low-tax jurisdictions, such as the "controlled foreign company" rules that require Russian companies to pay taxes on profits earned by their foreign subsidiaries that are deemed "controlled" by the Russian parent.

The Federal Tax Service's methodology for checking the conformity of transfer pricing with market prices consists of four steps:

1. The controlled transaction is analysed in terms of subject matter, functions, and accepted risks of the parties of the transaction.
2. The method of substantiation of the market price shall be determined, taking into account the identified characteristics of the controlled transaction.
3. Using the selected market price calculation method, the income from the transaction is determined on the basis of market prices and compared with the actual income of the parties to the transaction.
4. Based on the comparison results of transfer prices with market prices, the Federal Tax Service verifies the completeness of the calculation and payment of taxes and duties on the transactions carried out.

The methods for determining transfer pricing for tax purposes and the procedure for calculating the range of profitability are stipulated in the Tax Code in Chap. 14.3. Thus, according to the Tax Code, the following methods may be applied for determining transfer prices between related parties:

1. *Comparable market price method*—According to Article 105.9 of the Tax Code, this method is applied for "determining the conformity of the price of goods/works/services in the analysed transaction with the market price by comparing the price used in the analysed transaction with the market price range" (Article 105.9, Chap. 14.2, Section V.1, Tax Code of Russia).
2. *The resale price method*—According to Article 105.10 of the Tax Code, this is a "method of determining the conformity of the price in the analysed transaction with the market price by comparing the gross profitability realised by the person who carried out the analysed transaction on the subsequent sale (resale) of the goods purchased in the analysed transaction (group of similar transactions) with the market range of gross profitability" (Article 105.1, Chap. 14.2, Section V.1, Tax Code of Russia). This method is used if the reseller has no intangible assets that significantly affect its level of gross profitability.
3. *Cost-plus method*—According to Article 105.11 of the Tax Code, the cost-plus method is a "method of determining the conformity of the price of the analysed transaction with the market price by comparing the gross cost profitability of a person who is a party to the analysed transaction (group of similar analysed transactions) with the market range of gross cost profitability in the reference transactions" (Article 105.11, Chap. 14.2, Section V.1, Tax Code of Russia).
4. *Net margin method*—According to Article 105.12 of the Tax Code, this method is the comparison of the operating profitability of a person who is a party to the analysed transaction with the market range of operating profitability in the determined reference transactions (Article 105.12, Chap. 14.2, Section V.1, Tax Code of Russia).
5. *Profit split method*—According to Article 105.13 of the Tax Code, the profit split method is the comparison of the actual distribution of the total profit received by all parties to the transaction with the distribution of profit between the parties to the reference transaction (Article 105.13, Chap. 14.2, Section V.1, Tax Code of Russia).

This list is exhaustive, as the Federal Tax Service gives priority to the comparable market price method, which it also recommends. However, the legislation of Russia allows that if the application of the comparable market price method is impossible or does not allow reasonably concluding that the prices applied in the transactions correspond or do not correspond to market prices, other methods may be used for tax purposes, so that the most reasonable assessment can be made of whether the price applied in the transaction corresponds or does not correspond to the market price. The completeness and reliability of the initial data and the validity of the adjustments made to ensure the comparability of the transactions with the transaction under analysis should be taken into account in the choice of a method.

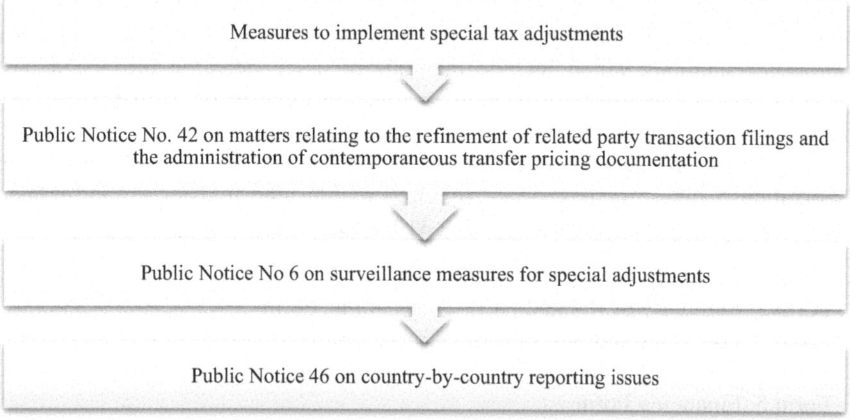

Fig. 4.10 Transfer pricing rules in China. *Source:* Elaborated by the author

India's accelerated development and increased investor interest in the economy, as well as the growth in the number of multinationals, have raised the issue of developing a new tax framework to reduce the number of offshore transactions and the erosion of the tax base. Thus, in 1999, the Indian legislators proposed to adopt the Income Tax Act 1961 to the new economic environment by supplementing the Act with Sections 92A and 92F, which delineate the concept of transfer pricing and the manner of intra-group transactions in line with Article 9 of the Organisation for Economic Cooperation and Development transfer pricing guidelines. The transfer pricing regime in India applies to both domestic and international transactions and is regulated under Sections 92A-F of the Income Tax Act 1961 and Rule 10A-E of the Income Tax Rules.

Transfer pricing in China is regulated by the Corporate Income Tax Law of 2017, Part 6, as well as by a series of tax notes and tax bulletins issued by the State Taxation Authority (Fig. 4.10). The Corporate Income Tax Law stipulates that states with tax rates lower than 12.5% are considered tax havens, and thus, enterprises controlled by Chinese residents in these states are susceptible to tax evasion. China's transfer pricing regulations and practices are both comprehensive and generic, leaving the tax authorities discretion when it comes to any particular transfer pricing case, as the outcome of a transfer pricing case is ultimately based on communication and negotiation between the tax authority and the taxpayer.

Chinese law defines seven types of stakeholder relationships. For example, according to Notice No. 42, a related party relationship is considered when one party directly or indirectly owns 25% or more of the shares of the other party or when a common third party directly or indirectly owns 25% or more of the shares of both parties.

In terms of transfer pricing methods, Chinese taxpayers are free to use any method that corresponds to the transaction profile and is advantageous to them, such as the comparable uncontrolled price method, the resale price method, the cost-plus method, the transactional net margin method, the profit split method, and other appropriate methods which include methods of asset valuation through a cost approach, market approach, or income approach or other methods that can reflect that profits are taxed where the economic activities take place and value is created.

According to Article 11 of Circular 2 and Circular 114 of the State Administration of Taxation, Chinese taxpayers are required to file nine transfer pricing-related returns each year, which are due by May 31 for each fiscal year:

- Form 1: Related Party Relationship Form
- Form 2: Summary of Related Party Transactions Form
- Form 3: Purchases and Sales Form
- Form 4: Services Form
- Form 5: Financing Form
- Form 6: Transfer of Intangible Assets Form
- Form 7: Fixed Assets Transfer Form
- Form 8: Foreign Investment Status Form
- Form 9: Foreign Payments Status Form

The main objective of transfer pricing regulations is to provide tax clarity and certainty on cross-border investment and trade and to avoid double taxation in critical periods. In this regard, China is simultaneously adjusting its regulations in line with the new OECD guidelines, bringing them in line with international standards in terms of combating tax avoidance and setting rules that correspond to economic realities. The extensive treaty network and the growing need for cross-border investment have prompted China to engage in bilateral negotiations with many countries to sign double tax treaties, so far having signed such treaties with over 105 countries.

Although South Africa is not a member of the OECD, it has transposed the OECD transfer pricing guidelines into national law. The transfer pricing legislative framework consists of the Income Tax Act No. 58 of 1962 and the SARS Income Practices Note No. 7 (1999), which have undergone numerous adjustments in line with the OECD guidelines. The South African legislation does not use the term related party transactions, referring to them as an "affected transaction". This is defined as any transaction, operation, scheme, arrangement, agreement, or understanding entered into directly or indirectly for the benefit of one or both parties: a resident and a non-resident; a non-resident and another non-resident who has a permanent establishment in South Africa; a resident and another resident who has a permanent establishment outside South Africa; a non-resident and a controlled foreigner (Sect. 31(1) of the Income Tax Act No. 58 of 1962).

Summarising the above, it can be noted that the emerging BRICS economies have made important steps in aligning and harmonising their transfer pricing tax policies and practices with OECD guidelines. However, how the transfer pricing issue is regulated in the BRICS countries is not consistent and there are arguably variations in the level of resolution and legal comprehensiveness (Table 4.9).

As the largest recipients of foreign direct investment, the BRICS economies are constantly concerned with assessing transfer pricing practices and valuation

Table 4.9 Summary of the tax treatment of transfer pricing in emerging BRICS economies

	Brazil	Russia	India	China	South Africa
Corporate tax rate	34%	20%	35%	25%	28%
Type of regulation	OECD-compliant national regulations	OECD-compliant national regulations	OECD	OECD-compliant national regulations	OECD-compliant national regulations
Do your domestic laws or regulations refer to the principle of freedom?	No	Yes	Yes	Yes	Yes
Does your domestic law or regulation define related parties?	Yes	Yes	Yes	Yes	Yes
Transfer pricing methods:					
Comparable uncontrolled price method	Yes	Yes	Yes	Yes	No
Selling price method	Yes	Yes	Yes	Yes	No
Cost-plus method	Yes	Yes	Yes	Yes	No
Net transaction margin	No	Yes	Yes	Yes	No
Profit split method	No	Yes	Yes	Yes	No
The criterion for the application of transfer pricing methods	Other methods	Method hierarchy	Closest method	Closest method	Closest method
Does your tax administration use secret comparable information for transfer pricing purposes?	No	No	No	Yes	No
Does your legislation allow or require the use of a competitive range and/or a statistical measure to determine competitive remuneration?	No	Yes	Yes	Yes	No
Do your domestic laws or regulations contain specific guidance for the pricing of controlled transactions involving intangible assets?	No	No	No	Yes	No

(continued)

Table 4.9 (continued)

	Brazil	Russia	India	China	South Africa
Does your national law or regulation provide for transfer pricing rules or special measures for hard-to-value intangible assets (HTVI)?	No	No	No	No	No
Do your internal laws or regulations provide specific guidance for intra-group service transactions?	No	No	No	Yes	No
Do your laws or regulations require the taxpayer to prepare transfer pricing documentation?	Yes	Yes	Yes	Yes	Yes
Are there requirements for preparing annual transfer pricing documentation?	Yes	Yes	Yes	Yes	Yes
Deadline for submission on request to the tax authorities	20 days	30 days	30 days	–	Immediately
Tax penalties for understatement of the tax base based on the use of transfer pricing	Undefined	40% of the determined surcharge	100–300% of the determined surcharge	–	Undefined

Source: Developed by the author based on TP country profiles

methods, with the avoidance of tax payment and double taxation as the main lines of action. The data in Table 4.9 shows that all BRICS countries have adopted the OECD transfer pricing guidelines in their national regulations. The main concern of the BRICS economies is to remain competitive in terms of FDI inflows and at the same time to avoid tax avoidance by continuously auditing the activities of multinationals. According to Hattingh (2015), limited resources of tax administrations in developing countries also limit the effectiveness of transfer pricing legislation. McNair et al. (2010) argue that "the lack of capacity of tax authorities in developing countries to monitor transfer pricing transactions entered into by multinationals provides them with the opportunity to shift profits from these countries to other countries also known as tax havens".

The problem of transfer pricing regulation and its use as a tool to erode the tax base contributes to the creation of economic and social discrepancies between countries. Due to the lack of specialised resources in the fair and equidistant application of transfer pricing and auditing methods, both international and national standards have a negligible impact on combating tax evasion. At the same time, while in developed countries there are forums where optimal transfer pricing solutions are discussed and tried to be found, in developing countries, they are lacking. Another problem for developing countries is access to comparable data, making it difficult to apply the principle of competition.

4.7 Summary Conclusions

Transfer pricing strategies and methods are quite complex and their application is associated with certain difficulties due to restrictive and diversified legislation from one country to another, as well as the lack of clear methodologies on how to prepare the transfer pricing file. The complex and restrictive transfer pricing legislation has a disruptive effect on the ability of multinationals to properly prepare transfer pricing documentation and to charge market prices.

Therefore, we believe that the OECD and G20 countries contributing to the implementation of the BEPS Action Plan should put in place a globally valid tax code whereby countries involved in international transactions ensure that profits are taxed where the activities have taken place and where they have created value, thus making it impossible to avoid or reduce tax avoidance. The use of transfer pricing implies control over the reasonableness of prices for export and import transactions. The definition of a comprehensive legislative framework, a comprehensive tax code and their correct application ensures the attraction of investment and establishes fair rules to maintain a balance between the state and the participants in the transactions. Undoubtedly, the desire for such a balance means reciprocal trade-offs, enshrined in regulatory and enforcement practice. At the same time, the new geopolitical shifts of recent times are shaping tax policies, which further emphasises the transfer pricing file. The withdrawal of capital from environments heavily affected by geopolitical risks, as well as the introduction of protectionist taxes and trade policies by several economies, is changing the outlook for companies' external activities, as they shift their operations to environments that offer them optimal certainty and predictability of invested capital. At the same time, changes in the international political and economic arena, as well as the enforcement of the economic and energy crisis, are increasing national interests in the taxes paid by multinationals, and the erosion of the tax base through the transfer pricing file has triggered a series of tax reforms.

References

Abidoye, R. B., & Chan, A. P. (2018). Improving property valuation accuracy: A comparison of hedonic pricing model and artificial neural network. *Pacific Rim Property Research Journal, 24*(1), 71–83. https://doi.org/10.1080/14445921.2018.1436306

Abu, M. M., Bello, U., & Mohammed, Z. (2020). Base erosion and profit shifting (BEPS) in low-income nations by the multinationals: A critical review of literature. *Journal of Critical Reviewers, 7*(5), 502–509.

Achim, V. M., Borlea, N. S., Văidean, L. V., Florescu, R. D., Mara, R. E., & Cuceu, C. I. (2021). *Economic and financial crimes and the development of society*. IntechOpen. https://doi.org/10.5772/intechopen.96269

Adu, S. (2016). 15 reasons why October 5th is a day to remember in the Nigerian tax terrain. *Tax Article on BEPS, 1*. Retrieved from: https://pwcnigeria.typepad.com/files/tax-article-on-beps.pdf

Agana, J. A., Mohammed, A., & Zamore, S. (2018). International transfer pricing and income shifting in developing countries: Evidence from Ghana. *International Journal of Emerging Markets, 13*(5), 181–219. https://doi.org/10.1108/IJoEM-05-2017-0181

Ainsworth, R. T., & Shact, A. (2012). Transfer pricing: The CUP—Case studies: Australia, US, UK, Norway, and Canada. *Tax Notes International*, 66(April 30), 465. Boston University School of Law, Law and Economics Research Paper No. 12-12. https://doi.org/10.2139/ssrn.2012721

Akinbowale, O. E., Klingelhöfer, H. E., & Zerihun, M. F. (2020). An innovative approach in combating economic crime using forensic accounting techniques. *Journal of Financial Crime, 27*(4), 1253–1271. https://doi.org/10.1108/JFC-04-2020-0053

Albanese, J. S. (2021). Organized crime as financial crime: The nature of organized crime as reflected in prosecutions and research. *Victims and Offenders, 16*(3), 431–443. https://doi.org/10.1080/15564886.2020.1823543

Álvarez-Martínez, M. T., Barrios, S., d'Andria, D., Gesualdo, M., Nicodeme, G., & Pycroft, J. (2021). How large is the corporate tax base erosion and profit shifting? A general equilibrium approach. *Economic Systems Research, 34*(2), 167–198.

Amidu, M., Coffie, W., & Acquah, P. (2019). Transfer pricing, earnings management and tax avoidance of firms in Ghana. *Journal of Financial Crime, 26*(1), 235–259. https://doi.org/10.1108/JFC-10-2017-0091

Anghelache, C., Anghel, M. G., & Iacob, Ş. V. (2020). Statistical-econometric methods and models used in the analysis of the capital market under the risk of inflation. *Economic Computation and Economic Cybernetics Studies and Research, 54*(2), 41–58.

Antràs, P. (2020). *De-globalisation? Global value chains in the post-COVID-19 age*. NBER Working Paper No. 28115.

Arafat, Y., & Haga, J. (2020). *Transfer pricing and its use for tax avoidance by corporations*. Master thesis in accounting, UMEA University.

Asongu, S. A., Uduji, J. I., & Okolo-Obasi, E. N. (2019). Transfer pricing and corporate social responsibility: Arguments, views and agenda. *Mineral Economics, 32*(3), 353–363. https://doi.org/10.2139/ssrn.3396641

Australian Taxation Office. (2022). *Country-by-country reporting*. Australian Government. Retrieved from: https://www.ato.gov.au/business/international-tax-for-business/in-detail/transfer-pricing/country-by-country-reporting/

Awodiran, M. A. (2014). Transfer pricing: A tax avoidance tool of multinational corporations. *SSRN Scholarly Paper*. https://doi.org/10.2139/ssrn.2463201

Baldenius, T. (2000). Intrafirm trade, bargaining power, and specific investments. *Review of Accounting Studies, 5*(1), 27–56.

Baldenius, T. (2009). *Internal pricing*. Now Publishers Inc.

Baldenius, T., & Reichelstein, S. (2006). External and internal pricing in multidivisional firms. *Journal of Accounting Research, 44*(1), 1–28. https://doi.org/10.1111/j.1475-679X.2006.00191.x

Baldenius, T., Reichelstein, S. J., & Sahay, S. (1999). Negotiated versus cost-based transfer pricing. *SSRN*. https://ssrn.com/abstract=180910

Baldenius, T., Melumad, N. D., & Reichelstein, S. (2003). Integrating managerial and tax objectives in transfer pricing. *SSRN*. https://doi.org/10.2139/ssrn.408260

Barrera, R., & Bustamante, J. (2018). The rotten apple: Tax avoidance in Ireland. *International Trade Journal, 32*(1), 150–161. https://doi.org/10.1080/08853908.2017.1356250

Barsch, S., Heckemeyer, J. H., & Olbert, M. (2019). Transfer pricing and the decision-making authority of the tax function in multinational companies. *Journal of Business Economics*, 1–53. https://doi.org/10.2139/ssrn.3271267

Beer, S., de Mooij, R., & Liu, L. (2018). International corporate tax avoidance: A review of the channels, magnitudes, and blind spots. Retrieved from: www.RePEc.org

Blouin, J., & Robinson, L. (2020). Double counting accounting: How much profit of multinational enterprises is really in tax havens? *SSRN Scholarly Paper*. https://doi.org/10.2139/ssrn.3491451

Boro, J. (2013). *Relationship between transfer pricing techniques and their level of implementation: A case of multinational companies in Kenya*. Master Thesis, Business Administration, Nairobi University. Retrieved from: http://erepository.uonbi.ac.ke/bitstream/handle/11295/58815/Boro_Relationship;jsessionid=EB61EB59741A8643F190FDC34C7D82E9?sequence=3

Bradley, W. (2015). Transfer pricing: Increasing tension between multinational firms and tax authorities. *Accounting & Taxation, 7*(2), 65–73.

Brugger, F., & Engebretsen, R. (2022). Defenders of the status quo: Making sense of the international discourse on transfer pricing methodologies. *Review of International Political Economy, 29*(1), 307–335. https://doi.org/10.1080/09692290.2020.1807386

Burgers, I., & Mosquera, I. J. V. (2017). Corporate taxation and BEPS: A fair slice for developing countries. *Erasmus Law Review, 10*(1), 29–47.

Burnett, C. (2019). Interest deductibility: Implementation of BEPS Action 4 and the future of transfer pricing of intragroup finance. *Bulletin for International Taxation, 73*(6/7), 325–331.

Callon, M., Courtial, J. P., & Laville, F. (1991). Co-word analysis as a tool for describing the network of interactions between basic and technological research: The case of polymer chemistry. *Scientometrics, 22*(1), 155–205. https://doi.org/10.1007/BF02019280

Challoumis, C. (2019). Transfer pricing methods for services and the policy of fixed length principle. *Economics and Business, 33*(1), 222–232. https://doi.org/10.2478/eb-2019-0016

Chitic, O., & Birman, A. (2012). Value, prices and the evolution to modern transfer pricing. *Hyperion International Journal of Econophysics & New Economy, 5*(2), 363.

Choi, J. P., Furusawa, T., & Ishikawa, J. (2018). *Transfer pricing and the arm's length principle under imperfect competition*. Discussion paper series HIAS-E-73, Hitotsubashi Institute for Advanced Study, Hitotsubashi University.

Choi, J. P., Furusawa, T., & Ishikawa, J. (2020a). Transfer pricing regulation and tax competition. *Journal of International Economics, 127*, 103367. https://doi.org/10.1016/j.jinteco.2020.103367

Choi, J. P., Ishikawa, J., & Okoshi, H. (2020b). *Transfer pricing of intangible assets with the arm's length principle*. European Economic Blog. Retrieved from: https://cepr.org/voxeu/columns/transfer-pricing-intangible-assets-arms-length-principle

Chong, K., Loy, Y., Masschelein, S., & Woodliff, R. (2018). The effect of performance evaluation schemes on predicted transfer prices: Do leadership tone and perceived fairness concerns matter? *Management Accounting Research, 41*, 11–19. https://doi.org/10.1016/j.mar.2018.02.003

Ciubotariu, M. S., & Petrescu, C. (2021). Aspects regarding the transfer pricing mechanism. *The USV Annals of Economics and Public Administration, 21*.

Clausing, K. A. (2003). Tax-motivated transfer pricing and US intrafirm trade prices. *Journal of Public Economics, 87*(9–10), 2207–2223. https://doi.org/10.1016/S0047-2727(02)00015-4

Cobham, A., & Janský, P. (2018). Global distribution of revenue loss from corporate tax avoidance: Re-estimation and country results. *Journal of International Development, 30*(2), 206–232. https://doi.org/10.1002/jid.3348

Cools, M., & Slagmulder, R. (2009). Tax-compliant transfer pricing and responsibility accounting. *Journal of Management Accounting Research, 21*(1), 151–178. https://doi.org/10.2139/ssrn.1520421

Cools, M., Emmanuel, C., & Jorissen, A. (2008). Management control in the transfer pricing tax compliant multinational enterprise. *Accounting, Organizations and Society, 33*(6), 603.

Cooper, M., & Nguyen, Q. T. K. (2020). Multinational enterprises and corporate tax planning: A review of literature and suggestions for a future research agenda. *International Business Review, 29*(3), 101692. https://doi.org/10.1016/j.ibusrev.2020.101692

Cooper, J., Fox, R., Loeprick, J., & Mohindra, K. (2016). *Transfer pricing and developing economies: A handbook for policy makers and practitioners public sector governance*. World Bank. Retrieved from: http://documents.worldbank.org/curated/en/230331483627135642/Transfer-pricing-and-developing-economies-a-handbook-for-policy-makers-and-practitioners

Cristea, A., & Nguyen, D. (2016). Transfer pricing by multinational firms: New evidence from foreign firm ownerships. *American Economic Journal: Economic Policy, 8*(3), 170–202. https://doi.org/10.1257/pol.20130407

Dallyn, S. (2017). An examination of the political salience of corporate tax avoidance: A case study of the tax justice network. *Accounting Forum, 41*(4), 336–352. https://doi.org/10.1016/j.accfor.2016.12.002

de Mooij, R., & Liu, L. (2018). At a cost: The real effects of transfer pricing regulations. WP/18/69. Retrieved from: www.RePEc.org

De Wulf, O. (2015). Les prix de transfert en droits Britannique et Français. *SSRN Scholarly Paper*. Retrieved from: https://papers.ssrn.com/abstract=2689815

Deloitte. (2016). Country-by-country reporting thought leadership FAQs. Retrieved from: https://www2.deloitte.com/content/dam/Deloitte/global/Documents/Tax/dttl-tax-country-by-country-reporting-faqs.pdf

Devereux, M. P., & Vella, J. (2018). Implications of digitalization for international corporate tax reform. *Intertax, 46*(6–7), 550–559.

Duong, T. V. A. (2018, April). Current situation of transfer pricing and anti-transfer pricing methods toward FDI enterprises in Viet Nam. *Magazine of Accounting and Auditing*. Retrieved from: http://vaa.net.vn/Tin-tuc/Tin-chi-tiet/newsid/4321/Thuc-trang-chuyen-gia-va-giai-phap-chong-chuyen-gia-doi-voi-cac-doanh-nghiep-co-von-dau-tu-nuoc-ngoai-FDI-tai-Viet-Nam

Duri, J. (2021). Transparency International Anti-Corruption Helpdesk Answer Corruption and economic crime. Retrieved from: https://www.transparency.org/en/what-is-corruption

Durst, M. C. (2010). It's not just academic: The OECD should reevaluate transfer pricing laws. *Tax Notes International, 57*, 247–256.

Eden, L. (2009). Taxes, transfer pricing, and the multinational enterprise. In A. M. Rugman (Ed.), *The Oxford handbook of international business* (2nd ed.). Oxford University Press. Retrieved from: https://www.voxprof.com/eden/TRANSFERPRICING/Eden-OHIB2-Ch21.pdf

Edlin, A. S., & Reichelstein, S. (1995). Specific investment under negotiated transfer pricing: An efficiency result. *Accounting Review*, 275–291.

European Commission. (2009). European Union accounting rule 15: Related party disclosures. Retrieved from: https://ec.europa.eu/info/sites/default/files/about_the_european_commission/eu_budget/eu-accounting-rule-15-related-party-disclosures_2009_en.pdf

Faccio, T., & Ghosh, J. (2021). Taxing multinationals: A fundamental shift is under way. *Intereconomics. Review of European Economic Policy, 56*(2), 62. https://doi.org/10.1007/s10272-021-0953-1

Falcão, T. (2021). Formula-based transfer pricing: How Brazil can improve the OECD's framework. *Tax Notes International, 101*. https://ssrn.com/abstract=3826904

Federal Law No 227-FZ of July 18, 2011.[Федеральный закон "О внесении изменений в отдельные законодательные акты Российской Федерации в связи с совершенствованием принципов определения цен для целей налогообложения" от 18.07.2011 N 227-ФЗ (последняя редакция)]. Retrieved from: https://www.consultant.ru/document/cons_doc_LAW_116968/

Fogarty, T., & Jones, D. A. (2014). Between a rock and a hard place: How tax practitioners straddle client advocacy and professional responsibilities. *Qualitative Research in Accounting and Management, 11*(4), 286–316. https://doi.org/10.1108/QRAM-06-2013-0024

Fun, J. A., & Raiahu, N. (2018). Analysis of the implementation of transfer pricing documentation policy in Indonesia. In *2nd international conference on administrative science, policy, and governance studies 2018 (ICAS-PGS 2018)* (p. 260). Faculty of Administrative Science, Universitas Indonesia.

Goetschalckx, M., Vidal, C. J., & Hernández, J. I. (2012). Measuring the impact of transfer pricing on the configuration and profit of an international supply chain: Perspectives from two real cases. In *Congreso Latino-Iberoamericano de Investigación Operativa* (pp. 1659–1669). Simposio Brasileiro de Pesquisa Operacional.

Gox, R., & Schiller, U. (2006). An economic perspective on transfer pricing. *Handbooks of Management Accounting Research, 2*, 673–695. https://doi.org/10.2139/ssrn.885480

Graham, J. R., Hanlon, M., Shevlin, T., & Shroff, N. (2017). Tax rates and corporate decision-making. *The Review of Financial Studies, 30*(9), 3128–3131.

Greil, S. (2021). The arm's length principle in the 21st century-a literature overview. *Journal of Tax Administration, 6*(2), 148.

Grondona, V. (2017). Transfer pricing: Concepts and practices of the "sixth method" in transfer pricing. In *South Centre tax cooperation policy brief, 2, Geneva, Switzerland.*

Grubert, H., & Mutti, J. (1991). Taxes, tariffs and transfer pricing in multinational corporate decision making. *The Review of Economics and Statistics, 73*(2), 285–293. https://doi.org/10.2307/2109519

Güvemli, B., Alpaslan, H. I., & Şuşoğlu, M. E. (2017). Balkanlarda transfer fiyatlaması. *Muhasebe ve Finansman Dergisi, 2017*, 152–164. https://doi.org/10.25095/mufad.402679

Halperin, R., & Srinidhi, B. (1987). The effects of U.S. income tax regulations' transfer pricing rules on allocative efficiency. *The Accounting Review, 62*, 686–706.

Halperin, R. M., & Srinidhi, B. (1991). US income tax transfer-pricing rules and resource allocation: The case of decentralized multinational firms. *Accounting Review, 66*(1), 141–157.

Hattingh, J. (2015, April 22). *Transfer pricing in South Africa*. Presentation to Portfolio Committee on Trade and Industry. Retrieved from: https://pmg.org.za/committee-meeting/20728/

Heckemeyer, J. H., Olbert, M., de Simone, L., Eichfelder, S., Heitzman, S., Lisowsky, P., Rane, S., Rego, S. O., Overesch, M., Spengel, C., & Sureth-Sloane, C. (2017). *Transfer pricing and the decision-making authority of the tax function in multinational companies*. Sven-Eric Bärsch Flick Gocke Schaumburg. Retrieved from: https://ssrn.com/abstract=3271267

Hiemann, M., & Reichelstein, S. (2012). Transfer pricing in multinational corporations: An integrated management- and tax perspective. In W. Schön & K. Konrad (Eds.), *Fundamentals of international transfer pricing in law and economics* (MPI studies in tax law and public finance) (Vol. 1). Springer. https://doi.org/10.1007/978-3-642-25980-7_1

Hirshleifer, J. (1956). On the economics of transfer pricing. *The Journal of Business, 29*(3), 172–184. https://doi.org/10.1086/294110

Holmstrom, B., & Tirole, J. (1991). Transfer pricing and organizational form. *The Journal of Law, Economics, & Organization, 7*(2), 201–228.

Huang, M. H., & Chang, C. P. (2014). Detecting research fronts in OLED field using bibliographic coupling with sliding window. *Scientometrics, 98*(3), 1721–1744. https://doi.org/10.1007/s11192-013-1126-1

Huh, W. T., & Soo, K. P. (2013). Impact of transfer pricing methods for tax purposes on supply chain performance under demand uncertainty. *Naval Research Logistics, 60*(4), 269. https://doi.org/10.1002/nav.21533

Irma, J. M. V. (2015). The OECD-BEPS measures to deal with aggressive tax planning in South America and Sub-Saharan Africa: The challenges ahead. *Intertax, 43*(10), 615–627.

Jost, S. P., Pfaffermayer, M., & Winner, H. (2014). Transfer pricing as a tax compliance risk. *Accounting and Business Research, 44*(3), 260–279. https://doi.org/10.1080/00014788.2014.883062

Kaur, J., & Gupta, V. (2010). Effective approaches for extraction of keywords. *International Journal of Computer Science Issues, 7*(6), 144–148.

KPMG. (2016). BEPS action plan 13 master file and country by country reporting: Navigating challenges with tax, accounting and IT service offerings. Retrieved from: https://assets.kpmg/content/dam/kpmg/pdf/2016/06/BEPS-Action-Plan-13.pdf

Kumar, S., Pandey, N., Lim, W. M., Chatterjee, A. N., & Pandey, N. (2021). What do we know about transfer pricing? Insights from bibliometric analysis. *Journal of Business Research, 134*, 275–287. https://doi.org/10.1016/j.jbusres.2021.05.041

Lang, M., Cottani, G., & Petruzzi, R. (2018). *Fundamentals of transfer pricing: A practical guide*. Kluwer Law International B.V.

Lecraw, D. J. (2017). Some evidence on transfer pricing by multinational corporations. In *Routledge library editions: Multinationals* (Multinationals and transfer pricing) (Vol. 5).

Lee, E., & Yi, K. M. (2018). Global value chains and inequality with endogenous labor supply. *Journal of International Economics, 115*, 223–241. https://doi.org/10.1016/j.jinteco.2018.09.006

Lips, W. (2019). Great powers in global tax governance: A comparison of the US role in the CRS and BEPS. *Globalizations, 16*(1), 104–119. https://doi.org/10.31219/osf.io/ewd3j

Lo, A. W. Y., Wong, R. M. K., & Firth, M. (2010). Tax, financial reporting, and tunneling incentives for income shifting: An empirical analysis of the transfer pricing behavior of Chinese-listed companies. *Journal of American Taxation Association, 32*(2), 1–26. https://doi.org/10.2308/jata.2010.32.2.1

Lohse, T., & Riedel, N. (2013). Do transfer pricing laws limit international income shifting? Evidence from European multinationals. CESifo Working Paper Series No. 4404. https://doi.org/10.2139/ssrn.2334651.

Marcuta, A., Popescu, A., & Marcuta, L. (2021). Study on the role of transfer prices in consolidation of the tax base and in determining the taxable profit of the group of companies. *Scientific Papers Series Management, Economic Engineering in Agriculture and Rural Development, 21*(1), 487.

Markina, S., Artemov, R., Nosachevskaya, E., & Panskov, V. (2021). Countering economic crime in the context of globalization. *SHS Web of Conferences, 92*, 07040. https://doi.org/10.1051/shsconf/20219207040

Marques, M., & Pinho, C. (2016). Is transfer pricing strictness deterring profit shifting within multinationals? Empirical evidence from Europe. *Accounting and Business Research, 46*(7), 703–730. https://doi.org/10.1080/00014788.2015.1135782

Mashiri, E., Dzomira, S., & Canicio, D. (2021). Transfer pricing auditing and tax forestalling by multinational corporations: A game theoretic approach. *Cogent Business and Management, 8*(1), 1907012. https://doi.org/10.1080/23311975.2021.1907012

Massimo, A., & Corrado, C. (2017). An R-tool for comprehensive science mapping analysis. *Journal of Informetrics, 11*(4), 959–975. https://doi.org/10.1016/j.joi.2017.08.007

Matei, G., & Pirvu, D. (2011). Prețurile de transfer în Uniunea Europeană, economie teoretică și aplicată (Transfer prices in the European Union). *Theoretical and Applied Economy, 4*(557), 99–111.

McNair, D., Dotley, R., & Cobham, A. (2010). Transfer pricing and the taxing rights of developing countries. Retrieved from: https://core.ac.uk/download/files/662/28878778.pdf

Melega, A., Grosu, V., Macovei, A. G., & Botez, D. (2022). *Clustering based bibliometric analysis of the business performance concept* (Economics edition, p. 35). Studies and Scientific Researches.

Miyosawa, T., Kitajyo, J., Hirose, H., & Tsuchiya, T. (2016). Keyword extraction of tourism information by using co-occurrence relations. *International Journal of Emerging Technology and Advanced Engineering, 6*(2), 156–163.

Mongeon, P., & Paul-Hus, A. (2016). The journal coverage of €Web of Science and Scopus: A comparative analysis. *Scientometrics, 106*, 213–228. https://doi.org/10.1007/s11192-015-1765-5

Nehoray, M., Lemmens, J., & Adachi, Y. (2015). *Transfer pricing documentation and country-by-country reporting*. Deloitte. Retrieved from: https://www2.deloitte.com/content/dam/Deloitte/us/Documents/Tax/us-tax-beps-changes-transfer-pricing-documentation-and-country-by-country-reporting.pdf

Nguyena, H. N., Thama, J., Khatibia, A., & Ferdous Azama, S. M. (2019). Enhancing the capacity of tax authorities and its impact on transfer pricing activities of ISD enterprises in Ha Noi, Ho

Chi Minh, Dong Nai, and Binh Duong province of Vietnam. *Management Science Letters, 9*, 1299–1310.

OECD. (1993). *Glossary of industrial organization economics and competition law*. Centre for Co-operation with European Economies in Transition.

OECD. (1995). Transfer pricing guidelines for multinational enterprises and tax administrations. In *Report of the OECD committee on fiscal affairs*. OECD Publishing. Retrieved from: https://one.oecd.org/document/OCDE/GD(95)31/En/pdf

OECD. (2010). Transfer pricing guidelines for multinational enterprises and tax administrations. In *Report of the OECD committee on fiscal affairs*. OECD Publishing. https://doi.org/10.1787/tpg-2010-en

OECD. (2015a). *Measuring and monitoring BEPS, Action 11–2015 final report, OECD/G20 base erosion and profit shifting project*. OECD Publishing. https://doi.org/10.1787/9789264241343-en

OECD. (2015b). *Transfer pricing documentation and country-by-country reporting, Action 13–2015 final report, OECD/G20 base erosion and profit shifting project*. OECD Publishing. https://doi.org/10.1787/9789264241480-en

OECD. (2017a). *Model tax convention on income and on capital: Condensed version 2017*. OECD Publishing. https://doi.org/10.1787/mtc_cond-2017-en

OECD. (2017b). OECD model tax convention on income and on capital. Retrieved from: https://read.oecd-ilibrary.org/taxation/model-tax-convention-on-income-and-on-capital-2017-full-version_g2g972ee-en#page1

OECD. (2017c). *OECD transfer pricing guidelines for multinational enterprises and tax administrations 2017*. OECD Publishing. https://doi.org/10.1787/tpg-2017-en

OECD. (2018). Country by country reporting—Compilation of peer review reports (phase 1). In *Inclusive framework on BEPS: Action 13*. OECD Publishing. https://doi.org/10.1787/9789264300057-en

OECD. (2019). Country by country reporting—Compilation of peer review reports (phase 2). In *Inclusive framework on BEPS: Action 13*. OECD Publishing. https://doi.org/10.1787/f9bf1157-en

OECD. (2020). Country by country reporting—Compilation of peer review reports (phase 3). In *Inclusive framework on BEPS: Action 13*. OECD Publishing. https://doi.org/10.1787/fa6d31d7-en

OECD. (2021a). *Activated exchange relationships for CRS information*. Automated Exchange Portal. Retrieved from: https://www.oecd.org/tax/automatic-exchange/international-framework-for-the-crs/exchange-relationships/

OECD. (2021b). Country by country reporting—Compilation of 2021 peer review reports. In *Inclusive framework on BEPS: Action 13*. OECD Publishing. https://doi.org/10.1787/73dc97a6-en

OECD. (2021c). *International framework for the CRS*. CRS Information. Retrieved from: https://www.oecd.org/tax/automatic-exchange/international-framework-for-the-crs/

OECD. (2022a). Activated exchange relationships for country-by-country reporting. Retrieved from: https://www.oecd.org/tax/beps/country-by-country-exchange-relationships.htm

OECD. (2022b). *OECD transfer pricing guidelines for multinational enterprises and tax administrations*. OECD Publishing. https://doi.org/10.1787/0e655865-en

Ohnuma, H., & Sakurada, J. (2017). Corporate governance issues regarding transfer pricing taxation: Evidence from Japan. *Asian Business Research, 2*(3), 58–73. https://doi.org/10.20849/abr.v2i3.238

Oliinyk, O., Bondarchuk, V., Kuchynska, I., & Koshel, O. (2021). Ways and mechanisms to combat organized crime, corruption and financial fraud in the economic and financial spheres: International experience. *Revista Relações Internacionais do Mundo Atual Unicuritiba, 3*(32), 113. https://doi.org/10.21902/Revrima.v3i32.5514

Omodero, C. O., & Ogbonnaya, A. K. (2018). Corporate tax and profitability of deposit money in Nigeria. *Journal of Accounting, Business and Finance Research, 3*(2), 47–55. https://doi.org/10.20448/2002.32.47.55

Overesch, M. (2006). *Transfer pricing of intrafirm sales as a profit shifting channel: Evidence from German firm data*. ZEW-Centre for European Economic Research Discussion Paper, 06-084. https://doi.org/10.2139/ssrn.955758

Padhi, S. K. (2019). Transfer pricing a review of literature. *International Journal of Advanced Research in Management, 10*(1), 1–7.

Petruzzi, R., & Buriak, S. (2018). Addressing the tax challenges of the digitalization of the economy—A possible answer in the proper application of the transfer pricing rules? *Bulletin for International Taxation, 72*(4a/Special Issue). Retrieved from: https://ssrn.com/abstract=3746882

Petruzzi, R., & Tavares, R. J. S. (2019). *Transfer pricing and value creation: Schriftenreihe IStR, Band 116 (Schriftenreihe zum Internationalen Steuerrecht)*. International Kindle Paperwhite.

Pleune, J., Peters, C. A. T., & Essers, P. H. J. (2017). *The desirability of the arm's length principle in the 21st century*. Master thesis International Business Tax Economics, Tilburg School of Economics and Management, Tilburg University. Retrieved from: https://arno.uvt.nl/show.cgi?fid=143966

Popko, V., & Popko, Y. (2021). Theoretical and legal characteristics of economic crimes of a transnational nature. *Baltic Journal of Economic Studies, 7*(1), 93–101. https://doi.org/10.30525/2256-0742/2021-7-1-93-101

Putra, A. L., & Saptono, H. W. (2021). Comparability analysis in transfer pricing: Problem and guideline in selecting the most appropriate method. *Journal of Research in Business and Management, 9*(1), 18–25.

Riedel, N., Zinn, T., & Hofmann, P. (2015). *Do transfer pricing laws limit international income shifting? Evidence from Europe* (CESifo working paper series) (Vol. 4404). CESifo Group Munich.

Rogers, H., & Oats, L. (2022). Transfer pricing: Changing views in changing times. *Accounting Forum, 46*(1), 83–107. https://doi.org/10.1080/01559982.2021.1926778

Rudzikiene, A. (2017). *Transfer pricing methods*. Royalty Range. Retrieved from: https://www.royaltyrange.com/home/blog/transfer-pricing-methods

Rus, A. (2020). *Ghidul OECD de "evaluare" a impactului pandemiei asupra prețurilor de transfer a fost emis*. Ce trebuie să facă companiile? Retrieved from: https://www.ey.com/ro_ro/tax/ghidul-OECD-de%2D%2Devaluare%2D%2Da-impactului-pandemiei-asupra-preturi

Sari, D., Utama, S., Fitriany, N., & Rahayu, N. (2020). Transfer pricing practices and specific anti-avoidance rules in Asian developing countries. *International Journal of Emerging Markets, 16*(3), 492–516. https://doi.org/10.1108/IJOEM-10-2018-0541

Schoen, W. (2015). Transfer pricing issues of BEPS in the light of EU law. *SSRN Scholarly Paper*. https://doi.org/10.2139/ssrn.2657998

Sebele-Mpofu, F., Mashiri, E., & Schwartz, S. C. (2021). An exposition of transfer pricing motives, strategies and their implementation in tax avoidance by MNEs in developing countries. *Cogent Business and Management, 8*(1), 1944007. https://doi.org/10.1080/23311975.2021.1944007

Septiani, D. H., Prawira, I. F. A., & Kustiawan, M. (2021). Transfer pricing, a tax avoidance tool (a review of literature). In *1st ICEMAC 2020: International conference on economics, management and accounting*.

Sheth, C. (2018). Transfer pricing in post BEPS world. Retrieved from: https://www.wirc-icai.org/images/material/Transfer-Pricing-post-BEPS-world.pdf

Shukla, G., Pandey, S. K., & Lingam, S. (2020). Tax effects of treaty shopping and OECD's BEPS implications. *FIIB Business Review, 9*(2), 85–93. https://doi.org/10.1177/2319714520907245

Sikka, P., & Willmott, H. (2010). The dark side of transfer pricing: Its role in tax avoidance and wealth retentiveness. *Critical Perspectives on Accounting, 21*(4), 342. https://doi.org/10.1016/j.cpa.2010.02.004

Small, H. (1999). Visualizing science by citation mapping. *Journal of the American Society for Information Science, 50*(9), 799–813. https://doi.org/10.1002/(SICI)1097-4571(1999)50:9%3C799::AID-ASI9%3E3.0.CO;2-G

Smolarski, J. M., Wilner, N., & Vega, J. G. (2019). Dynamic transfer pricing under conditions of uncertainty: The use of real options. *Journal of Accounting and Organizational Change, 15*(4), 535. https://doi.org/10.1108/JAOC-08-2018-0083

Sørensen, K. (2021). The governance of company groups. In *OECD corporate governance working papers* (Vol. 22). OECD Publishing. https://doi.org/10.1787/6302f79a-en

Stuart, A. (2009). *Transfer pricing: A world of pain*. CFO Magazine. Retrieved from: https://www.cfo.com/news/transfer-pricing-a-world-of-pain/669783/

Susanti, A. (2018). Determinants of transfer pricing decisions in Indonesia manufacturing companies. *Jurnal Akuntansi dan Auditing Indonesia, 22*(2), 81. https://doi.org/10.20885/jaai.vol22.iss2.art1

Tax Code of the Russian Federation. [Налоговый кодекс Российской Федерации, часть первая от 31 июля 1998 г. N 146-ФЗ (с изм. и доп. от 30 марта, 9 июля 1999 г., 2 января 2000 г.) и часть вторая от 5 августа 2000 г. N 117-ФЗ. (n.d.)]. Retrieved from: https://www.nalog.gov.ru/html/nk.htm

Tax Justice Network. (2020). Country by country reporting. Retrieved from: https://taxjustice.net/topics/country-by-country-reporting/

Tax Justice Network. (2022). What is a tax haven? FAQ. Retrieved from: https://taxjustice.net/faq/what-is-a-tax-haven/#:~:text=Although%20there%20isn't%20a,they%20should%20in%20those%20countries

Tørsløv, T. R., Wier, L. S., & Zucman, G. (2018). The missing profits of nations. Retrieved from: http://gabriel-zucman.eu/missingprofits/

TPG. (2017). Introduction to transfer pricing. Evolution of transfer pricing. Retrieved from: https://tpguidelines.com/b-1-introduction-to-transfer-pricing/

Transfer Pricing Asia. (2017). What is a local file? Retrieved from: https://transferpricingasia.com/2017/06/08/transfer-pricing-local-file/

Transfer Pricing Asia. (2018). What is a master file? Retrieved from: https://transferpricingasia.com/2018/01/10/master-file/

United Nations. (2021). *Practical manual on transfer pricing for developing countries* (3rd ed.). United Nations. Retrieved from: https://tpcases.com/wp-content/uploads/UN_2021_TP_Manual.pdf

Valentiam Group. (2021). Understanding the master & local file for transfer pricing. Retrieved from: https://www.valentiam.com/newsandinsights/understanding-master-local-file-transfer-pricing.

Van Eck, N. J., & Waltman, L. (2018). *Vosviewer manual*. CWTS Meaningful Metrics, Universiteit Leiden.

Velikorossov, V. V., Chaykovskaya, L. A., & Filin, S. A. (2019). Transfer pricing for taxation of transnational corporations under innovative economy conditions. In *2nd international conference on contemporary education and economic development (CEED 2019)*.

Vissio, A. N., & Samperna, S. (2022). *Blockchain and its impact on transfer pricing control*. Master thesis, Universita Politecnica delle Marche. Retrieved from: https://tesi.univpm.it/bitstream/20.500.12075/7700/1/Vissio%2C%20Alberto%20-%20Master%20thesis%20-%20Final%20Version%20%281%29.pdf

Ylönen, M., & Teivainen, T. (2018). Politics of intra-firm trade: Corporate price planning and the double role of the arm's length principle. *New Political Economy, 23*(4), 441–457. https://doi.org/10.1080/13563467.2017.1371124

Zetter, M., Blumenfeld, B., Butler, K., & Singahl, B. (2009, November). Transfer pricing and the new economics. *International Tax Review, 20*, 17–19.

Conclusions

After an extensive review of the research results drawn from the literature, correlated with the sudden changes in the geo-economic paradigm in recent times, it was found that the business environment is becoming sensitive to geopolitical changes, which is why it is necessary to develop mechanisms to assess and prevent these threats, so that the impact is minimised. At the same time, geopolitical risks have been observed to pose a potential threat to the international accounting framework, specifically its ability to meet stakeholders' information needs by providing accurate, meaningful, comparable, verifiable, timely, and understandable information.

The increased role of the emerging BRICS economies in the international political and economic arena, and their separation from major international economic bodies, raises questions about the progress made in harmonising their national accounting standards with the International Financial Reporting Framework (IFRS).

The BRICS economies have established themselves as a counterweight to traditional Western-dominated institutions, advocating a more inclusive and multipolar world order in terms of the division of economic power and influence. However, it is worth noting that the BRICS countries are not a monopolistic group and that they have different political systems, interests and levels of development, which sometimes create divergent positions on some issues. But despite the challenges, BRICS is seen as an important platform for promoting cooperation among member countries. At present, there is still no information on whether the BRICS economies will develop a unified financial reporting system in the future, as the process of achieving this goal is complex and lengthy. However, this scenario should not be disregarded, especially against the backdrop of intensifying political and economic tensions between Russia and the West.

The accounting systems of the BRICS economies are different, each following their own accounting principles or international financial reporting standards. In order to make it easier for companies to do business across borders and for investors to compare the financial performance of companies from different countries, the

A. Melega, *Geopolitical Risks in Financial Reporting and Transfer Pricing*, Contributions to Finance and Accounting,
https://doi.org/10.1007/978-3-031-76600-8

BRICS economies are promoting greater compatibility and convergence between national accounting systems. Therefore, given the complexity of compatibility of accounting and reporting standards, as well as the regulatory and cultural environments in each country, the development of a unified financial reporting system would entail substantial costs, and is a complicated and lengthy process, but one that should not be ignored, but on the contrary, should be considered especially by investors.

The theoretical and practical aspects addressed throughout this book are materialised in own contributions that are also reflected in the results obtained, such as:

1. Identifying paradigm shifts in the internationalisation of companies: outlining the perimeter affected by visible changes in international business (from the perspective of internationalisation of companies) influenced by emerging geopolitical risks. At the same time, the effects of these risks on the sources of financing, the volatility of financial assets and stock markets, as well as on the performance and sustainability of internationalised companies were analysed. It was also considered appropriate to introduce a new paradigm, in terms of "geo-accounting" that takes into account the need to adapt the international financial reporting system to the changes in the global geopolitical arena and to avoid the risk of divergence.
2. The analysis of the stakeholder theory and the role of financial reporting in attracting foreign direct investment highlighted the relationship between stakeholders and financial reporting, correlated with the objectives of financial statements and the information needs of stakeholders. The results of this analysis identified the limitations and obstacles encountered by stakeholders in meeting their information needs and fostering sustainable business relationships. Also in this context, it has been possible to assess the contribution of the quality of financial disclosures in attracting FDI, by looking closely at the impact of accounting policies on the quality of financial statements and the possibilities to reduce information asymmetry between stakeholders.
3. The comparative analysis of the financial reporting framework specific to the BRICS group of companies made it possible to highlight the specific peculiarities of accounting policies and practices, the objectives and structure of financial reporting and, last but not least, the strengths and weaknesses of the economic-financial communication process influenced by political, social, environmental, regional, and cultural factors.
4. Synthesise and analyse the transfer pricing tax policies applied by companies in BRICS countries. For this purpose, a bibliometric and statistical analysis of the transfer pricing literature was carried out, complemented by a conceptual and applied approach from an accounting, legal, and tax perspective of transfer pricing. It also emphasised the importance of the transfer pricing file as a tool for assessing the legality and compliance of intra-group transactions, while identifying the determinants in the construction of the transfer pricing file and the attraction of foreign direct investment.

Due to the fact that the book focuses more on the process of internationalisation of companies and on the analysis of the existing threats to the current IFRS international financial reporting framework and the impact of emerging geopolitical risks, the limits of the research are drawn by the high level of economic, political, and security uncertainty that characterises national economies and the entire global context, in the sense that the changes that may occur are unpredictable and difficult to manage.

The heightening of geopolitical risks in recent times and the visible and easily quantifiable effects on the business continuity of multinational companies by affecting investment activity have created a series of unprecedented crisis situations, which raise a number of unanswered questions at present, such as: What will be the future of multinational companies, given that many governments will adopt a policy of nationalising resources and obviously limiting access for foreign operators in favour of resident ones? If business relationships will be limited and made conditional on membership of a particular interest group, will the international financial reporting framework still be applied in its current form in countries that are today in open conflict with the Anglo-Saxon system, such as Russia for example; to what extent will the accentuation of current geopolitical conflicts be able to prevent the risk of divergence of national/regional accounting standards from international ones? This book provides valuable information for companies, regulators, investors, and other stakeholders, as it gives them the opportunity to navigate the ever-changing global geopolitical landscape and to be able to identify new opportunities to attract foreign direct investment. At the same time, they have the opportunity to learn how to prevent tax avoidance through the correct use of transfer pricing accounting and tax policies (perceived as a tool to erode the tax base).

The manufacturer's authorised representative in the EU is Springer Nature Customer Service Centre GmbH, Europaplatz 3, 69115 Heidelberg, Germany. If you have any concerns regarding our products, please contact ProductSafety@springernature.com

Printed and bound by CPI Group (UK) Ltd, Croydon, CR0 4YY
30/09/2026
02225607-0011